THE ENCYCLOPEDIA OF

Roses

An Organic Guide to Growing and Enjoying America's Favorite Flower

Judith C. McKeon

Rodale Press, Inc.
Emmaus, Pennsylvania

A FRIEDMAN GROUP BOOK

Copyright © 1995 by Michael Friedman Publishing Group, Inc.

Published in 1995 by Rodale Press, Inc.

If you have any questions or comments concerning this book, please write to:

Rodale Press
Book Readers' Service
33 East Minor Street
Emmaus, PA 18098

THE ENCYCLOPEDIA OF ROSES
was prepared and produced by
Michael Friedman Publishing Group, Inc.
15 West 26th Street
New York, NY 10010

Michael Friedman Publishing Group Editorial and Design Staff:
Editor: Susan Lauzau
Art Director: Jeff Batzli
Designer: Andrea Karman
Photography Editor: Colleen Branigan

Rodale Editorial Staff:
Editor: Ellen Phillips
Senior Associate Editor: Nancy J. Ondra
Designer: Darlene Schneck
Studio Manager: Mary Ellen Fanelli
Copy Editor: Carolyn Mandarano
Editorial Director, Home and Garden: Margaret Lydic Balitas
Art Director, Home and Garden: Michael Mandarano
Copy Director, Home and Garden: Dolores Plikaitis
Editor-in-Chief, Rodale Books: William Gottlieb

Library of Congress Cataloging-in-Publication Data

McKeon, Judith C.
    The encyclopedia of roses: an organic guide to growing & enjoying America's
favorite flower / Judith C. McKeon.
        p. cm.
    Includes bibliographical references (p. 189) and index.
    ISBN 0–87596–656–X (hardcover)
    1. Rose culture. 2. Roses. 3. Rose culture—United States.
4. Roses—United States.   I. Title.
SB411.M46   1995
635.9'33372—dc20   95–2174

Distributed in the book trade by St. Martin's Press

Color separations by Fine Arts Repro House Co., Ltd.
Printed in China by Leefung-Asco Printers Ltd.

2 4 6 8 10 9 7 5 3 1 hardcover

To my mentors Léonie Bell and Robert Ballantine III, to my colleague Charles Holman, and to my comrades of the Philadelphia Rose Society; thanks to each of you for sharing your knowledge and love of roses with me and for supporting my efforts to grow beautiful roses.

Acknowledgments

I am grateful to Paul W. Meyer, director, and Rick J. Lewandowski, curator, Morris Arboretum of the University of Pennsylvania, for supporting my leave to write the book. I appreciate the professional advice of Arboretum colleagues: Dr. Ann F. Rhoads, director of botany, Shelley Dillard, propagator, and Paul W. Meyer.

Special thanks to Catherine McKeon for her support. I am eternally grateful to Agatha Hughes, who provided valuable editorial commentary and counsel. Thanks to Susan Byrnes for technical assistance with my PC; and to Mike Lowe, John Elsley, and Steve Hutton for contributing photographs. I am grateful to friends who read parts of the manuscript: Harriet Cramer, Laura Flandreau, Diana Post, Nina Schneider, and Elayna Singer.

Thanks to Ellen Phillips of Rodale. I appreciate the fine work of the staff of the Michael Friedman Group: Sharyn Rosart, Susan Lauzau, Andrea Karman, and Colleen Branigan.

Finally, I'd like to acknowledge my companion, Jack Russell terrier 'Beanbag', retired Morris Arboretum hero, who valiantly protected the rosebuds from marauding deer.

CONTENTS

Part

One

Growing Roses

'MARJORIE FAIR'

'LOUISE ODIER'

'GOLD MEDAL'

◀ *Roses are the perfect way to welcome family and friends to your garden. Adorn an entrance with masses of showy, fragrant flowers, or train a climber up a pillar to create a charming garden scene. Here, the opulent blooms of 'America' cover an arbor.*

Chapter One

WHAT IS A ROSE?

Sooner or later, every gardener gives in to the urge to plant some roses. Somewhere in the back of our minds is the idea that the garden won't really be complete without a rose bed, an arbor, or a fence ablaze with fragrant blooming roses.

Roses are the most irresistible of all flowers. There's no other plant with the history, allure, and mystique of roses. They bring to the garden the sublime combination of everything we could want from a flower: color, fragrance, form, and class.

◀ *Few flowers are more appealing to the senses than the rose. An old-fashioned rose like this stunning*
'Crested Moss' bud invites us to enjoy its sweet scent, delicate color, and soft silky texture.

History is full of allusions to roses. Legend tells us that they were present at the birth of Venus. It's said that Antony and Cleopatra reclined on sofas stuffed with rose petals. Taken as the emblems of British noble houses, roses have even precipitated a war. (That's why it was called the War of the Roses.) The image of the rose is found on ancient coins and in paintings by the masters. Its praises are sung in the verse and prose of almost every author, including Chaucer, Shakespeare, Dante, and Burns. Roses are glorified in song, from Tin Pan Alley tunes to stirring anthems such as "The Yellow Rose of Texas."

The rose represents romance. It seduces us with its fragrance and delicate petals. It intrigues us with its prickly stems. It reminds us that sometimes we have to put up with sharp barriers when we reach out for beauty.

Above all, the rose is known for its perfect flower form. Its blooms are at home in a formal border or a cottage garden, clambering up the side of a house or barn, and, especially, indoors in a vase. There its fragrance may perfume an entire house. It's a practical plant as well. Roses have been used as an herbal remedy for ages. Its fruits, called hips, are rich in vitamin C.

The hips of the Moyes rose

Yellow Lady Banks rose

Whenever you plant a rose, you bring some of its history and mystique to your landscape. Roses are versatile. They can be used as climbers, ramblers, bushes, hedges, and groundcovers. They can even be used in rock gardens. Some are best in the perennial, shrub, or mixed border. Others are at home in the herb, cutting, or cottage garden.

So why doesn't everyone grow roses? Unfortunately, these gorgeous plants have another reputation, too. They're known as finicky, difficult children—prima donnas, suited only for formal settings. They're said to need constant attention and tricky pruning. Fortunately, none of that is true.

Roses are easier to grow than you might think. Many are virtually care-free. Some are hardy to Zone 3 or 4, the northernmost plant hardiness zones of the United States, and disease-resistant roses are not difficult to find. Some need very little pruning.

The secret to successful rose growing is taking the time to find out which rose is which and then picking the right plant for the right place. That may seem to be a daunting job. Rose classification appears to be a briar patch of classes and subclasses. But it's not as complex as you might fear. In this chapter, we'll sort out the classes of roses to help you find good candidates to suit your climate, soil, and taste.

Botanically speaking, roses belong to the plant family Rosaceae, the rose family, which is comprised of more than 100 genera, or types, of small trees, shrubs, and herbs. Characteristic family traits include flowers with five separate petals— often appearing in showy masses—and edible or eye-catching fruits. Familiar members of the rose family include such well-known fruit-bearing relatives as apples, pears, apricots, plums, cherries, peaches, strawberries, raspberries, and blackberries, as well as ornamental fruit trees such as

'Rosa Mundi'

flowering cherry, crab apple, and Bradford pear. Yet the member of the family most prized for its fragrance and ornamental, medicinal, economic, and symbolic properties is the rose.

The rose family derives its name from its largest genus, *Rosa*, which is represented by approximately 150 species of wild roses distributed throughout the Northern Hemisphere, where they have prodigiously produced flowers and set fruit for thirty-two million years. With the exception of species, or wild, roses, which are referred to by botanical as well as common name—rugosa rose (*Rosa rugosa*), for example—most roses are cultivars, often called horticultural varieties. Rose cultivars generally result from selective hybridization, or breeding. New varieties also occasionally arise from a genetic mutation, or sport—usually a shoot from a single bud different in some way from the rose variety that produced it. Rose cultivars are referred to by their registered trade, or accepted, name and placed in single quotes, such as the 'Peace' rose. In addition, because trade names often change from country to country, rose cultivars are also given a code name, represented by a few upper-case letters of the hybridizer's name, followed by a few lowercase letters indicating the specific cultivar. For instance, 'Tropicana', known as 'Superstar' in Europe, is registered with the code name TANorstar, because the hybridizer is Mathias Tantau of Holstein, Germany. These code names are the same the world over. Finally, trade names of roses are often registered with a trademark, such as Pearl Meidiland™ and Sunbright®.

Classified according to their ancestry, roses are divided into classes and subclasses. Species, or wild, roses and old roses with their many subclasses belong to the antique group, also called old roses. The continuous-blooming hybrid tea rose celebrated its debut in 1867, when tea roses were bred with hybrid perpetual and China roses, and that year marks the inauguration of the modern rose era. Other classes of modern roses include polyantha, rambler, climber, miniature, floribunda, grandiflora, and shrub roses.

Species Roses

Species roses and their hybrids enhance the garden with scent, color, texture, and seasonal interest. The easy-care shrubs and scramblers are valued for their delicate single flowers and colorful hips. They look attractive with full-flowered old roses and perennial companions in an informal setting. Undemanding species roses and their hybrids are among the easiest flowering shrubs to grow. The adventurous gardener will find much to appreciate, savor, and enjoy about the wild roses.

Whether gracefully arching, mounding, or scrambling, species roses are deciduous shrubs characteristically armed with prickles, which are commonly called thorns. Five-petaled or single flowers cover the shrubs in late spring, often fol-

'Tausendschon'—You can see why this flower's name means "thousand beauties." For more on this lovely rose, see page 160.

lowed by colorful rose hips that attract birds into the garden in late summer and autumn. Individual flowers vary in size. With fragrant, deep pink flowers and scarlet autumn foliage, the low-growing New England shining rose (*Rosa nitida*) is a rounded shrub that seldom exceeds 3 feet in height. Whereas *Rosa filipes*, a Himalyan rambler, can easily climb 30 feet into a neighboring tree.

Most species roses are tough, hardy, disease-resistant shrubs. Plant them with perennials and flowering shrubs in mixed borders, cottage gardens, and herb gardens. Species roses are also suitable for naturalizing in the wild garden. Native American species, including the pasture rose (*Rosa carolina*), New England shining rose, the swamp rose (*Rosa palustris*), the Virginia rose (*Rosa virginiana*), and *Rosa woodsii*, are at home in the wild garden, interplanted with wildflowers and native shrubs or placed to arch gracefully over edges of ponds or streams. Most provide autumn interest with their superb foliage display and colorful hips. Although all roses are sun lovers, many species roses, including redleaved rose (*Rosa glauca*), eglantine (*Rosa eglanteria*), and Scotch rose (*Rosa spinossissima*), will readily accept a position in the high or dappled shade of deciduous trees.

Species roses are tailor-made for difficult landscape situations such as erosion-prone banks, beds flanking paving, boggy areas, and poor rocky sites in full sun. Many species roses and their hybrids are good choices for these conditions. Bog roses such as the swamp rose and New England shining rose grow and flourish in wet sites, while the prairie rose (*Rosa setigera*) and wingthorn rose (*Rosa sericea* var. *pteracantha*) readily tolerate rocky, barren soils. Virginia rose and naturalized rugosa rose (*Rosa rugosa*) colonize the seaside, and few shrubs are better adapted to urban "hot spot" plantings that border paving and parking lots than hybrid rugosa roses such as the compact 'Frau Dagmar Hartopp'.

Old Roses

The antique group, or old roses, with its many subclasses basically divides into the mostly once-blooming roses with a common ancestor, *Rosa gallica*—gallica, damask, alba, centifolia, and moss—and the China and China-influenced roses of the nineteenth century, which are mostly repeat-flowering, and include the Bourbon, Noisette, perpetual damask (Portland), hybrid perpetual, and tea roses. Although the old roses available to gardeners today represent only a fraction of the thousands of cultivars once catalogued, gardeners in each generation cultivated and thereby preserved some of the heritage roses.

Today, with a renewed appreciation for antique flowers associated with informal gardening styles, a growing interest in the fragrant, long-lived old roses, and a greater awareness of organic gardening techniques, care-free old roses appeal to ever-widening circles of gardeners. A heritage rose renaissance continues to increase the availability of old roses to gardeners.

Modern Roses

Asian tea roses descended from Rosa odorata were bred with hybrid perpetual and China roses to create continuous-blooming hybrid tea roses. The hybrid tea rose celebrated its debut sometime after 1850. 'La France' was introduced in 1867 and is considered by many to be the first hybrid tea; the year 1867 was later chosen to mark the inauguration of the modern rose era. The hybrid tea, however, did not suddenly replace the hybrid perpetual; both lines continued, weaving a trail often difficult to follow, until 1900, when the final stage of hybrid perpetual development, represented by 'Frau Karl Druschki', 'Georg Arends', and similar cultivars, became indistinguishable from hybrid

'Persian Yellow'

teas. At this point, the hybrid perpetual line was abandoned. In the twentieth century, the popularity of hybrid tea roses increased because they possess superior characteristics: They make excellent, everblooming bedding plants and florist flowers and are treasured for their elegant, high-centered blooms borne on long stems.

Over the course of nearly a century, modern roses were influenced by important developments in rose breeding that set the stage for new classes of roses. The introduction of the multiflora *(Rosa multiflora)* and memorial roses *(Rosa wichuraiana)* from China in the late nineteenth century, for example, led to the creation of polyantha, rambler, and large-flowered climbing roses. Everblooming China roses continued to play an important role in modern breeding, particularly of polyantha and miniature roses. The hardiness of hybrid tea roses was improved, and their attributes of continuous flowering and elegant flower form were bred into the major modern rose

classes. From 1867 to the mid-twentieth century, modern classes of hybrid tea, polyantha, rambler, climber, miniature, floribunda, grandiflora, and shrub roses were introduced.

Until the turn of the century, color in garden and florist roses was limited to shades of white, pink, and crimson. An explosion of the color range to include yellow and flame hues bestowed by the Austrian briar *(Rosa foetida)* was successfully engineered in 1900, when French hybridizer Joseph Pernet-Ducher crossed *Rosa foetida* 'Persian Yellow' with a hybrid perpetual to produce the hybrid tea 'Soleil d'Or' with rich, yellow-orange blooms. The full spectrum of clear yellow, gold, and apricot to brilliant orange and flame colors is now represented in twentieth-century roses. The first yellow-blend hybrid tea to capture the hearts of generations of rose-lovers was 'Peace'. It was introduced by the Conard-Pyle Company of West Grove, Pennsylvania, at the close of World War II.

M a k e   Y o u r   O w n   P o t p o u r r i

Potpourri is a French term for a simple process: drying rose petals and other flowers and herbs to preserve their scent. Dried centifolia and damask rose petals are the most fragrant potpourri ingredients. Scented gallica, alba, and moss rose petals can also be dried and used in potpourri, but their perfume is not as strong. Fragrant modern roses do not retain their scent when dried. Dried lavender, rosemary, and other fragrant herbs can also be included for a more complex fragrance and to add more color and texture.

Damask, centifolia, and alba rose petals are traditionally used in making potpourri. Some of the best include the damask cultivars 'Celsiana', 'Ispahan', and 'Leda'; centifolia roses 'Centifolia' ('Rose des Peintres'), 'Variegata' ('Cottage Maid'), 'Bullata', and 'La Noblesse'; and albas 'Alba Semi-Plena', 'Maxima', and 'Suaveolens'. You can also use other old rose flowers, such as the fragrant moss roses 'Nuits de Young', 'Common Moss', and 'Salet'; and gallicas 'Apothecary's Rose' and 'Rosa Mundi'; or choose your favorite fragrant old roses.

Recipe for Potpourri

8 cups of dried centifolia, damask, or alba rose petals

2 tablespoons of ground mace

2 tablespoons of ground nutmeg

2 tablespoons of ground allspice

2 tablespoons of ground cloves

1 cinnamon stick, crushed

⅔ cup of orris root powder, for a fixative

5 drops of rose oil, optional (if petals used are not strongly scented when dried)

Cut roses for potpourri in the morning after dew has dried on the petals. Select flowers that are two-thirds open, trim off the stems, and pull off the petals. Spread them in a single layer on a screen and dry them in a cool, dark location. Store the dried petals in an airtight jar. To make potpourri, combine the dry ingredients in a large bowl, sprinkle with fixative and essential oil (if used), and mix well. Place the potpourri mixture in a large, airtight jar and place in a dark location. Periodically, shake the jar to blend the ingredients.

Describing Rose Flowers

Rose flowers vary in petal number, color combination, and shape. Presented here is the special terminology used to describe the variations. When referring to rose flowers, also keep in mind that they are arranged on the stem as either solitary, terminal blooms or grouped in clusters or sprays. In addition, roses are termed either once-blooming or repeat-blooming. Once-blooming roses, typically the old roses, have one big flush of bloom, like the flowering shrubs they are. Repeat-blooming roses, typically the modern roses, have flushes of bloom all season.

Semidouble

Semidouble: Eight to twenty petals in two or three rows. *Examples:* 'Celsiana', *Europeana*®, 'Apothecary's Rose'.

Loosely double: Twenty-one to twenty-nine petals in three or four rows. *Examples:* 'Harison's Yellow', 'Pristine', 'China Doll'.

Fully double: Thirty to thirty-nine petals in four or more rows. *Examples:* 'Frau Karl Druschki', 'Iceberg', 'Queen Elizabeth'.

Very full double: Forty or more petals in numerous rows. *Examples:* 'Madame Hardy', 'Yankee Doodle'.

Single

FLOWER FULLNESS

Single: Five to seven petals in a single row. *Examples:* 'Ballerina', 'Betty Prior', 'Dainty Bess', Dortmund®.

Fully Double

FLOWER COLOR

Single: Petals have similar color throughout. *Example: 'Iceberg' (white).*

Bicolored: The reverse, or back, of each petal is a distinctly different color from the front. *Example: 'Love' (red with white reverse).*

Blend: Two or more distinct colors on the front of each petal. *Examples: 'Peace' (yellow with pink edges), 'Secret' (light pink with deep pink edges).*

Striped: Two or more distinct colors on each petal, with at least one in distinct stripes or bands. *Example: 'Camaieux' (cream flowers striped with violet and crimson).*

FLOWER SHAPE

Globular: Very double flower with petals curving inward to form a globelike shape. *Example: Constance Spry®.*

Open-cupped: Double or semidouble flower forming a distinctly rounded, cuplike shape. *Examples: 'Ferdinand Pichard', Graham Thomas™.*

Pompon: Very double flower with short petals evenly arranged into a rounded bloom. *Examples: Alba Meidiland™, 'Sea Foam', 'The Fairy'.*

Reflexed: Outer petals reflex (curve back and down) as they open. Very double types almost form a ball, while other double and semidouble cultivars form a looser, less pronounced ball shape. *Examples: 'Félicité Parmentier', 'Salet'.*

Rosette: A double flower with short petals evenly arranged into a flat, low-centered bloom. *Example: 'Cornelia'.*

Saucer: Single, semidouble, or double flower with outer petals curving slightly upward in a saucerlike shape. *Examples: 'Betty Prior', 'Harison's Yellow'.*

FLOWER CENTER

Open Center

Button center: A round green center, or eye, in a fully open rose bloom, formed in very double roses. *Examples: 'Fantin-Latour', 'Madame Hardy'.*

High center: The long, inner petals of the bud arranged in a pointed cone. The form most often found in hybrid teas, grandifloras, and floribundas. *Example: 'Iceberg'.*

Muddled center: Double or semidouble flower with inner petals forming an irregular central area that conceals the stamens when the flower is fully open. *Example: 'Rose de Rescht'.*

Open center: Stamens are prominent when the flower is fully open; single, semidouble, and double forms may have this characteristic. *Example: 'Iceberg'.*

Quartered center: Inner petals folded into three, four, or five distinct sections (or quarters) in a fully open flower. *Examples: 'Baronne Prévost', 'Konigin von Danemark', 'Souvenir de la Malmaison'.*

Adapted from Maggie Oster, *The Rose Book* (Emmaus, Pa.: Rodale Press, 1994), 8–9.

Chapter Two

SITE, SOIL, AND PLANTING

All your careful planning leads to one moment: planting time. This is where life begins for the second time for your rosebushes.

Your plant may be one of thousands or perhaps tens of thousands of a cultivar grown at a nursery. But it's only when the plant comes home to your yard that a rosebush becomes an individual. This is where it will reach its full potential.

This is also where you as the gardener and rose lover have the most impact. Your gardening skill and knowledge will combine with the plant's genetic potential to make it the best rose it can be. That's why just putting the rose in the ground with good intentions and best wishes isn't enough. Like all plants, roses have certain simple requirements. As stars of the flower world, roses need the spotlight.

◀ *Shrub roses are easy to plant and make excellent specimens, screens, and foundation plantings. These colorful hybrid roses encircling a lawn create a drift of showy seasonal blooms. They produce flowers freely in spring and ask little of the gardener in return.*

They thrive in full sun, though some species grow quite well in dappled shade from a deciduous tree. They shouldn't be crowded in among other plants. Roses need elbow room to stretch and fill out until they reach their mature size. Finally, roses prefer a rich, well-drained soil to put down roots.

There's nothing inherently new or tricky about preparing a garden site to grow great roses. The following pages present all the information you need to get the soil ready and plant roses in your landscape.

Choosing a Site

Because roses are sun lovers that adapt more easily to a hot spot than to a shady location, choose a well-drained, sunny site that receives at least a half day, or about six hours, of direct sunlight. An ideal site for growing roses gets full sunlight in morning and early afternoon but is shaded in the heat of midafternoon. Both everblooming and reblooming roses need a minimum of six hours of full sun to produce their abundant display of flowers. When everblooming roses are placed in shady situations, they're a real disappointment, since they'll produce spindly, elongated growth and few flowers.

When choosing a site for roses, also keep in mind that roses resent having to compete with tree roots for moisture and nutrients. It's best to situate beds for roses or mixed borders away from greedy tree roots. In addition, give young rosebushes room to establish themselves in sunny mixed borders. Initially, the immature shrubs may be much smaller than their vigorous perennial companions, which can shade out the shrubs if they're planted too close. Antique and modern shrub roses need three years to reach maturity. But once established, they hold their own with even the most aggressive neighbors.

Almost all cultural conditions in the garden can be adjusted to grow roses, but if sunlight is at a premium or nonexistent, your efforts will be wasted. If your garden is shaded by deciduous trees, try limbing up or opening the canopy by selective pruning to provide more sunlight. Grow species and old alba roses that flower in late spring or early summer and tolerate dappled light or high shade from deciduous trees. These easy-care roses require less summer sunlight because they set flower buds in early spring before the leaves emerge on shade trees. However, even tough species roses won't tolerate heavy shade from maple trees or a site in the shadow of a building or evergreen trees. If yours is a shady yard, however, a deck or patio may get enough sun to grow a few miniature and shrub roses in containers. See page 26 for more on container growing.

Soil for Roses

Getting to know your garden soil may be the most important and interesting challenge that confronts you as a gardener. Soil is a living environment that anchors plants and sustains them with the water and nutrients required for growth. It's made up of decomposed rock and humus, or decayed organic matter. Typically, soil consists of about 45 percent mineral particles, 50 percent oxygen and water (or the space between the particles), and 5 percent organic matter. The mineral particles are composed of sand, silt, and clay.

The particle size of the soil determines its texture. Sand particles are the largest. Soils made up of sand are well drained, porous, and infertile because nutrients are quickly leached away from the root area. Silt particles are smaller, medium-textured, and tend to make a slightly fertile soil of light to medium density. Clay particles are the smallest, and soil of this type tends to be fine-textured, heavy, and sticky, but fertile because nutrients adhere more readily to the particles. But few gardens have pure sand, silt, or clay. Most are combinations of all three particle types, creating soils that are both more fertile and better drained.

When the soil has a balance of sand, silt, and clay particles, it is called loam. The crumbly, friable texture of loam allows water to percolate evenly while retaining moisture and nutrients for plant roots to absorb. Unfortunately for gardeners, most soils could use some help. But with a lot of organic matter and a little elbow grease, you will end up with good garden soil.

You can discover the composition of your soil with a simple experiment. Take a fistful of wet soil and form it into a ball. Then try to roll it into a rod. Clay loam easily rolls into a sticky, thin ribbon; silt loam makes a rod that is slightly sticky; sandy loam breaks apart.

Improving Your Soil

Adding organic matter in the form of compost, rotted manure, Milorganite, shredded leaves, or peat moss will improve the structure of sandy, silty, and even heavy clay soils. Organic matter improves drainage and aeration and bulks up the soil's moisture-holding capacity. It acts like a sponge to hold water, nutrients, and oxygen, and then releases them as the soil dries.

Annual incorporation of compost or rotted manure replenishes the organic content of your soil; it also builds and conditions it. A crumbly, porous soil is created by the action of microorganisms and earthworms feeding on the organic matter in compost and rotted manures. Organically rich soil is dynamic, teeming with organisms that work to get nutrients into a form that plants can use. Roots absorb nutrients with water from the soil.

A well-drained garden soil with good organic content—the kind of soil that's typical of vegetable gardens—is ideal for growing roses. Roses do not require a perfect loamy soil. They will thrive in clay, silt, and sandy loams, as long as the soil has been amended with enough organic matter to be adequately drained and able to provide ample nutrients. Roses, particularly continuous- and repeat-blooming types, are heavy feeders and grow best in soils that are conditioned with plenty of organic matter and supplemented with organic fertilizers. An organically rich soil

takes some time to build, but it is worth the effort. It encourages the quick establishment and growth of rosebushes and eventually makes the gardener's job of digging much easier.

In wet, boggy, or poorly drained soils or on sites that are extremely alkaline or rocky, consider making raised beds to accommodate the soil requirements of most roses, flowering shrubs, and perennials. Raised beds are simply made by mounding soil or by building a frame using wood, brick, or stone to hold an organically rich soil mixture.

Soil pH

Soil pH measures the level of acidity or alkalinity of your soil. Soil pH is measured on a scale from 1.0 to 14.0. The lowest number is the most acidic, the highest is most alkaline, and 7.0 is neutral. Although tolerant of soil pH between 5.5 and 7.0, roses, like most herbaceous ornamental plants and vegetables, grow best in a slightly acidic soil with a pH of about 6.0 to 6.5. At that level, nutrients are more readily available for root absorption. Acidic or sour soils can be "sweetened" with the addition of lime. Sweet, limy, or alkaline soils can be made more acidic with agricultural granular sulfur. Adding organic matter like compost will bring both acidic and alkaline soils closer to neutral. The use of organic fertilizers generally has an acidifying effect on the soil.

Before planting roses, have your beds tested to determine soil pH. Your local Agricultural Cooperative Extension Service offers soil testing through its lab. Send for soil test mailers, then follow directions for collecting soil samples from your garden. The test results indicate soil pH, evaluate fertility, and recommend fertilizer adjustments. There is usually a small fee for the mailers. When you send in your soil samples, tell the lab that you want organic recommendations; otherwise you'll get a set of directions on how to use chemicals to correct your soil problems.

B e d
P r e p a r a t i o n

You can begin bed preparation for spring planting in autumn and for autumn planting in spring. To maintain good soil structure, dig beds while they're moist but not wet. Take care not to leave open ground or exposed beds of soil because organic matter is quickly eroded by the wind, sun, and freezing and thawing, and soils can become compacted. In autumn, you can plant winter rye as a cover crop to be turned under in spring or mulch beds with shredded leaves or compost, then allow the soil to settle for a few months before planting. The advantage of using a fine organic mulch like compost or shredded leaves is that roses and perennials can be planted through it in spring, whereas a coarser mulch such as wood chips must be pulled aside or removed.

Condition the soil in established beds in autumn or early spring. Top-dress the beds with compost or rotted manure, incorporating the organic matter around your rosebushes to replenish nutrients and build healthy soil. All rosebushes benefit from an annual application of about 2 inches of organic matter.

Double Digging

Double digging is a method of bed preparation that works organic matter deep into the root area of the soil. When establishing a new bed, it's good practice to turn over the soil and add organic material to improve structure and drainage, even if you have loamy soil. But if you have compacted soil or heavy clay, you should try double digging. Double digging lightens heavy clay garden soils and improves the structure of compacted soils.

To start, dig a trench about one spade deep and transport the topsoil in a wheelbarrow or garden cart to the other end of the plot, reserving it for later. Loosen the subsoil in the bottom of the trench by plunging a spading fork into the soil and pushing it back and forth. Work your way along the trench until the subsoil is loosened from one end to the other. Then add several

Double Digging

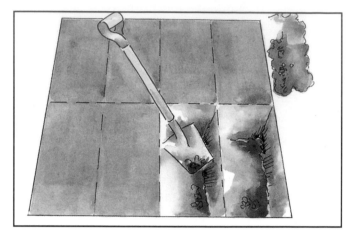

Prepare the bed by working one trench at a time.

Step 1. *Dig a trench one spade deep across half the width of the bed. Transport the soil to the end of the plot (as shown above).*

Step 2. *Loosen subsoil in the bottom of the trench to a depth of 1 foot by plunging a digging fork in the soil and rocking it back and forth.*

Step 3. *Dig the next trench one spade deep and move the topsoil from it into the first trench. Repeat these steps until the entire bed is dug.*

M a k i n g   C o m p o s t

Because it supplies plant nutrients in a balanced, ready-to-use form and is such a great soil conditioner, compost is one of the best forms of organic matter. You can make it by simply recycling garden debris. You can quickly make a freestanding compost pile in a space as small as 3 square feet. As debris such as grass clippings, chopped leaves, and weeds become available, add them to the pile in layers about 8 inches deep. Top each layer with a sprinkling of soil and an organic nitrogen source such as kitchen scraps, manure, fresh grass clippings, blood meal, or alfalfa pellets. Continue building the heap in this manner—sprinkling a thin layer of topsoil and organic matter over every 8 inches of garden debris—until it reaches a height of 3 feet. Smaller particles break down faster, which is a good reason to use chopped leaves.

Heat will build up as organisms in the layers of soil go to work breaking down the fibrous garden debris and feeding on the nitrogen and carbon in the organic matter. You can monitor the rising temperature of your pile with a compost thermometer or by sticking your hand into the pile. If it feels hot, it's working! Turn the pile twice a week to aerate it and to move less-decomposed material into the hottest area at the center of the pile. Compost can be made in three to four weeks in warm weather. (Moisten the pile if it dries out—it should be as damp as a wrung-out sponge.) When your compost is dark, crumbly, and has cooled down, use it right away. If you can't, cover the pile with plastic to prevent nutrients from leaching.

inches of organic matter. Dig a second trench, spading its topsoil into the first trench on top of the organic matter. Try not to mix the soil layers while digging. Slide the soil into place instead of turning it over and dumping it. Continue in this manner until the whole plot has been double-dug. When the final trench has been loosened and refilled, you will wind up with a garden plot that's slightly higher than when you started and filled with loosened, fluffy soil.

P l a n t i n g

Planting roses is no harder than planting a perennial or small shrub. Basically, you just dig a good-sized hole, keep the roots watered, and plant carefully. But each type of rose plant—bareroot, packaged, and container-grown—requires its own customized treatment. Here's what to do.

Handling Dormant Bareroot Bushes

If you order dormant bareroot bushes by mail, they will be shipped directly to your home at the right time for spring or autumn planting in your region. Caring for bareroot bushes is not difficult, but they will need some immediate attention upon arrival. It's really like taking a few minutes to place perishable dairy products in the refrigerator after shopping.

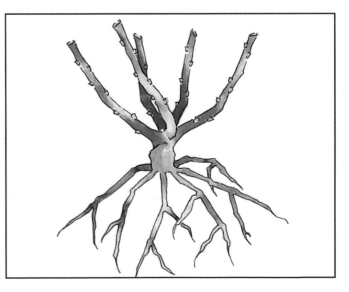

Dormant bareroot rosebush

Open the carton, inspect the bushes, and make sure you have received premium No. 1 grade bushes with three or four stout canes and a healthy, well-branched root system. Canes should look smooth, with a green or reddish color and fresh white wood or pith showing where the tops of the canes were pruned by the nursery. If the canes are spindly, broken, rotted, or shriveled, or if the root mass is dried out, damaged, or one-sided, call the grower and request replacements or a refund. Reputable nurseries will give credit or replacement bushes.

Also check to be sure that you have received the number of plants and the cultivars you ordered. Each plant should be labeled with the name of the grower, rose cultivar name, and grade. Call the nursery if you have not received the cultivars you ordered.

Dormant bareroot bushes are often wrapped in plastic, with a packing material such as moist sphagnum moss added to prevent drying. After inspection, mist the roots with a spray of water, rewrap them, and store your roses in a cool place, safe from freezing temperatures, until you

Planting Dormant Bareroot Rosebushes

Step 1. *Soak the roots in a bucket of water overnight or for at least a few hours before planting. Dig a planting hole 24 inches wide and 18 inches deep.*

Step 2. *Inspect the bush and prune off any broken canes or roots. Cut back the canes by about one-half to two-thirds their length. This encourages the growth of vigorous new canes from the crown.*

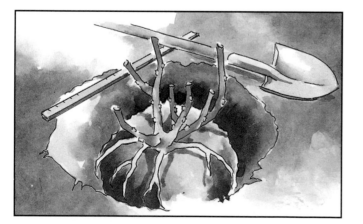

Step 3. *Form a mound of soil in the bottom of the hole and spread the roots out on it. Set plants with the knuckle (graft union) at soil level, or 2 to 3 inches below soil level in regions where winters are severe.*

Step 4. *Backfill topsoil around the roots. Water well. Complete backfilling and water again. Hill soil up around the canes to prevent them from drying out.*

have time to plant them. Moisture is the most important requirement for bareroot plants, so take care that the roots do not dry out. Wrapped roses can be safely stored in a refrigerator or cool garage for about ten days. Periodically open the carton and wrapping to mist the roots with water.

If you need to hold bareroot roses for longer than ten days, it is best to heel them into the garden (a temporary planting method commonly used with bareroot plants). To do this, dig a trench about 12 inches deep in a prepared bed or in the vegetable garden. Lay the bushes in the trench at a 45-degree angle, cover the roots and most of the canes with soil, and water well. In early spring, roses that are heeled in can be held for weeks with little ill effect as long as temperatures remain cool. Autumn shipments can be held in the same way and even heeled in for winter if necessary.

Planting Dormant Bareroot Bushes

Planting bareroot bushes is a simple task. Soak the roots in a bucket of water overnight or for several hours before planting. You can take a trash can to your planting site and fill the bottom with water, submerge the roots of the bushes, and plant each bush directly from the trash can. Take care that bareroot bushes are not exposed to drying winds and sun in the garden. Keep the roots submerged in water or wrapped in wet burlap while you dig the planting holes.

Inspect the bushes before planting and prune off any broken canes or roots with sharp hand shears. Cut back the canes by about one-half to two-thirds of their length, leaving about two or three buds. This encourages vigorous shoots from the crown. Do not be tempted to leave the canes unpruned in hopes of getting more flowers. In fact, the reverse is true. Over the entire season and the life of the bush, many more flowers will ultimately be produced if plants are pruned hard at planting. That's because the tops of dormant bareroot bushes always dry out on their long journey from harvest, cold storage, and shipping to you. It is best to get rid of the

top two-thirds of the canes so the plant puts energy into getting its roots established and producing vigorous new canes. This pruning method applies to all budded bushes, including once-flowering roses that do not set flower buds their first season in the garden. Pruning them encourages the production of vigorous canes that carry next year's bloom.

Remove any metal wire identification tags that would eventually girdle the cane. They're inevitably lost or detached from their bush anyway. Attach permanent labels with the plants' cultivar names, using plastic-coated wire and leaving some room between the coated wire and the cane. Check the labels annually to make sure they're still readable, and make sure you reattach them after pruning. It is also helpful to use a garden plan to map and identify the roses in your beds. That way you'll know what's out there even if a label gets lost.

Make sure to amend the soil in the bed with organic matter before planting. Then dig planting holes about 24 inches wide and 18 inches deep. If beds have not been prepared in advance, discard a few shovels of subsoil and add a few shovels of compost to the planting hole, backfilling with the topsoil. Form a small mound of soil in the bottom of the hole and spread the roots over it. Set each budded plant with its bud union (or knuckle) at soil level. In Zones 3 to 5, where winters are severe, set the bud union 2 or 3 inches below soil level.

Deep planting protects tender roses from frost and also allows the cultivar to establish its own root system and not be so dependent on its understock. However, in heavy clay soils, deep planting may contribute to the growth of crown gall. Parts of the submerged crown may eventually rot and allow crown gall bacteria easy entry. Therefore, when planting in heavy clay soils in moderate climates (Zones 6 to 9), set the bud union at soil level so that it is exposed to air and light.

Once you have set the plant in the hole, backfill around the roots with enough soil for the plant to stand up. Then irrigate thoroughly, allowing water to fill in air pockets in the hole. Finish filling in the soil

Planting Container-Grown Roses

Step 1. *Water container-grown bushes before planting. Dig a planting hole 24 inches wide and 18 inches deep.*

Step 2. *Remove the rosebush from its container before planting. Loosen the soil at the bottom of the root ball. Set the bush in the hole at same depth it was in the container.*

Step 3. *Fill in topsoil around the root ball, firm soil around the plant, and water well. Lightly fertilize with a complete organic fertilizer. Mulch to maintain soil moisture.*

to the top of the hole, firm soil around the bush, and irrigate again. Finally, hill soil up around the canes to keep them from drying out. In about four to six weeks, when leaves emerge, remove the soil mounds with a stream of water. When planting in autumn, leave the soil mound in place until spring. Dormant bareroot bushes planted in well-drained, amended soils are ready to grow and need no fertilizer until after their first blooming period.

Planting Packaged Dormant Bushes

Remove dormant bushes packed in moist sphagnum moss from the box and treat them like bareroot bushes. Soak the roots in a bucket of water overnight or for a few hours before planting. Sometimes the directions recommend planting the entire box; ignore these directions. Roots will never push through the cardboard container.

Planting Container-Grown Bushes

Container-grown roses can be planted any time the ground is not frozen. First, water the plants well before planting. Dig planting holes about 24 inches wide and 18 inches deep. Be sure that each planting hole is large enough to easily accommodate the container. Give the rosebush plenty of room and avoid crowding the roots into a small planting hole. If beds have not been prepared in advance, add organic matter like compost to the planting hole and backfill with soil. Remove rosebushes from any type of container before planting. Loosen the soil at the bottom of the root ball. Plant each rose with the top of the root ball at the same level as it was in the container. Fill in soil around the root ball and water well. Finish filling in soil, firm it around the plant, make a saucer around the bush with soil, and water again. After planting, lightly fertilize container-grown roses with a balanced organic fertilizer to help them get established and keep their foliage green and healthy.

Transplanting Established Roses

Besides planting new roses, you may want to move a rose that's already growing on your property. Or a friend or neighbor may offer you a rosebush that's growing in their yard. The optimum time for moving rosebushes is in autumn or early spring, while plants are dormant. Before you begin digging, cut back the canes of everblooming roses such as hybrid teas and floribundas to about 12 to 18 inches. Cut back climbers and ramblers to about half their length and tie their canes together. Tie canes of species and old roses so that you can dig around them comfortably; some pruning may be needed to make moving easier. Any rose can be pruned hard to facilitate moving, but remember that climbers and once-blooming bushes take at least a year to build up blooming wood again.

After pruning, carefully dig a trench around the bush about 12 inches out from it and about 18 inches deep. Gently coax the plant out of the soil with a spading fork and comb the soil from its roots. Inspect the bushes and prune off any stubs of old canes and broken roots. Soak the roots in a bucket of water while preparing planting holes, then treat each plant as a dormant bareroot bush.

Planting Roses to Climb on Trees

One of the loveliest sights in any yard is a blooming rose spilling out of the branches of a tree. It's easy to create this gorgeous spectacle in your own yard with a climbing or rambling rose cultivar. Dig a planting hole 3 to 4 feet out from the tree trunk, where competition from large tree roots is somewhat reduced. Lay the bush in the hole so that its roots are pointing away from the trunk and its canes are angled toward it. Fill in with soil and water well. As the canes grow, guide them along bamboo sticks until they reach the trunk. Guide them up the trunk to the first crotch. After this, the climber or rambler will pull itself up by its prickles.

Training Roses to Climb into Trees

About 3 feet from the base of the tree, dig a planting hole 24 inches wide and 18 inches deep. Plant the rosebush with its canes angled toward the tree trunk. Fill in the soil and water well. Train canes along bamboo stakes set against the trunk at a 45° angle.

As plants grow, train canes by guiding them up the trunk on stakes until they reach the first crotch. After this, canes pull themselves up by their thorns and grow toward the light.

Chapter Three

ROSE CARE
AND MAINTENANCE

Rose care and maintenance is simpler than you think. For all their mystique, roses are basically flowering shrubs. Even planting rosebushes is pretty straightforward. If you've planted any shrub or other large plant, you know how to plant a rose. (For details on planting roses, see Chapter 2.) You'll learn everything you need to know about tending your roses in the following pages.

◀ *Lush, healthy roses are a pleasure to behold in any garden. The soft pink blooms of this thriving rambler are the perfect complement to the ornate, old-fashioned bench. With the proper care, your roses will look just as beautiful.*

Straw mulch

'Apothecary's Rose'

Mulch

Mulch beds with wood chips, shredded leaves, or straw in spring, spreading a 3-inch layer over the bed. The benefits of an organic mulch can't be overstated. The mulch retains soil moisture, suppresses weeds, and adds organic matter to the soil as it breaks down.

Irrigation

Water young plants and everblooming roses deeply at a rate of 1 inch per week if no rain falls. If you irrigate with sprinklers, water early enough for foliage to dry completely before nightfall, or you'll encourage fungal diseases. Overhead irrigation does have one benefit: It suppresses the mite population. Established species and old roses are relatively drought-resistant and generally can fend for themselves without additional water.

Fertilizer

Roses are heavy feeders, and they benefit from annual applications of complete organic fertilizers in early spring. Everblooming and reblooming roses should also be fertilized again after early-summer bloom to encourage repeat bloom.

A balanced organic fertilizer contains the three basic elements required for plant nutrition: nitrogen, phosphorus, and potassium (N-P-K). Nitrogen stimulates stem growth. Phosphorus aids in root establishment, photosynthesis, and flower production. Potassium provides plants with strong stems or canes, winter hardiness, and vigor. Plants also require calcium and magnesium in smaller amounts and trace elements typically found in soils that are rich in organic matter.

You can read the fertilizer analysis on the bag or box. It's listed as three numbers representing the percentage of N, P, and K in that fertilizer. For example, alfalfa meal has a fertilizer value of 5-1-2. In this case 5 percent is nitrogen, 1 percent is phosphorus, and 2 percent is potassium. Bonemeal has a fertilizer value of 0-12-0: It has no nitrogen or potassium but provides 12 percent phosphorus and also contains calcium. A complete fertilizer provides a supply of each element.

Packaged organic fertilizers that contain all three elements are available from garden centers, but you can easily mix your own. For example, mix 3 parts fish meal, 6 parts rock phosphate, and 6 parts greensand for a complete fertilizer. Spread 1 to 2 cups around each rosebush. You can also apply organic fertilizers separately. Many rose gardeners start off the growing season by applying 1 cup each of alfalfa meal, fish meal, bonemeal, and gypsum around each plant. Gypsum supplies calcium and conditions the soil. Spread the fertilizer around each bush in early spring and scratch it in with a hoe. Organic fertilizers are valuable sources of nutrients for roses; mix and match them, and watch your roses grow and bloom as never before.

Manure, Alfalfa, and Seaweed Teas

In addition to granular organic fertilizers, reblooming and everblooming roses benefit from monthly applications of liquid fertilizer. Seaweed or fish emulsion can be mixed with water and applied to each bush or sprayed on the foliage as directed on the label. Manure and alfalfa teas also make excellent liquid fertilizers. To make tea, put some manure in a cheesecloth or burlap bag and soak it in a trash can full of water overnight. Or soak several handfuls of alfalfa pellets to make a nutrient-rich tea. Water your rosebushes with 1 to 2 gallons of manure or alfalfa tea monthly.

Winter Protection

Protect roses in regions where winter temperatures drop below −10°F (Zones 4 to 5). Many gardeners in Zone 6 (where winter lows range between 0°F and −10°F) also protect their roses. (If you're not sure which hardiness zone you live in, check the map on page 188. Cold, drying winter winds and the freezing and thawing of the soil cause injury to roses such as hybrid teas, grandifloras, and most English and floribunda types. The graft union, or knuckle, which forms the crown of the plant, is the most important part of the bush to protect from winter injury. In addition, you should protect at least 8 to 12 inches of the rose canes.

Before applying winter protection to your plants, let the final blooms form seed heads (or hips) to signal the rose plant to begin dormancy. In late autumn, hybrid tea and grandiflora bushes can be cut back to a height of 4 feet, but no other pruning is recommended. Shortening the canes on tall cultivars prevents breakage from whipping winds during the winter months.

The simplest method of protection is to mound shredded bark, oak leaf mulch, pine needles, compost, or soil over the base of the plant to a height of 8 to 12 inches. But avoid materials that tend to become soggy, such as peat moss or maple leaves. Soil is probably the best insulator, but it must be hauled into the bed and removed in the spring. Double-shredded hardwood bark or oak leaves work well and can be spread as a mulch in the spring, adding valuable organic matter to the bed.

Make sure to protect tender old roses, including Chinas, Noisettes, and Bourbons such as 'Souvenir de la Malmaison'. Fasten climbers securely to their supports. Standards, or tree roses, should be wrapped in burlap to protect the aboveground graft union.

Protection against Common Pests and Diseases

Using Nontoxic Pesticides

Today there are many alternatives to toxic chemical pesticides, which pollute the environment and endanger the health of home gardeners. Nontoxic products, including insecticidal soap, neem extract, garden sulfur, baking soda, horticultural oil, and antitranspirants, are all safe, useful controls in the organic arsenal. Neem extract or insecticidal soap will effectively control most rose pests. Neem extract, sold as Margosan-O, Bioneem, or Benefit, is an insect growth regulator that prevents larvae from developing into adults; it is also an effective repellent for adults such as Japanese beetles. Used on rose foliage, it offers the added benefit of reducing powdery mildew and rust infections.

You can control black spot effectively with applications of baking soda combined with horticultural oil. Studies conducted at Cornell University show that weekly applications of Sunspray E6 horticultural oil (2½ tablespoons per 1 gallon of water) combined with

baking soda (3 teaspoons) control black spot and mildew on hybrid tea roses. Scientists think that the baking soda works because it raises the pH on the leaf surface, causing the environment to become more alkaline and therefore hostile to the germinating fungal spores. The oil helps the baking soda stick to the leaves. Use the horticultural oil at a reduced rate during hot, dry periods. Spray only in the early morning or on an overcast day, and keep plants well irrigated. You'll get even better control by replacing the horticultural oil with an antitranspirant.

Sulfur has been used as a fungicide on grapes and other fruit crops for generations; it is more effective than baking soda in controlling black spot. Apply flowable sulfur at rates recommended on the label and combine it with an antitranspirant. Using an antitranspirant, which spreads and holds the sulfur on the leaf surface, will improve and extend the effectiveness of this organic fungicide. Protect the foliage of black spot–susceptible roses by spraying at least twice monthly, beginning as soon as leaves emerge in spring. A disadvantage of sulfur is that it can cause leaf burn in hot, dry weather. In hot weather, apply the antitranspirant alone or add baking soda. Read all labels carefully and follow directions for application.

'Tausendschon' trained on a brick wall

Rose Pests

Here are ten of the worst rose pests, with simple organic controls for each pest.

Aphids on a rosebud

Aphids

Aphids are tiny, winged, pear-shaped, typically light green pests that cluster on flower buds and young shoot tips. Spray with neem extract or insecticidal soap.

Bristly Rose Slugs

These ½-inch green caterpillar-like sawfly larvae skeletonize rose leaves in spring. Spray with neem extract or insecticidal soap.

Cane Borers

These tiny, dark blue bees tunnel into the pith of pruned canes and lay eggs. In spring, prune back damaged canes to unharmed pith. Always make clean pruning cuts on rosebushes, and seal them with nail polish, white glue like Elmer's, or grafting wax to prevent egg laying.

Collecting Japanese beetles

Japanese Beetles

Metallic blue-green adults are ½ inch long. They feed on flowers and buds, and skeletonize leaves. Pick them off when they appear, or apply neem extract as a preventive spray to repel beetles. The repellent lasts for two to four weeks. Control beetle larvae, which are white grubs that live in the soil, by applying neem extract, predatory nematodes, or milky disease (also called milky spore) to lawns at recommended rates listed on the labels.

Leafhoppers

These small, greenish-yellow insects cause shoot tips and buds to appear discolored, slightly wilted, or seared. Spray with neem extract or insecticidal soap.

Mites

Tiny two-spotted spider mites cluster on the undersides of leaves and look like sugar crystals to the naked eye. The upper side of the leaves appears stippled with red or yellow; webs may be visible. Mite activity usually begins in early summer with the onset of hot weather. Dislodge the mites with a sharp spray of water. Spray with insecticidal soap, making sure you cover the undersides of leaves.

Rose Chafers

These ⅓-inch, slender, tan beetles feed on flowers during early-summer bloom. Pick them off or spray with neem extract or pyrethrin.

Rose midge damage

Rose Midges

Rose midges are tiny, white maggots. When midges infest roses, flower buds and shoots appear seared, and turn brown. Prune off buds and destroy them. Spray with insecticidal soap or use pyrethrin if insects persist.

Rose Stem Girdlers

These small, green beetles lay eggs under the bark. The grubs girdle the rose canes, causing swelling and splitting of the bark. Cut out the infected canes as you notice them. Susceptible species include the rugosa rose (*Rosa rugosa*) and Father Hugo's rose (*Rosa hugonis*).

Thrips

These tiny, black to brownish yellow, winged insects damage rosebuds and flowers—buds are bent and fail to open. Flowers look streaked and spotted. Typically, thrips prefer white and pink flowers. Apply neem extract or insecticidal soap to buds and flowers.

Rose Diseases

These diseases are the most troublesome on roses. As you can see, there are only four, and they're all fungal. By choosing resistant cultivars, using good cultural techniques, and becoming familiar with symptoms and controls, you'll have gone a long way toward disease-free roses.

Black Spot

This is the most serious disease problem affecting garden roses. Leaves develop black spots that turn yellow, and eventually the leaves drop from the bush. Because the fungal spores that cause this infection overwinter on the canes, pruning susceptible bushes (especially everblooming types) hard in early spring removes the spores. As soon as the leaves emerge in spring, protect the foliage with an organic fungicide. This early-season treatment is really effective at reducing the problem. Use sulfur, usually sold as wettable or flowable sulfur fungicide, or fungicidal soap, and follow the directions on the label. You can add an antitranspirant to extend the effectiveness of the fungicide. For disease-susceptible rose cultivars, reapply organic fungicide at least twice monthly to control black spot, or grow disease-free cultivars like 'Alba Semi-Plena', 'Stanwell Perpetual', and 'Madame Plantier'. Others are listed in the encyclopedia section, beginning on page 73.

Canker

This fungal disease produces sunken, brown areas on the canes that cause dieback to stems above. Prune off the canes that have become infected by canker and destroy them.

The Black Spot Story

Black spot is the most serious disease problem of garden roses. In order to combat this fungal disease, you must know your enemy and its life cycle in the garden.

Studies show that black spot spores overwinter on rose canes at the leaf nodes. Night temperatures in spring of about 60° to 65°F and spring rains are ideal conditions for spore germination. The spores are spread to emerging leaves by rainwater, but the spores must be continuously wet for at least seven hours for any infection to occur. In early summer, if no preventive spray has been applied to protect the leaves, distinctive black spots will appear on leaf surfaces of lower leaves. Thousands of spores will be released from these fruiting bodies, and the infection will spread to the upper leaves of the bushes and to neighboring bushes by splashing rainwater.

One of the best methods of control is hard pruning in spring to rid the bushes of disease spores overwintering on the canes. In addition, the application of an antifungal agent like baking soda or sulfur as soon as leaves emerge in spring is the most important and effective preventive treatment of the growing season. These two simple measures will effectively control rose black spot disease. Other tips to reduce black spot infection include avoiding planting in shaded locations because it takes longer for leaves to dry, allowing adequate space between bushes for air to circulate, and digging up and destroying black spot–prone cultivars that harbor spores and spread the disease to neighboring roses.

Susceptibility to black spot varies among individual rose cultivars and is affected by regional climatic conditions, particularly rainfall and humidity. All modern roses and many of the old roses are potentially susceptible to black spot. The term disease-resistant does not mean disease-free. Even disease-resistant roses can lose some leaves to black spot, particularly in a wet season, but typically they don't lose all of them. With minimal care, these roses will look good and perform well in an average garden.

If you are growing black spot–susceptible roses, including Bourbons, hybrid perpetuals, hybrid teas, grandifloras, and many floribunda,

(continued)

The Black Spot Story (continued)

English, China, and miniature roses, use a preventive program to get control. Prune bushes hard in spring, apply flowable sulfur combined with an antitranspirant when leaves emerge, and twice monthly thereafter, or use weekly applications of baking soda combined with horticultural oil. Once you have gained good control of the disease, it is possible to allow greater intervals between sprays. Monthly applications should allow even the most susceptible cultivars to hang on to most of their leaves and perhaps rebloom in autumn.

Black spot–prone climbers and bushes such as 'Peace', *Rosa foetida* var. *bicolor*, and the Bourbon 'Zephirine Drouhin' can't be severely pruned each spring like everblooming bush roses. The only method of control is application of a preventive spray as soon as leaves emerge in spring and at regular intervals.

Some gardeners take no preventive measures and allow disease-susceptible roses to drop all of their leaves. This is not a solution to the black spot problem. In fact, it aggravates it by harboring a source of the fungus that can continuously spread the infection to neighboring roses. If you do not intend to protect bushes from infection, it is best to remove the disease-prone culprits. For roses that exhibit good resistance, this minimal-care program provides a practical method to combat the disease.

Powdery mildew on hybrid tea rose leaves

Powdery Mildew

Leaves appear to be covered with white or gray powder. Climate and culture affect the spread of this fungal disease. Powdery mildew is generally more serious on greenhouse roses and on susceptible cultivars grown in southern gardens. Planting your roses in a part of the garden with good drainage and good air circulation, pruning to keep the rosebushes open, and not working around your roses when the leaves are wet will go a long way toward mildew control. Powdery mildew is also easy to control by spraying weekly with baking soda combined with horticultural oil while the disease is active. Neem oil also controls mildew and offers the added benefit of systemic protection lasting two to four weeks.

Rust

Orange bubbles appear on undersides of leaves and eventually spread to upper surfaces. This fungal disease is a regional problem generally confined to the western United States. Spray at regular intervals with garden sulfur as directed on the label. Neem oil also reduces rust infection.

Weed Control

Edge rose beds to prevent grass from creeping into them. A 3-inch layer of mulch really helps to suppress weeds. Hand pull weeds in small areas and hoe weeds in large areas to prevent them from flowering and setting seed. Persistent hand weeding or hoeing will

D e a l i n g   w i t h   D e e r

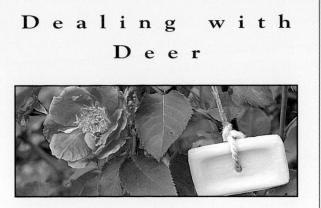

Bar of deodorant soap used as a deer deterrent

Roses are a favorite food of deer. During the growing season, deer eat rose shoots and buds, causing dwarfing and lack of flowering. Fencing is often recommended as a temporary solution to the deer feeding problem. Fencing is an effective measure to prevent deer from feeding on commercial field crops, fruits, nursery plants, botanical collections, and home garden vegetables and ornamentals.

At the Morris Arboretum of the University of Pennsylvania in Philadelphia, herds of deer decimate roses and yew hedges and threaten botanical collections throughout the 166-acre public garden and nursery fields. In an attempt to deter deer feeding in the 1-acre Arboretum rose garden, the staff experimented with the application of repellents, installed motion-sensitive lighting and alarms, and even put a Jack Russell terrier on patrol. All of these methods worked for a while, but eventually failed as a growing deer population exerted more and more pressure on the land. Finally, a 10-foot mesh fence proved to be an effective barrier for the 1-acre garden.

eventually rid the garden of all annual weeds and most noxious perennial weeds as well. You can also apply the organic herbicide Safer SharpShooter at recommended rates to control the most difficult perennial weeds, particularly in paving and when establishing new beds.

P r u n i n g
R o s e s   R i g h t

There is one rose-growing job that intimidates gardeners and often causes them to settle for some other plant. It's the prospect of pruning—the fear of cutting, wounding, or even killing your precious plant. Rose growers know, however, that when it comes to roses, pruning is the kindest cut. It rejuvenates the plants and helps reduce disease. Once we start, you'll quickly see that it isn't so bad.

Rose pruning becomes a manageable task once you understand why it needs to be done. The amount of pruning a rose requires, and the right time to do the job, differs from one type of rose to the next. In fact, there are some rose species that need virtually no pruning. There's nothing like the feeling of strolling through the rose bed armed with a pair of hand pruners, a folding saw, and the confidence that you'll use them correctly. Once you've reviewed the next few pages, you'll be ready.

Pruning is the best way to keep any rosebush healthy. Removing the oldest canes every year encourages the bush to produce vigorous young ones. With regular pruning, all canes will be replaced in three or four years for most roses. This rejuvenation cycle is much quicker with vigorous everblooming roses such as hybrid teas, floribundas, and miniatures, because severe annual pruning produces vigorous new canes that bear the flowers for the current growing season. It's always better to prune vigorous roses to keep them growing strongly than not to prune them. No matter what type of rose you're growing, don't be afraid of damaging the bushes by pruning them—roses are forgiving shrubs.

When to Prune

Timing is essential in rose pruning. The proper timing varies, depending on which kinds of roses you're growing.

Spring Pruning

Prune everblooming and reblooming roses while they are dormant in late winter or early spring, because their flowers are carried on the vigorous new wood that is produced each season. In the East and Midwest, spring pruning typically coincides with the flowering of forsythia.

Everblooming Roses

Everblooming bush roses include hybrid teas, grandifloras, floribundas, miniatures, polyanthas, and small Chinas and noisettes. These vigorous bushes benefit from severe pruning in late winter or early spring. Spring pruning encourages vigorous new growth, produces better flowers, and rids plants of many overwintering diseases and pests. The object is to rejuvenate bushes annually by removing dead, damaged, and diseased canes while opening up the center of the bush to air and sunlight.

General pruning techniques are similar for all everblooming and reblooming roses. Start by completely removing any protective mulch from the crowns of the bushes. Prune all canes damaged by winter injury or borers or from rubbing by neighboring canes. Damaged canes appear blackened, often with sunken areas, and are dried out. Cut them back to a lateral branch or to clean, healthy wood below the damaged area. Using sharp hand pruners, make clean cuts about ¼ inch above an outward-facing bud, slanting the cut slightly away from the bud. If a cane is dead to the base, you should remove it at the base by making a clean flush cut with hand pruners or a sharp saw.

As you work, you should begin to picture the pruned bush with its open, vase-shaped form made up of several strong canes. Select the best canes to support the season's flower display. Stout, healthy one- or two-year-old canes are the best scaffolding for your flowers. The bark of young, healthy canes looks smooth and green (or light reddish on deeply colored cultivars). The pith, or center of the cane, is white and crisp. Older canes are usually thicker, with weathered, rough, brown bark. Always favor stout one-year-old canes, and remove older ones. Clean out the center of the bushes, and remove any twiggy growth smaller than a pencil.

Tools

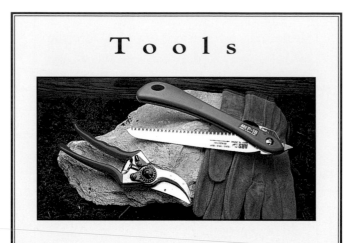

Always begin by assembling your pruning tools and accessories. These should include: a pair of leather or pigskin gloves to protect your hands from thorn pricks; a sharp pair of Felco No. 2 hand shears, or similar quality scissors-type pruner; a sharp ARS folding saw or equal-quality saw equipped with a short blade about 6 inches long that is easy to maneuver in dense bushes; jute for tying climbers; and a bottle of clear nail polish or white glue, like Elmer's, to seal pruning cuts. Pruning cuts provide the major entry for cane borers. The hard surface of the dried polymer coats the exposed pith or wood left after pruning and prevents entry of cane borer wasps.

In northern gardens, Mother Nature often decides how far canes need to be pruned back to rid the bush of winter-killed wood. Yet even in mild climates, all everblooming roses benefit from severe annual pruning. At that time, you should shorten canes to about three or four buds to promote new basal growth. When you're finished, your bushes should have an open, vase-shaped, balanced appearance made up of several stout, healthy one- or two-year-old canes. They should have been pruned hard to clean healthy wood, with the top bud facing outward so that growth is directed away from the center of the bush.

After pruning, seal all pruning cuts with nail polish or white glue to prevent cane borers from damaging the pith that's been exposed by pruning. This simple preventive measure works wonders. Clean up canes and old leaves and destroy them. Do not add them to your compost pile because they may harbor overwintering diseases and pests.

Keep in mind that the dormant pruning of hybrid tea and grandiflora roses is usually only the first pruning cut. Late frost may hit some of the upper buds and canes, but this damage won't show up until plants leaf out. Damaged canes produce spindly growth that quickly yellows, so prune these canes back to healthy wood.

Reblooming Shrub Roses

Prune reblooming shrubs to fit the space designed for them. Upright shrubs such as 'Carefree Wonder', and many English roses such as 'Graham Thomas', resemble grandiflora roses and are pruned the same way. If canes are not winter-injured and you want them to fill a space at the back of the border, prune them higher. Once you get a feel for how roses respond to pruning, you can decide how hard to prune them.

Reblooming shrubs such as hybrid rugosas, hybrid musks, damask perpetuals, Bourbons, and hybrid perpetuals benefit from moderate to hard pruning in late winter or early spring. Thin the mature bushes by

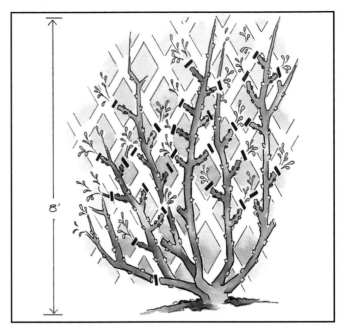

Pruning reblooming shrubs

removing about one-third of the older wood, reducing the canes to about one-half to two-thirds their length. Prune to outward-facing buds so that growth is directed away from the center of the bush.

With the more arching shrub roses, you can be flexible with your pruning to suit the space in your garden. For example, the hybrid musk rose 'Ballerina' is a floppy-stemmed shrub that can be pruned and trained to fill a variety of sites. 'Ballerina' is pruned back to 12 inches each spring at the Morris Arboretum of the University of Pennsylvania in Philadelphia to fill about a 3-foot position near the front of a border, where it mingles with perennials in an English-style cottage garden. But at the New York Botanical Garden in the Bronx, 'Ballerina' is given its head and reaches about 4 or 5 feet high and wide. And at the Brooklyn Botanic Garden in New York, 'Ballerina' is grown wrapped around a pillar and reaches 6 feet tall.

Rose Hedges

Roses make fine informal hedges. The shape of the hedge depends on the cultivar selected. For example, 'Carefree Wonder' makes an upright hedge, while the hybrid rugosa 'Frau Dagmar Hartopp' makes a lower, more spreading hedge. If you're training reblooming and once-blooming roses as hedges, prune them in late winter.

Begin training hedges when the plants are young, removing shoots that don't fit the desired hedge shape. As plants mature, remove a few of the oldest canes each year to encourage vigorous new growth. Try to keep the bottom of the hedge wider than the top so that light reaches the bottom branches. Clip the hedge each year in late winter or early spring to maintain its desired shape and size, and go over it again after flowering to remove any shoots that don't conform to the shape of the hedges.

Repeat-Blooming Climbers

Prune repeat-blooming climbers in early spring or late winter. Remove deadwood and enough of the older canes to make space for younger ones. Prune the lateral or side branches back to four buds. Tie up in new canes through the growing season, and continue to shorten laterals after each bloom.

Pruning repeat-blooming climbers

How to Cut Flowers

Hybrid tea, grandiflora, floribunda, and miniature roses make excellent cut flowers because they have relatively long stems. You will know that buds are ready to be cut when the sepals—the green leafy covering on flower buds—have folded down and some of the flower color is showing. Cut stems as if you were deadheading: Find a five-leaflet node and cut the flower stem to the desired length, making the cut about ¼ inch above an outward-facing leaflet. Cut flowers for the house in the early morning, and immediately place them in a bucket of water. Recut the stems underwater before placing them in a vase; dissolve a teaspoon of floral preservative or sugar in the water to provide carbohydrates and thereby extend the life of the flowers.

S u m m e r
P r u n i n g

Summer pruning for repeat-blooming roses mostly involves removing spent flowers. Once-blooming roses, species roses, and ramblers need their main pruning in early summer, soon after their bloom season is over.

Deadheading

After flowering cut off, or deadhead, the spent flowers of everblooming and reblooming roses to encourage repeat flowering. Prune back to at least the second five-leaflet node, making the cut ¼ inch above it. The strong buds at the remaining five-leaflet nodes will produce new flowering stems in about four to six weeks. Try to remove spent flower stems at an outward-facing leaflet to direct new growth away from the center of the bush. Tall cultivars can be pruned harder when deadheading to maintain a shapely bush. Treat miniature and polyantha roses like herbaceous perennials, shearing them back after each flowering period.

Once-Blooming Old Roses

Once-blooming old roses, including gallica, damask, alba, centifolia, and moss roses, are generally pruned after their flowers fade in early summer. Thin out about one-third of the older canes, and shorten stems that have just flowered by two-thirds their length. Dead, diseased, and damaged wood should be removed as soon as you see it. In spring, neaten bushes by removing wayward growth.

Species Roses

Mature species roses are easy to maintain by thinning out the oldest canes to make room for new shoots. After bloom, thin out one-third of the older canes and shorten canes by one-third their length. Allow arching shrubs such as wingthorn four-petal rose (*Rosa sericea* var. *pteracantha*) to grow in their characteristic vase-shaped form. Hybrids of species or shrub roses that

behave like species roses should be pruned the same way. Upright species and hybrids, such as *Rosa foetida* 'Harison's Yellow', can be pruned the same way as old roses. Suckering shrubs such as swamp rose (*Rosa palustris*), New England shining rose (*Rosa nitida*), and Virginia rose (*Rosa virginiana*) can be left to grow as they please or pruned to fit the space designed for them; rejuvenate these species by removing all of the canes to the crown and allowing the bushes to resprout.

Ramblers

The long, flexible canes of ramblers are best treated as biennials because new canes are produced each season from the crown. Prune canes that have already bloomed in summer after flowering. Shorten lateral or side branches that grow off the main canes to four buds. The vigorous new canes will bear next season's flowers. Tie the young canes to their supports with jute or other natural-fiber string. The flexible canes can be trained over arches or a split rail fence, wrapped around pillars, fanned out on trellises or walls, or trained into trees. Always leave enough canes to fill the space given to the rambler.

Once-Blooming Climbers

Prune once-blooming climbers as you prune ramblers— after flowering in early summer. Remove deadwood along with the oldest canes. Thin enough older wood to

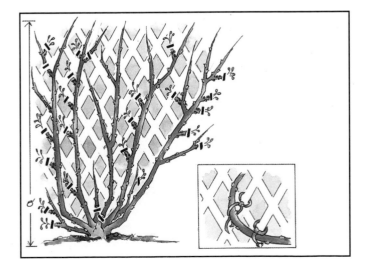

make space for younger healthy canes to take their place. Shorten the side branches or laterals that grow off the main canes to four buds. Train climbers horizontally or fan the canes out for best flower production. Tie the canes to their structure.

Pillar Roses

Many short climbers and floppy-stemmed old and modern shrubs can be trained on pillars. Make the support by sinking 10-foot-long rot-resistant posts or cedar logs 3 feet into the ground. Train roses as they grow by wrapping the canes around the pillar and tying them in place. Prune repeat-blooming pillar roses in late winter and once-blooming roses after their flowers fade in summer. Remove deadwood and older canes, and cut lateral shoots back to four buds. Deadhead reblooming pillar roses after blooms fade, cutting stems back to four buds.

Pegging Roses

Pegging is a training method in which the canes of arching or floppy-stemmed shrubs are pulled down and secured to the ground to form an arching, fountainlike effect. Bending the canes causes more lateral shoots to form and produces more flowers. Peg the flexible canes beginning in spring, and by the end of summer, strong upright shoots will appear. Cut out the older canes and train the young shoots in their place as the shrub matures. Each year, continue the process, bending and pegging new shoots to train them.

Pegged roses bloom heavily, so they appreciate a liberal topdressing with compost or well-rotted manure every year. Many of the old roses with floppy habits, including damask, centifolia, Bourbon, and hybrid perpetual roses, respond well to pegging. Roses such as 'Madame Isaac Pereire', 'Louise Odier', and 'Reine des Violettes' are also good subjects for pegging.

Caring for Roses: A Monthly Guide

This calendar lists months 1 through 12 rather than January through December, since the actual date will vary depending on your USDA Plant Hardiness Zone. (If you're not sure which hardiness zone you live in, check the map on page 188.)

For example, month 1 equals Zone 9, January; Zone 8, late January to February; Zone 7, late February to March; Zone 6, late March to April; Zone 5, April; and Zone 4, late April to May.

With this ingenious care guide, you'll always know exactly what to do, wherever you garden!

Month 1

Late Winter to Spring Pruning

Remove mulch or other protective materials completely, and expose crowns of rosebushes to light and air.

Hybrid teas, grandifloras, and floribundas: Prune out dead and damaged canes. Leave three to six healthy canes spaced in an open vase shape. Cut them back to clean wood, leaving three or four buds or about 6 to 10 inches. Prune to outward-facing buds, making cuts about ¼ inch above the bud. Clean up canes and old leaves that harbor overwintering diseases and pests, and destroy them.

Miniatures and polyanthas: Prune back to three or four buds or about 3 to 6 inches. Remove all twiggy growth, especially from the center.

Repeat-flowering old roses and shrubs: Remove deadwood and about one-third of the older canes; reduce by about one-third their length.

Repeat-flowering climbers: Remove deadwood and about one-third of the older canes. Reduce lateral branches to four buds. Tie canes to their support with jute.

First Fertilization

Spread 1 to 2 cups of prepared or homemade organic fertilizer around each bush and scratch it into the soil. Use a complete organic fertilizer equivalent to 4-6-3, or spread Milorganite at a rate of 5 pounds per 100 sq. ft., and greensand at a rate of 3 pounds per 100 sq. ft.

Spring Planting

Improve your soil by adding about one-third organic matter—well-rotted manure, compost, or Milorganite—to the planting hole and backfill.

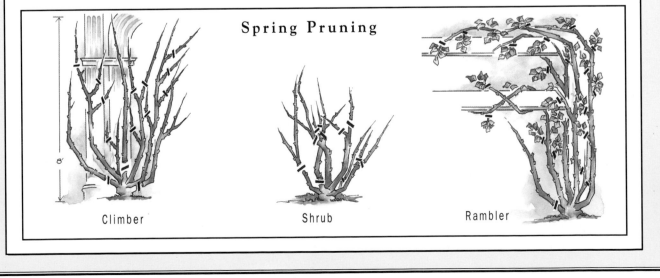

Spring Pruning

Climber   Shrub   Rambler

(continued)

Caring for Roses
(c o n t i n u e d)

Bareroot roses: Soak roots overnight in a bucket of water. Dig planting holes 24 inches wide and 18 inches deep. Form a mound of soil in the bottom of the hole and spread roots over it. Plant budded plants with the knuckle (graft union) at soil level (2 to 3 inches lower in cold climates). Backfill and water in well. Hill soil up around canes until new leaves emerge, then remove soil with a stream of water.

Months 2 to 12
Planting Container Roses
Plant container roses anytime the ground is not frozen. Dig planting holes about 24 inches wide and 18 inches deep. Amend soil with organic matter. Remove the bush from its container and plant it with the crown at the same level as in the container. Backfill and water in well. Spread about 1 cup of organic fertilizer around each bush.

Month 2
Mulch
Mulch with shredded leaves, wood chips, or pine needles to retain soil moisture.

Months 2 to 12
Disease and Pest Control
Black spot: Apply a preventive organic fungicide spray to black spot–susceptible roses as soon as leaves emerge. This is the most important and effective black spot control measure of the growing season. Black spot is effectively controlled with applications of Safer's fungicidal soap, flowable sulfur combined with an antitranspirant like Vapor-Gard, or baking soda combined with Sunspray E6 horticultural oil.

Inspect plants: Monitor plants for insect damage. Apply neem extract or insecticidal soap to control most rose pests.

Irrigation
Water young plants and everblooming roses deeply at a rate of 1 inch per week if no rain falls. If overhead watering is used, allow time for foliage to dry completely before nightfall. Most established species and old roses are relatively drought-resistant; mulch them and let them fend for themselves.

Foliar and Liquid Fertilization
Irrigate everblooming and reblooming roses with 1 to 2 gallons of manure or alfalfa tea monthly. Fish emulsion and seaweed also make excellent liquid fertilizers, or they can be applied as a foliar feed monthly.

Weed Control
Edge beds to prevent grass from creeping into them. Apply mulch 3 inches thick to smother weeds. Weed or hoe small weeds to prevent them from flowering and setting seed. Apply Safer SharpShooter at recommended rates to control perennial and annual weeds.

Month 3
Second Fertilization
Fertilize everblooming and reblooming roses and all newly planted bareroot bushes with an organic fertilizer equivalent to 4-6-3. Spread 1 to 2 cups around each bush and scratch it into the soil.

Summer Pruning

Once-blooming old roses such as gallicas, albas, damasks, centifolias, and moss roses: After flowering, thin out the bushes by cutting the oldest canes from the base, removing weak growth and shortening flowering shoots by one-third to leave a tidy appearance.

Ramblers and once-blooming climbers: After flowering, remove canes that have already bloomed. Tie in vigorous young canes that will bear next season's floral display and reduce lateral shoots to four buds.

Months 3 to 12

Deadheading and Cut Flowers

Deadheading: Remove spent blooms to at least the second five-leaflet node on the flower stem. Make cuts about ¼ inch above the leaflet. Strong buds at these nodes will produce another flower stem in five to six weeks. Discontinue deadheading about four weeks before hard frost. Simply pull off spent petals and leave the seed head (rose hip), signaling the plant to begin dormancy.

Cut flowers: Buds are ready for cutting when the green sepals covering the buds unfold and some color is showing. Cut long stems about ¼ inch above a five-leaflet node. Cut roses in the morning and immediately place the cut flowers in a bucket of water. Recut the stems underwater before placing in a vase with a floral preservative for longer vase life.

Deadheading

Month 8

Autumn Planting

Double dig beds or improve soil by adding about one-third organic matter to the planting hole and backfilling with soil. Well-rotted manure, compost, and Milorganite are all excellent soil conditioners.

Bareroot roses: Soak roots overnight in a bucket of water. Plant budded plants with the knuckle at soil level (lower in cold climates). Water well. Hill soil up around canes and leave it in place for winter.

Condition Soil

Top-dress beds with organic matter: Spread about 2 to 3 inches of compost, Milorganite, or rotted manure around the bushes and work it into the soil. Double dig the beds to prepare for spring planting.

Month 9

Winterizing

For gardens in Zones 4 to 6, where tender roses are susceptible to winter injury: Cut back hybrid tea and grandiflora roses to 4 feet to avoid damage to canes from whipping winter winds. Tie climbers securely to their supports.

Winter protection: In December, protect tender bushes including hybrid tea, grandiflora, floribunda, China, noisette, and Bourbon roses. Cover crowns with mulch, shredded oak leaves, pine needles, compost, or soil. Hill up to about 12 inches around the mulched crowns.

Months 10 to 12

During the winter months, order roses for spring planting. Plan new beds. Purchase tools and gardening supplies in preparation for spring.

Part
Two

Designing with Roses

'BRIDE'S DREAM'

'ALCHYMIST'

'CHINA DOLL'

◄ *The old roses mix beautifully with other roses and with many popular perennials, making garden design a breeze.*
Their exuberant flower displays are also handsomely set off against a simple backdrop of green foliage.

Chapter Four

USING ROSES IN YOUR LANDSCAPE

Whether antique or modern, roses provide rich color, delightful fragrance, and appealing texture to the home landscape. Roses can give a touch of elegance or a charming cottage appeal to your garden. Roses are such tough plants that they will shine in just about any sunny, well-drained spot. And there are beautiful roses for every

climate, so you can grow these favorite flowers no matter where you live.

You can bring out the best in roses by working them into your total landscape design or by building a garden bed around them. In fact, just a handful of well-placed roses can completely transform any landscape.

◄ *With sprays of blooms from spring to frost, modern floribunda roses provide a bright spot of color in mixed borders all season long.*
The showy bushes are covered with blooms and look great with companion perennials. Here, the pure white petals of 'Iceberg'
create a stunning display at the edge of a lawn.

"Tree" roses trained as standards

The trick to using roses in the landscape is to learn what makes each type of rose look best and to take advantage of the varied feelings different roses can bring to your garden. For example, you can create romantic scenes by using climbers and ramblers to cascade over walls or to cover sunny banks, hills, and slopes. Shrub roses can add mass and color to mixed borders and flower beds, or add beauty to your yard as hedges or foundation plantings. Try antique roses in herb beds, where their fragrance will mix with the many scents of the herbs. For a wilder look, naturalize species roses in meadows or plant them with wildflowers at the edge of woodlands. Or add a touch of class to decks and porches with displays of miniature roses cascading from baskets or urns.

As you plan and plant, you'll see your garden in a new light—a light that lets roses shine. You'll find that there are simple ways to show off your roses' best fea-

tures and minimize their shortcomings. Along the way, you'll gather the confidence you need to make the most of your roses.

Choosing Where to Plant Your Roses

It doesn't take a lot of studying to master the art of rose placement. In just a few pages, you'll learn the basics of how to evaluate your site and soil to enable you to choose the proper place for your roses. Then you'll find out which rose types are best for different uses, including mass plantings, as groundcovers for hillsides, on decks and patios, and more. If you're still stumped as to which type of rose will meet your landscaping needs, I've added tips on places you can go for ideas and inspiration.

Roses Need Sun

If there's one thing roses need, it's sunlight. Light is the critical element for healthy, vigorous rose growth. In shady situations, roses sulk, produce spindly canes, and don't set many flower buds. But give roses a half day (about six hours) of full sun and they'll reward you with peak performance and flower production. Full sun combined with good air circulation reduces disease problems because the foliage has a chance to dry after it rains. Not sure if you have enough sun for roses? If you're already growing a respectable crop of tomatoes, basil, and flowers such as marigolds, then those areas have enough light for roses. If your sunny deck, patio, or balcony is decorated with colorful pots of healthy, blooming geraniums, there's enough sunlight there for miniature roses in containers.

Of course, you can estimate the amount of sunlight by observing your yard in summer. Take note of which areas receive full sun, and count the hours of unimpeded sunshine. An ideal location for roses receives sun from morning through early afternoon, with shade deepening in the heat of mid- to late-afternoon.

If your yard is shaded by deciduous trees and receives lots of dappled light, it's worth taking a chance with some of the roses that tolerate shade. Try growing species and alba roses in dappled-shade situations similar to the edge of a woodland. These roses set their flower buds in spring before the trees leaf out and bloom in early summer. Or try training a rambler into one of your trees and let it make its way toward the light.

Soil for Roses

Once you have determined which areas of your garden provide enough light for successful rose growing, you are ready to think about the soil. Roses aren't fussy about soil type, as long as the soil is well drained and rich in organic matter like compost, shredded leaves, or well-rotted manure. Roses tolerate a pH of between 5.5 and 7.0, but like most flowers and vegetables they grow best in a slightly acidic soil with a pH of about 6.5. To find out more about creating a soil pH that's right for roses, see Chapter 2.

Sometimes the problem with your site is water—too much of it. To deal with a low, wet area where water collects, you can create raised beds to elevate the soil level until it drains properly. Or plant a bog garden using the swamp rose (*Rosa palustris*) or New England shining rose (*Rosa nitida*), both of which tolerate wet soil. Raised beds are also a good way to deal with very dry, rocky sites, where it is difficult to dig without the aid of earth-moving equipment.

Matching Roses to Your Landscape Needs

Once you have made the hard choices and have done the difficult work, it's time for the fun part—choosing the right roses. There are plenty of choices for both formal and informal gardening styles. Informal uses of roses abound: training climbers or ramblers into trees or over tool sheds and garages, pegging floppy-stemmed roses to the ground to create a fountain of bloom, massing landscape shrubs to create drifts of color, and using cascading groundcover roses to carpet sunny slopes and tumble over walls. In informal gardens, roses are great for turning eyesores into attractions.

Roses are often used as informal shrubs, but used as hedges, trained over stately arches and pergolas, or massed in parterres and neatly edged beds, they become part of the formal architecture of the garden. You can create colorful seasonal "walls" by planting a hedge or screen of shrub roses. Climbers and ramblers will drape and beautify existing garden structures, enclose a secret hideaway, or create a feeling of romantic lushness. Roses can be used to compose, enhance, and adorn outdoor spaces, garden rooms, and sitting areas to provide a private retreat from the bustle of daily life.

'Baronne Prévost'

Choosing the Right Roses for Your Garden

The following pages offer some suggestions of roses you can use to create different effects. You'll be happiest with your roses if you choose cultivars that meet your space and landscape needs.

Getting Ideas

One of the best ways to begin selecting roses for your home garden is to visit public gardens and municipal parks. Many public gardens display roses in demonstration gardens geared to the scale of the backyard. Even in municipal parks and gardens that display large masses of roses, you can often get excellent ideas on how to use roses in your own garden. Just take those plans and reduce them.

One good reason to visit public gardens and municipal parks is to see the mature size of the roses that you want to grow. Although hybrid tea and floribunda roses tend to stay put, especially with annual pruning, many species and old roses grow into very large shrubs. Knowing the mature size of particular roses is an important first step in basic garden design. Consult the encyclopedia section of this book, beginning on page 73, for the mature size of individual rose cultivars.

Adding Roses to Existing Beds

A simple way to get started with roses is to add them to existing beds. Many gardeners interplant fragrant old roses with vegetables, herbs, and flowers. This is a traditional use of roses that reminds us of medieval gardens. Fragrant blooms of gallica, damask, and alba roses, and the fragrant leaves and blooms of eglantine (*Rosa eglanteria*) add a touch of elegance even in the vegetable garden. The rose petals can be dried for use in potpourri, and dried hips make a tea that is rich in vitamin C.

Specimen roses make romantic accents in mixed borders. Some of the aristocratic species roses—*Rosa sericea* var. *pteracantha*, redleaved rose, and Moyes rose (*Rosa moyesii*)—also add structure and substance to the border in all seasons.

China roses are a must for mixed borders. The small, cupped flowers (usually in shades of pink or crimson) can always be counted on to contribute a spot of color to the fall border. The compact damask perpetuals 'Jacques Cartier' and 'Rose de Rescht' and the small Bourbon 'Souvenir de la Malmaison' are also easy to incorporate. Plant them in groups of three or more to create a mass or drift of fragrant, showy, seasonal blooms. These roses produce fragrant flowers in spring and repeat their bloom in late summer and fall. These charming shrubs mix well with other roses, perennials, and herbs.

Everblooming modern roses are available in a wide range of colors. Repeating their bloom throughout the season, they are fun and easy to include in flower borders. For nonstop bloom, use dwarf polyantha and miniature roses, grouping them in drifts of three to five plants near the front of the border. Informal, versatile floribundas are among the best of the everblooming types for home landscapes. You can choose cultivars in brilliant flame and scarlet hues for use in hot-colored "sunset" borders, or old-fashioned singles in light to deep pink tones that will blend nicely in soft, cool pastel borders, especially with antique roses.

Gardeners are continually challenged when trying to incorporate varying heights in beds and borders. Roses trained on pillars provide instant height without taking a lot of space. Simply install 10-foot posts made of rot-resistant wood and plant roses to wrap around them. Some of the floppy-stemmed old albas and damasks make excellent candidates for pillars. Plant clematis or honeysuckle vines to extend the bloom period. Train them to climb the pillar with the rose. For repeat bloom, swathe pillars with choice Bourbon, noisette, and tea roses. Modern, tough,

hardy Kordesii shrub roses, with their eye-catching brilliant red and yellow flowers, also make wonderful repeat-blooming pillar roses.

Climbers and Ramblers for Height

One of the easiest ways to get started with roses is to plant a few climbers or ramblers. All you need is a fence, wall, trellis, arbor, or even a tree. In full bloom, climbing and rambling roses provide a curtain of color in the garden. Trained over garden structures and walls, climbing roses can soften hard architectural lines, contribute height, or hide unsightly structures.

Climbers are excellent landscape roses for all gardens. Short repeat-blooming climbers can be trained on walls, tied to fences, and grown over arches to create height and interest while conserving space in small gardens.

Ramblers and some of the once-blooming climbers are best for larger spaces. Their long canes can easily reach the second story of a house. Most are rampant growers that scramble 12 to 20 feet or more. Besides adding interest to house walls, these roses are perfect for growing on medium-sized trees and covering unsightly garages, sheds and other buildings.

Groundcovers for Hillsides, Terraces, and Slopes

Mowing grass on a slope is both difficult and dangerous. On sunny slopes, vigorous groundcover roses provide a colorful, low-maintenance alternative to lawn. Choose spreading, creeping, and trailing roses such as memorial rose and its hybrids, the Meidiland™ series of landscape shrubs, the Pavement series of hybrid rugosa roses, climbing miniatures, and 'The Fairy'.

Hedges, Screens, and Mass Plantings

Roses make excellent, colorful informal hedges, mass plantings, screens, and foundation plantings. The rugged rugosa rose and its many superior hybrids make outstanding hedges and mass plantings because of their dense, arching, bushy habit; repeat bloom; showy hips; and salt

'Rosa Mundi' and 'Will Scarlet' edging a walkway

tolerance. Eglantine *(Rosa eglanteria)*, with its apple-scented foliage and scarlet hips, is traditionally used in hedgerows in Britain. Many other dense species roses and their hybrids make sturdy once-blooming hedges.

Old roses, particularly the dense, bushy albas and gallicas, are also good for hedges and mass plantings. For reblooming hedges and foundation plantings, use tall, bushy floribundas, hybrid musks, and care-free, hardy shrub roses such as 'Bonica', 'Carefree Wonder', 'William Baffin', and 'John Davis'.

Roses for Decks and Patios

All of the smaller roses can be grown in containers on a sunny deck, patio, or balcony. Miniature roses are especially good in containers, and they're available in a rainbow of colors. Other roses that do well in containers include polyanthas, small floribundas, groundcovers, and dwarf China roses. Choose a planter that suits the style of your deck, patio, or house—from rustic wood or terra-cotta planters to formal stone urns. With a group of containers, you can create an instant, easy-to-grow rose garden.

Roses for Entrances and Edgings along Paths and Drives

Add impact to your landscape by using roses around walks and entryways. Garlands of climbing roses tumbling, spilling, and cascading over a fence, arbor, gate, or porch provide a colorful welcome to your yard. Roses flowing out of urns, or a pair of weeping standard roses at an archway or doorway, create a focal point to mark the entry. Roses can also carpet sunny beds along walks, drives, and pathways to make a colorful edging. Miniature and polyantha roses are best for edgings. Other low, compact shrub roses for edging and massing include floribundas, groundcovers, and dwarf Chinas.

No matter what the size of your yard or the shape of your gardening dreams, you can find the right roses once you know how to look for them. For more inspiration turn to Chapter 5, where you'll find ready-made designs for different types of gardens that showcase gorgeous, hardy roses. Then take a look through the encyclopedia section, beginning on page 73, note your favorites, and set off on your way to a rosy future!

Growing Roses in Containers

If you want to grow roses in containers, choose a smaller type, especially miniature and polyantha roses. Climbing miniatures 'Jeanne Lajoie' and 'Red Cascade' will spill out of a pot or urn to provide a shower of blooms. Low-growing floribundas 'Showbiz', 'Class Act', and 'Sunsprite' are also good choices for planters. Maintain these bushes with a hard spring pruning each year to encourage a graceful habit in proportion to the planter size.

You can also use compact polyanthas such as 'Yesterday', 'The Fairy', 'Lavender Dream', and other groundcover roses if the planter is large enough. These larger roses should be pruned hard each spring to maintain a compact habit.

Choose a planter big enough to allow for root development throughout the season. A pot-bound plant is an unhappy plant that constantly dries out. Maintaining enough moisture is critical. A well-drained soil mix with plenty of organic matter and nutrients provides the best growing medium. For best results, use a thoroughly mixed combination of one-third pasteurized soil, one-third peat moss or compost, and one-third perlite.

Make sure the pot has several drainage holes, but cover them with clay pot shards or screening to prevent the medium from escaping. Fill the container with potting mixture, leaving about 2 inches of space below the rim for a top layer of mulch and room to irrigate. Water well. (Mulch will help to maintain soil moisture.) Fertilize monthly with a complete liquid fertilizer as directed on the label. Check the soil moisture frequently in hot, dry weather, and water as needed throughout the growing season. For best drainage and air circulation, raise pots by placing bricks under them.

In areas where temperatures drop below 0°F (Zone 6 and colder), sink the pots of roses into loose soil in the garden. Move larger pots into a cold frame, or protect them in place with the microfoam wrap used by nurseries. Before wrapping the planters or covering the cold frames, irrigate the soil well. On warm winter days, when the temperature climbs above 40°F, prop open the cold frames so that the planters do not heat up. Check the soil moisture throughout the winter. In spring, prune hard, mulch the planters, place them on the deck, patio, or balcony, and resume regular applications of liquid organic fertilizer.

Thornless and Nearly Thornless Climbers and Ramblers

'Zéphirine Drouhin'

'Tausendschon'

These roses will save wear and tear on your hands (or gloves). Because they don't have thorns to anchor them to their support, they'll need more help than other roses to stay put. Make sure to tie them every few feet to hold them on.

'Goldfinch'

Lady Banks rose (*Rosa banksiae* var. *banksiae*)

'Reine des Violettes'

'Tausendschon'

'Zéphirine Drouhin'

Best Groundcover Roses for Hillsides, Terraces, and Slopes

'Nozomi'

Blush/Pink
'Dwarf Pavement'
'The Fairy'
'Foxi Pavement'
'Frau Dagmar Hartopp'
Fuchsia Meidiland™
'Max Graf'
'Nozomi'
'Paulii Rosea'
Pearl Meidiland™
'Petite Pink'
'Pierette Pavement'
Pink Meidiland™
'Running Maid'
'Smarty'
'Stanwell Perpetual'
'Two Sisters'

Yellow
'Rise 'n' Shine Climbing'

Red/Orange
'Fiona'
'Ralph's Creeper'
'Red Cascade'
Red Meidiland™
Scarlet Meidiland™
'Scarlet Pavement'

A sloping spot covered with cascades of low-growing, spreading roses is an unforgettable sight. Groundcover roses can form thick, weed-suppressing clumps, protecting the soil and creating a beautiful landscape feature as well.

White
Alba Meidiland™
Memorial rose (*Rosa wichuraiana*)
'Paulii'
Rosa wichuraiana var. *poterifolia*
'Sea Foam'
'Snow Carpet'
'Snow Pavement'
'Temple Bells'
'White Bells'
White Meidiland™
'White Pavement'

Mauve
'Dart's Dash'
'Jeanne Lajoie'
'Lavender Dream'
'Purple Pavement'

Perennial Companions for Roses

Perennials with silver or purple foliage provide interesting contrast to both old-fashioned rose flowers in cool pink, white, and maroon shades and modern flame-colored flowers. Blue-flowered perennials look lovely with all roses and are especially attractive when grown in front of roses. Use low-growing perennials as flowering groundcovers around rosebushes, and plant larger perennials for tall accents. Here are some of the best perennials to grow with roses.

Perennials with Silver/White Foliage

Allium (*Allium senescens* 'Glaucum')

Artemisias (*Artemisia* 'Powis Castle', 'Huntingdon', 'Silver Mound', 'Valerie Finnis', 'Lambrook Silver', 'Silver Brocade')

'Bath's Pink' pinks (*Dianthus* 'Bath's Pink')

'Blue Beauty' rue (*Ruta graveolens* 'Blue Beauty')

'Bressingham Pink' thyme (*Thymus* 'Bressingham Pink')

Garden sages (*Salvia officinalis* 'Berggarten', 'Compacta')

'Hall's Woolly' woolly thyme (*Thymus pseudolanuginosus* 'Hall's Woolly')

Japanese painted fern (*Athyrium goeringianum* 'Pictum')

Jurisici's sage (*Salvia jurisicii*)

Lamb's-ears (*Stachys byzantina* 'Big Ears', 'Silver Carpet')

Lavender cotton (*Santolina chamaecyparissus*)

Rose campion (*Lychnis coronaria*)

Silver sage (*Salvia argentea*)

'Wisley Primrose' rock rose (*Helianthemum* 'Wisley Primrose')

Yarrows (*Achillea* 'Moonshine', 'Schwellenburg')

Perennials with Purple Foliage

Ajugas (*Ajuga* 'Bronze Beauty', 'Metallica Crispa', 'Catlin's Giant', 'Jungle Beauty')

'Herrenhausen' oregano (*Origanum laevigatum* 'Herrenhausen')

'Husker Red' foxglove penstemon (*Penstemon digitalis* 'Husker Red')

'Mohrchen' sedum (*Sedum* 'Mohrchen')

Delphiniums

'Palace Purple' heuchera (*Heuchera micrantha* var. *diversifolia* 'Palace Purple')

Purple-leaved setcreasea (*Setcreasea pallida* 'Purple Heart')

Purple sage (*Salvia officinalis* 'Purpurea')

Perennials with Blue/Violet Flowers

Arkansas blue star (*Amsonia hubrectii*)

Asters (*Aster* 'Alert', 'Lady in Blue', 'Purple Dome', 'Royal Opal')

Bluebell (*Campanula rotundifolia*)

Calamint (*Calamintha nepeta*)

Carpathian harebell (*Campanula carpatica*)

Catmints (*Nepeta × faassenii* 'Dropmore', 'Six Hills Giant')

Delphiniums (*Delphinium* spp.)

English lavenders (*Lavandula angustifolia* 'Hidcote', 'Munstead')

Frikart's aster (*Aster × frikartii*)

Great bellflower (*Campanula latifolia*)

'Homestead Purple' verbena (*Verbena* 'Homestead Purple')

Japanese iris (*Iris ensata*)

'Longin' Russian sage (*Perovskia atriplicifolia* 'Longin')

'Mariesii' balloon flower (*Platycodon grandiflorus* var. *mariesii*)

Meadow sage (*Salvia pratensis*)

Milky bellflower (*Campanula lactiflora*)

Moss verbena (*Verbena tenuisecta*)

Peach-leaved bellflower (*Campanula persicifolia*)

'Purple Rain' sage (*Salvia verticillata* 'Purple Rain')

Rabbit-ear iris (*Iris laevigata*)

Roof iris (*Iris tectorum*)

Serbian bellflower (*Campanula poscharskyana*)

Siberian irises (*Iris sibirica* 'Big Blue', 'Blue Brilliant', 'Caesar's Brother', 'Persimmon', 'Sky Wings')

'Souvenir d'André Chaudron' catmint (*Nepeta sibirica* 'Souvenir d'André Chaudron')

Spike lavender (*Lavandula latifolia*)

Veronicas (*Veronica* 'Goodness Grows', 'Sunny Border Blue')

Violets (*Viola* spp.)

Violet sages (*Salvia × superba* 'Blue Hill', 'Blue Queen', 'Lubeca', 'May Night')

Low-Growing Perennials

Allwood pinks (*Dianthus × allwoodii*)

Armenian cranesbill (*Geranium psilostemon*)

'Ballerina' grayleaf cranesbill (*Geranium cinereum* 'Ballerina')

'Biokovo' cranesbill (*Geranium × cantabrigiensis* 'Biokovo')

Blood-red geraniums (*Geranium sanguineum* 'Album', 'Max Frei', 'Purple Flame')

'Butterfly Blue' pincushion flower (*Scabiosa* 'Butterfly Blue')

Cheddar pinks (*Dianthus gratianopolitanus*)

Chinese anemone (*Anemone hupehensis*)

Dalmatian cranesbill (*Geranium dalmaticum*)

'Johnson's Blue' cranesbill (*Geranium ×* 'Johnson's Blue')

Lady's mantle (*Alchemilla mollis*)

Lilac cranesbill (*Geranium himalayense*)

(continued)

Perennial Companions
for Roses
(continued)

'Crete' pink lily

'Moonbeam' coreopsis
(*Coreopsis* 'Moonbeam')
Mountain mantle (*Alchemilla
alpina*)
Pinks (*Dianthus* 'Bath's Pink',
'Essex Witch', 'Kelsey Blue')
Pink-flowered showy
evening primrose (*Oenothera
speciosa* 'Rosea')
Rose verbena (*Verbena
canadensis*)

Snowdrop anemone
(*Anemone sylvestris*)
Sweet William (*Dianthus
barbatus*)
Thymes (*Thymus* spp.)
Violets (*Viola* spp.)
'Wargrave Pink'
cranesbill (*Geranium endressii*
'Wargrave Pink')
White-flowered mazus
(*Mazus reptans* var. *alba*)

White-flowered mourning
widow (*Geranium phaeum*
var. *album*)
Wild cranesbill (*Geranium
maculatum*)

Tall Perennials
Boltonia (*Boltonia asteroides*)
Brazilian vervain (*Verbena
bonariensis*)
Colewort (*Crambe cordifolia*)
Garden phlox (*Phlox panicu-
lata* 'David', 'Eva Cullum',
'Franz Schubert', 'Katherine')
Giant sea holly
(*Eryngium giganteum*)
Joe-Pye weed (*Eupatorium
purpureum*)
Kalimeris (*Kalimeris pinnafitida*)
Lavender mist (*Thalictrum
rochebrunianum*)
Lilies (*Lilium* cultivars)
Mulleins (*Verbascum* spp.)
'Nigra' hollyhock
(*Alcea rosea* 'Nigra')
Rattlesnake master (*Eryngium
yuccifolium*)
Sunflower heliopsis (*Heliopsis
helianthoides*)
'Taplow Blue' globe thistle
(*Echinops ritro* 'Taplow Blue')
White-flowered foxglove
(*Digitalis purpurea* 'Alba')

Shrubs and Vines to Grow with Roses

Shrubs and vines make excellent companions for roses. Choose flowering shrubs to complement the colors of your roses or to provide interest when the roses aren't in bloom. Vines also look wonderful when allowed to scramble up through rosebushes. Here are some of the best companion shrubs and vines for you to combine with your roses.

Shrubs

'Avalanche' Lemoine mock orange (*Philadelphus × lemoinei* 'Avalanche')

Bluebeards (*Caryopteris × clandonensis* 'Dark Knight', 'Longwood Blue')

'Blue Billow' bigleaf hydrangea (*Hydrangea macrophylla* 'Blue Billow')

'Blue Mist' dwarf fothergilla (*Fothergilla gardenii* 'Blue Mist')

Burkwood viburnum (*Viburnum × burkwoodii*)

Fountain buddleia (*Buddleia alternifolia*)

Fragrant viburnum (*Viburnum carlesii*)

Judd viburnum (*Viburnum × juddii*)

Orange-eye butterfly bushes (*Buddleia davidii* 'Lochinch', 'Nanho Blue', 'Nanho Purple', 'Black Knight')

Rose-of-Sharon (*Hibiscus syriacus* 'Diane', 'Blue Bird')

Silky dogwood (*Cornus amomum*)

'Silver and Gold' variegated golden-twig dogwood (*Cornus sericea* 'Silver and Gold')

Snowball hydrangea (*Hydrangea opulus*)

Sweet mock orange (*Philadelphus coronarius*)

Thunberg bush clovers (*Lespedeza thunbergii* 'Albiflora', 'Gibraltar')

Vanhoutte spirea (*Spiraea × vanhouttei*)

'Velvet Cloak' purple smoke tree (*Cotinus coggygria* 'Velvet Cloak')

Vines

Clematis (*Clematis*—large-flowered cultivars)

Golden clematis (*Clematis tangutica*)

Italian clematis (*Clematis viticella* cultivars)

Scarlet clematis (*Clematis texensis*)

'Nellie Moser' clematis

Trumpet honeysuckles (*Lonicera sempervirens* 'Cedar Lane', 'Magnifica', 'Sulphurea', 'Superba')

Virgin's bower (*Clematis virginiana*)

Chapter Five

SEVEN GREAT GARDEN DESIGNS

Even after you've decided to make roses part of your landscape, you might need a little help getting started. All of the possibilities can seem overwhelming. But you can simplify the process by deciding what kind of garden you want and using the plans in this chapter as guides. They'll give you specific ideas of what plants to use and where to place them. The designs have been created with color, plant form, and easy care in mind. But there's no need to slavishly follow them. Feel free to substitute your favorite plants in any of the following designs.

These seven designs are scaled to the small garden or backyard. They all include easy-care, hardy, disease-resistant roses of all types. Along with them you'll find suggestions for perennials, flowering shrubs, vines, and grasses that look particularly attractive with roses.

◀ *Garlands of roses cascading over a gazebo provide a lovely focal point in the summer garden. Roses add beauty to any type of garden, from sunny backyards to boggy streamsides. They can serve a practical purpose as well by screening sitting areas from nearby neighbors and the bustle of passersby.*

All of the designs (except the shade-tolerant wood-land garden) should be planted in full-sun sites that receive at least six hours of sunlight every day.

Choose a design that suits your garden site and your tastes. To make designing your garden as simple as possible, start with the roses suggested here, then move on to other roses and plants that strike your fancy. Go ahead and customize these plans however you like—you'll never lose with roses.

That's because roses are bursting with potential. Whether it's their gorgeous flowers, enchanting fragrance, or handsome plant form, roses are tailor-made for just about every garden style, as you'll see from the seven shown here. Roses are also extremely versatile: climbers spilling over a wall add the crowning touch to this cottage garden; shrub roses bring a relaxed, natural style to the mixed border; some of the antique "medicinal" roses (such as 'Apothecary's Rose') add a medieval cloister appeal to the herb garden; and dwarf and trailing roses mix beautifully with compact plants in the rock garden.

Roses can be tough and tenacious plants, too. Many of them are good candidates for difficult situations. Roses that tolerate heat and poor soils are perfect for city gardens, like the one shown on page 69. Salt-resistant species like rugosas fit naturally into the seaside garden. Species and once-blooming roses will often grow well in dappled shade and add early summer color to the woodland garden.

The Cottage Garden

A classic cottage garden may seem like an unplanned profusion of flowers spilling over each other. But there is an invisible order in the best cottage gardens. And that order starts with a strong backbone of roses. The following cottage garden plan is full to overflowing with easy-to-grow roses, clematis, perennials, biennials, and annuals.

Start with a vertical accent. Use the scented climbing roses 'Parade' and 'Eden Climber' to drape an existing wall, arch, or trellis. Or build a lattice tripod, as shown in the design, and combine creamy white roses with 'Henryi' clematis woven through for long-season bloom. For an extra-elegant look, erect pillars and wrap one with a 'White Cockade' rose, train Golden Showers® on another, and grow clematis over both.

Some of the best reblooming roses for small gardens are included in the plan. All of them combine beautifully with foxgloves, star of Persia alliums, and colewort, with its huge, billowing baby's-breath-like flower clusters. If you interplant the allium with fall-blooming Japanese anemones, the attractive foliage of the anemone plants will grow up and cover the allium leaves, which die back in summer. 'Honorine Jobert' is an excellent, late-blooming, pure white Japanese anemone. Annual cosmos and 'Miss Jekyll' love-in-a-mist also add their old-fashioned flowers to the late-spring and early-summer show, and they self-sow readily. The cottage garden style lets you allow for this element of chance and simply pull out or move seedlings to encourage a natural effect. To enhance the look, randomly plant seeds or seedlings of poppies in fall or early spring.

Some traditional, summer-blooming annuals belong in the cottage garden too. Colorful choices are cosmos tall Brazilian vervain, and low, spreading 'Imagination' verbena. Use the summer annuals to fill in for plants that die back after bloom, such as early cool-season annuals. For example, a spring planting of 'Miss Jekyll' love-in-a-mist followed by an early summer planting of 'Imagination' verbena will carry the show until frost. Similarly, cosmos planted around foxglove will give summer-long bloom. Perennials for late-summer and autumn flowers—when all of the roses are again giving a good show—include bluebeard, Japanese anemones, and tall, asterlike white boltonia. Spilling out of the bed are ground-hugging perennials, including fragrant cranesbill, 'Blue Hill' salvia, and 'Big Ears'—a lovely, giant-leaved, nonblooming lamb's-ears.

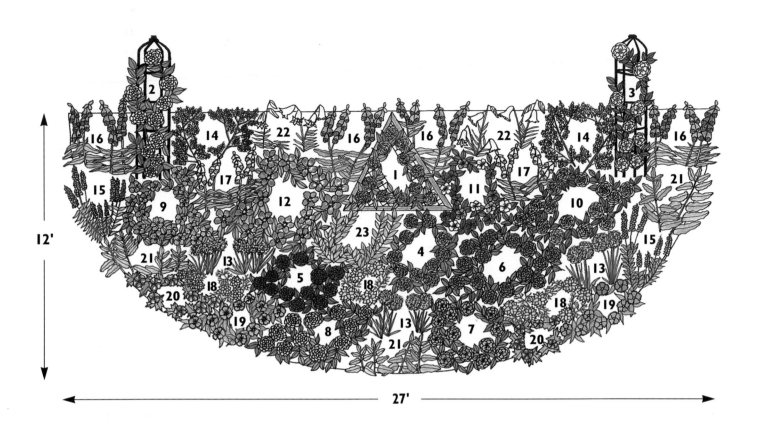

Plant List for the Cottage Garden

1. 'Eden Climber' rose (*Rosa* 'Eden Climber') or 'Parade'
rose (*Rosa* 'Parade')

2. 'White Cockade' rose (*Rosa* 'White Cockade')

3. Golden Showers® rose (*Rosa* Golden Showers®) or
'Venosa Violacea' Italian clematis (*Clematis viticella* 'Venosa
Violacea')

4. 'Jacques Cartier' rose (*Rosa* 'Jacques Cartier')

5. 'Rose de Rescht' rose (*Rosa* 'Rose de Rescht')

6. 'Gruss an Aachen' rose (*Rosa* 'Gruss an Aachen')

7. 'Baby Faurax' rose (*Rosa* 'Baby Faurax')

8. 'Marie Pavie' rose (*Rosa* 'Marie Pavie')

9. 'Betty Prior' rose (*Rosa* 'Betty Prior')

10. 'Stanwell Perpetual' rose (*Rosa* 'Stanwell
Perpetual')

11. 'Mutabilis' rose (*Rosa* 'Mutabilis')

12. Redleaved rose (*Rosa glauca*)

13. Star of Persia allium *(Allium christophii)* followed by
'Honorine Jobert' Japanese anemone (*Anemone
japonica* 'Honorine Jobert')

14. Colewort *(Crambe cordifolia)* followed by 'Snowbank'
boltonia (*Boltonia asteroides* 'Snowbank')

15. 'Blue Hill' salvia (*Salvia nemorosa* 'Blue Hill')

16. Foxglove (*Digitalis purpurea*) followed by 'Sensation
Mixed' cosmos (*Cosmos bipinnatus* 'Sensation Mixed')

17. White foxglove (*Digitalis purpurea* 'Alba') followed by
Brazilian vervain *(Verbena bonariensis)*

18. 'Miss Jekyll' love-in-a-mist (*Nigella damascena* 'Miss
Jekyll') followed by 'Imagination' verbena (*Verbena
*'Imagination')

19. 'Bath's Pink' pinks (*Dianthus* 'Bath's Pink')

20. 'Lancastriense' cranesbill (*Geranium sanguineum*
'Lancastriense')

21. 'Big Ears' lamb's-ears (*Stachys byzantina* 'Big Ears')

22. Regal lily *(Lilium regale)*

23. 'Dark Knight' bluebeard (*Caryopteris* × *clandonensis*
'Dark Knight')

The Herb Garden

You might not think to plant roses in an herb garden, but roses have been used as herbal plants for centuries. Coincidentally, they look right at home mixed in with culinary and ornamental herbs. In turn, the blue flowers and silver or colored foliage of herbs complement roses while providing additional fragrance and texture.

If you look at old herbals, you'll find the names of certain roses again and again. These are the ones you'll want to start with in your garden. 'Apothecary's Rose', an ancient medicinal plant, provides a delightful fragrance. The alba rose 'Suaveolens' has tradi-tionally been planted for its attar, or essential rose oil. 'Celsiana' was cherished for its sweet scent. The eglantine, or sweetbriar rose, has delightful, apple-scented foliage and a crop of small but showy red hips.

Train eglantine on a fence to manage its long canes. Underplant all of the roses with a tapestry of ornamental and culinary herbs, including 'Hopleys' marjoram, lemon thyme, purple sage, 'Hidcote' laven-der, lady's-mantle, 'Huntingdon' artemisia, bronze fennel, 'Blue Beauty' rue, and fragrant cottage pinks. Harvest the petals of sweetly scented roses along with lavender and leaves of sage and thyme to dry for pot-pourri. (See page 15 for complete instructions and a recipe for making potpourri.) For a smaller garden, just plant half of this design.

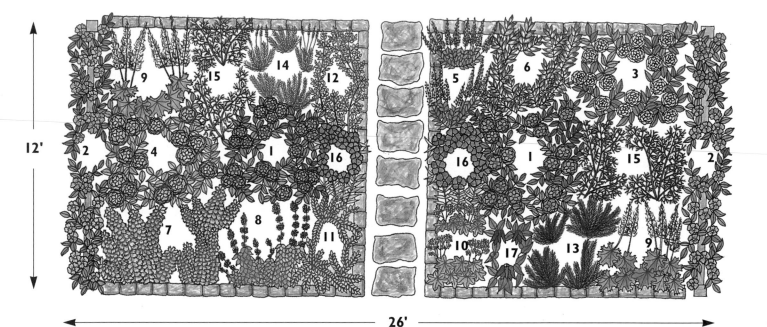

Plant List for the Herb Garden

1. 'Apothecary's Rose' (*Rosa gallica* var. *officinalis*)

2. Eglantine rose (*Rosa eglanteria*)

3. 'Suaveolens' rose (*Rosa* 'Suaveolens')

4. 'Celsiana' rose (*Rosa* 'Celsiana')

5. Calamint (*Calamintha nepetoides*)

6. Purple sage (*Salvia officinalis* 'Purpurea')

7. 'Huntingdon' artemisia (*Artemisia* 'Huntingdon')

8. 'Hopleys' marjoram (*Origanum laevigatum* 'Hopleys')

9. Plume poppy (*Macleaya cordata*)

10. Lady's-mantle (*Alchemilla mollis*)

11. Lemon thyme (*Thymus* x *citriodorus*)

12. 'Blue Beauty' rue (*Ruta graveolens* 'Blue Beauty')

13. 'Arp' rosemary (*Rosmarinus officinalis* 'Arp')

14. 'Hidcote' lavender (*Lavandula angustifolia* 'Hidcote')

15. Bronze fennel (*Foeniculum vulgare* var. *purpureum*)

16. 'Essex Witch' pinks (*Dianthus* 'Essex Witch')

17. Thai pepper (*Capsicum annuum* 'Thai Pepper')

T h e   R o c k G a r d e n

If you're intrigued and captivated by the diminutive flowers and form of miniature roses, there's no better way to show them off than in a rock garden. Dwarf roses grow well in the extremely well-drained soil of the rock garden. There, most seem to have fewer disease and pest problems. But miniatures aren't the only roses that are well suited to rock gardens. Polyantha, China, and groundcover roses—all of which are dwarf and prostrate types—are good choices to mix with rock garden plants. Many of the roses cascade and look particularly fine draped over a rock.

You have plenty of choices of perennials to grow with roses in a rock garden situation. Some of the most common rock garden plants are the most beautiful and easy to grow, including mountain pinks, candytuft, baby's-breath and rock rose. The small blooms and compact size of the rosebushes in this design match the scale of the other plants and provide all-season bloom.

This rock garden design is planned for a terrace. To customize it for a smaller space, you can plant one-half or even one-quarter of the design. For a flat but well-drained site, plant the whole garden or the top or bottom half as a low-growing border—perhaps at the top of a rock wall.

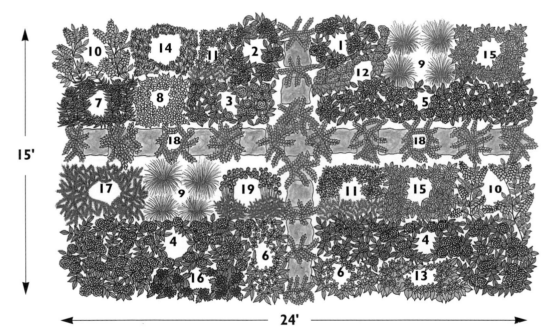

Plant List for the Rock Garden

1. 'Roulettii' rose (*Rosa* 'Roulettii')

2. 'Cinderella' rose (*Rosa* 'Cinderella')

3. 'Gourmet Popcorn' rose (*Rosa* 'Gourmet Popcorn')

4. 'The Fairy' rose (*Rosa* 'The Fairy')

5. Pearl Meidiland™ rose (*Rosa* Pearl Meidiland™)

6. 'Blue Hills' moss pinks (*Phlox subulata* 'Blue Hills')

7. 'Autumn Snow' candytuft (*Iberis sempervirens* 'Autumn Snow')

8. 'Wisley Primrose' rock rose (*Helianthemum* 'Wisley Primrose')

9. 'Elijah Blue' fescue (*Festuca cinerea* 'Elijah Blue')

10. 'Rose Carpet' indigo (*Indigofera tinctoria* 'Rose Carpet')

11. Anthemis (*Anthemis cupaniania*)

12. 'Vera Jameson' stonecrop (*Sedum* 'Vera Jameson')

13. Serbian bellflower (*Campanula poscharskyana*)

14. 'Viette's Dwarf' baby's-breath (*Gypsophila paniculata* 'Viette's Dwarf')

15. Cushion spurge (*Euphorbia polychroma*)

16. 'Homestead Purple' verbena (*Verbena* 'Homestead Purple')

17. Dwarf garden juniper (*Juniperus procumbens* var. *nana*)

18. Woolly thyme (*Thymus pseudolanuginosus*)

19. Lavender cotton (*Santolina chamaecyparissus*)

The Mixed Border

The mixed border is where your gardening imagination can run wild. There's a nearly unlimited realm of plants to choose from. And you can certainly find a wide variety of roses that fit right in. The mixed border can include a variety of shrubs, perennials, annuals, and bulbs selected to give a long season of bloom, interesting foliage, and architectural form. You can plant a hot-colored border where red, orange, and yellow flowers are set off by burgundy foliage, or go cool with white and pastel flowers. When considering roses, select those with an extended bloom period. Try 'Westerland' rose, trained on a tripod with sky blue 'Will Goodwin' clematis, along with the shrub rose 'Robusta' and everblooming flori-

bundas 'Showbiz' and 'Sunsprite'. The 'Geranium' Moyes' rose will be a centerpiece of the border with its blood red blooms followed by orange-red hips. 'Red Cascade' is a good choice for the edge of the border, where it will form an everblooming low mass.

In this mixed border, the perennial 'Kashmir Purple' Clark's geranium, yarrow, phlomis, oriental poppy, and Siberian catmint will bloom in early summer; daylilies, lilies, and goldenrod will flower through late summer. The annuals—musk mallow, annual butterfly weed, and dahlias—bloom after oriental poppies and lilies and continue flowering until frost. This garden requires little maintenance, but you'll need to keep the shrubs—purple smokebush, butterfly bush, and large-leaved elaeagnus—from outgrowing their space by pruning them back to the ground each spring.

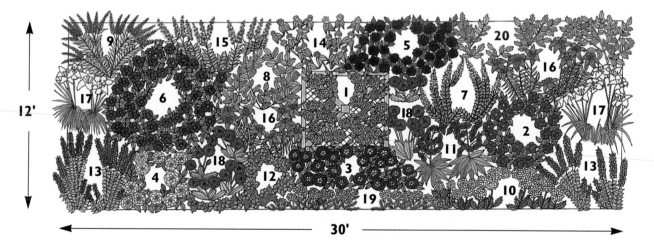

Plant List for the Mixed Border

1. 'Westerland' rose (*Rosa* 'Westerland') with 'Will Goodwin' clematis (*Clematis* 'Will Goodwin')
2. 'Robusta' rose (*Rosa* 'Robusta')
3. 'Showbiz' rose (*Rosa* 'Showbiz')
4. 'Sunsprite' rose (*Rosa* 'Sunsprite')
5. 'Red Cascade' rose (*Rosa* 'Red Cascade')
6. 'Geranium' Moyes' rose (*Rosa moyesii* 'Geranium')
7. 'Royal Purple' smokebush (*Cotinus coggygria* 'Royal Purple')
8. Large-leaved elaeagnus (*Elaeagnus macrophylla*)
9. 'Black Knight' butterfly bush (*Buddleia davidii* 'Black Knight')
10. 'Bishop of Llandaff' dahlia (*Dahlia* 'Bishop of Llandaff')
11. 'Fireglow' Griffith's spurge (*Euphorbia griffithi* 'Fireglow')
12. 'Kashmir Purple' Clark's geranium (*Geranium clarkei* 'Kashmir Purple')
13. 'Souvenir d'André Chaudron' Siberian catmint (*Nepeta sibirica* 'Souvenir d'André Chaudron')
14. Jerusalem sage (*Phlomis russelliana*)
15. 'Fireworks' goldenrod (*Solidago rugosa* 'Fireworks')
16. 'Enchantment' lily (*Lilium* 'Enchantment') followed by annual butterfly weed (*Asclepias curassavica*) or 'Red Shield' hibiscus (*Hibiscus acetosella* 'Red Shield')
17. 'Happy Returns' daylily (*Hemerocallis* 'Happy Returns')
18. 'Sundance' oriental poppy (*Papaver orientale* 'Sundance') followed by annual butterfly weed (*Asclepias curassavica*) or musk mallow (*Abelmoschus moschatus*)
19. 'Schwellenberg' yarrow (*Achillea* 'Schwellenburg')
20. 'Huntingdon' artemisia (*Artemisia* 'Huntingdon')

The City Garden

A center-city garden may seem like no place for a sensitive, bushy rose, but that couldn't be further from the truth. One or two rose plants can absolutely make an urban garden. There, both flowers and foliage are showcased.

In just a small, sunny space, you can create all-season interest with a planting of fragrant 'Frau Dagmar Hartopp' and a carpet of 'Snow Pavement' hybrid rugosa roses. Both are tough, hardy roses that bloom continuously, produce orange-red hips, and provide golden-bronze autumn foliage color. Add 'Karl Foerster' feather reed grass and drifts of 'Blue Spire' Russian sage, 'Autumn Joy' stonecrop, and deep violet-blue 'Persimmon' Siberian iris, and you've got an almost instant garden. For added color, use the scented climbing tea rose 'Sombreuil' to drape a background wall, fence, trellis, or pillar. In Zones 4 to 5, substitute the hardy alba rose 'Madame Plantier' for the climbing tea.

Plant List for the City Garden

1. 'Frau Dagmar Hartopp' rose (*Rosa* 'Frau Dagmar Hartopp')
2. 'Snow Pavement' rose (*Rosa* 'Snow Pavement')
3. 'Sombreuil' rose (*Rosa* 'Sombreuil') or 'Madame Plantier' rose (*Rosa* 'Madame Plantier')
4. 'Karl Foerster' feather reed grass (*Calamagrostis arundinacea* 'Karl Foerster')
5. 'Blue Spire' Russian sage (*Perovskia atriplicifolia* 'Blue Spire')
6. 'Autumn Joy' stonecrop (*Sedum* 'Autumn Joy')
7. 'Persimmon' Siberian iris (*Iris sibirica* 'Persimmon')

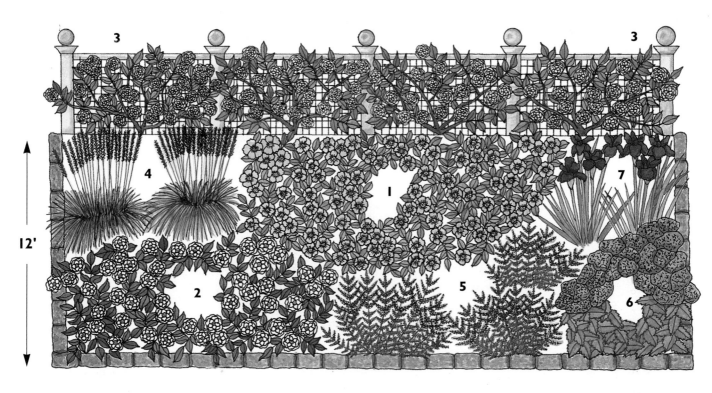

The Seaside Garden

There's no doubt that roses and salt air go together well. Just take a look at roses growing wild and flourishing along coastal dunes. In seaside gardens and where soils are mostly sandy, the "sea tomato rose" (*Rosa rugosa*)—named for its large, rounded, orange-red hips—and its excellent hybrids provide continuous flowers, autumn foliage color, and showy hips. In this plan, white rugosa roses are used as a hedge. Another good choice is Virginia rose, which naturally grows at the edge of salt marshes. In addition to summer flowers, the Virginia rose provides autumn foliage color and hips that contribute brilliant splashes of red through the winter months.

You can also use the red-flowered climbing roses 'John Cabot', Dortmund®, and 'Blaze' to drape a seaside fence. Include companions such as 'Morning Light' Japanese silver grass, with its fine-textured, silver leaves, and upright, blue-leaved 'Heavy Metal' switchgrass. Interplant flowering hydrangea and scented bayberry, and underplant with evergreen bearberry, everblooming coreopsis 'Moonbeam', and purple-leaved 'Mohrchen' stonecrop for all-season interest.

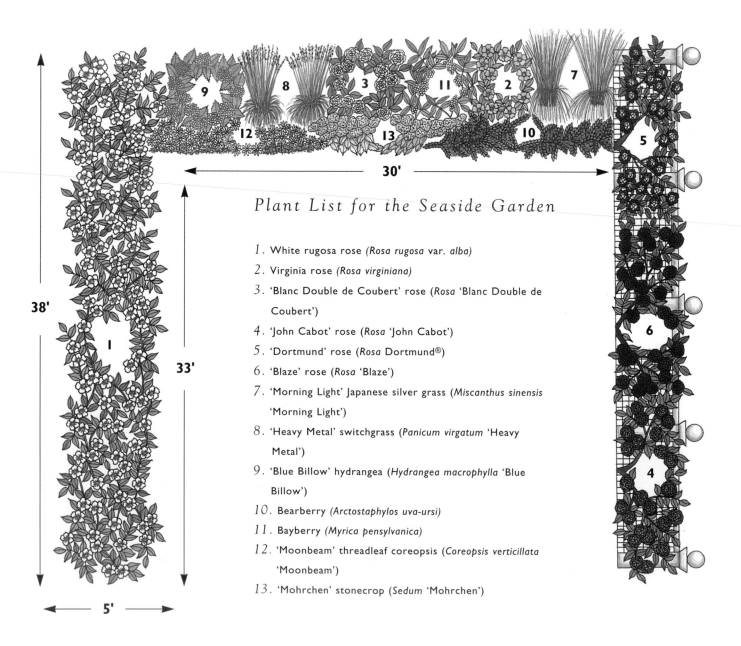

Plant List for the Seaside Garden

1. White rugosa rose (*Rosa rugosa* var. *alba*)

2. Virginia rose (*Rosa virginiana*)

3. 'Blanc Double de Coubert' rose (*Rosa* 'Blanc Double de Coubert')

4. 'John Cabot' rose (*Rosa* 'John Cabot')

5. 'Dortmund' rose (*Rosa* Dortmund®)

6. 'Blaze' rose (*Rosa* 'Blaze')

7. 'Morning Light' Japanese silver grass (*Miscanthus sinensis* 'Morning Light')

8. 'Heavy Metal' switchgrass (*Panicum virgatum* 'Heavy Metal')

9. 'Blue Billow' hydrangea (*Hydrangea macrophylla* 'Blue Billow')

10. Bearberry (*Arctostaphylos uva-ursi*)

11. Bayberry (*Myrica pensylvanica*)

12. 'Moonbeam' threadleaf coreopsis (*Coreopsis verticillata* 'Moonbeam')

13. 'Mohrchen' stonecrop (*Sedum* 'Mohrchen')

The Woodland Garden

There's nothing quite like the perfect bloom of a rose peeking out from the edge of the woodland in the shade cast from tall trees in dappled light. Species roses naturalize easily in this environment. The color seems even richer in the shade. The flowers seem more alluring seen against a deep green, leafy background. Combine incense rose, redleaved rose, and New England shining rose for a colorful show. Or train fragrant alba rose 'Madame Plantier' into a tree. (To find out how to train a climbing rose into a tree, see page 27.) For repeat bloom, include one shade-tolerant hybrid musk such as 'Penelope', 'Cornelia', or 'Ballerina'. These roses burst into bloom with pink flowers to provide a bright spot of color in shaded gardens.

Your woodland garden will approach perfection if you choose a succession of other shade-loving plants. Use royal azalea for colorful early bloom and mountain laurel for its showy June flowers. Surround shrubs with Japanese painted fern, Christmas fern, foamflower, and hellebores. In turn, underplant the ferns with wood hyacinths. Include kirengeshoma for late-summer flowers and bold foliage. Don't forget autumn foliage when making your choices. Royal azalea and New England shining rose provide the most stunning scarlet autumn color of all.

Plant List for the Woodland Garden

1. Incense rose (*Rosa primula*)
2. Redleaved rose (*Rosa glauca*)
3. New England shining rose (*Rosa nitida*)
4. 'Madame Plantier' rose (*Rosa* 'Madame Plantier')
5. 'Penelope', 'Cornelia', or 'Ballerina rose' (*Rosa* 'Penelope', 'Cornelia', or 'Ballerina')
6. Royal azalea (*Rhododendron schlippenbachii*)
7. Mountain laurel (*Kalmia latifolia*)
8. Japanese painted fern (*Athyrium nipponicum* 'Pictum')
9. Wherry foamflower (*Tiarella wherryi*)
10. Wood hyacinth, also called Spanish bluebell (*Hyacinthoides hispanicus*, formerly *Scilla campanulata* or *Endymion hispanicus*)
11. Christmas rose (*Helleborus niger*)
12. Kirengeshoma (*Kirengeshoma palmata*)

9'

23'

Part
Three

Encyclopedia
of Roses

'PLAYBOY'

'IMPATIENT'

'BARONNE PRÉVOST'

◀ *Roses add color, fragrance, texture, and a touch of elegance to the landscape. These lush, salmon-colored blooms growing up a wooden pergola create a lovely place to read or just relax. Whether you want a climber to adorn a trellis, a hedge to divide garden spaces, or a shrub to add to a mixed border, there's a rose that's right for you.*

'Agnes'

Cultivar Name:	'Agnes'
Classification:	Hybrid rugosa
Parentage:	*Rosa rugosa* × *Rosa foetida* var. *persiana*
Introduced:	Saunders, Canada; 1922
USDA Plant Hardiness Zones:	4 to 8

DESCRIPTION: 'Agnes' is one of the most beautiful and fragrant hybrid rugosa roses. Well-formed, soft yellow buds open to double, buff flowers with a delightful lemon fragrance. Plants bloom for several weeks in late spring with no repeat. Prickly canes are upright to arching, with small, leathery, dark green foliage that often appears bronzed and tattered by midsummer. Shrubs reach 5 feet tall and nearly as broad, although bushes can be maintained in an upright vase shape with pruning.

LANDSCAPE USES: To appreciate its flowers and perfume, plant 'Agnes' in the middle in a mixed border. Plant shrubs, reblooming roses, and later-blooming perennials in the foreground to hide the tattered foliage of 'Agnes' from view. One of the few hardy yellow roses, 'Agnes' is worth growing for its unique flower color and delicious scent.

CULTURE: 'Agnes' and other rugosa roses tolerate arid and poor soils as long as they are well drained. For best results, plant in a sunny location. Prune in late winter to shape and neaten: Reduce about one-third of the height and periodically remove older canes to keep plants growing vigorously. 'Agnes' is not recommended for Midwest gardens based on studies conducted at the University of Wisconsin-Madison, where black spot and winter dieback were reported.

DISEASE AND PEST PROBLEMS: 'Agnes' is susceptible to black spot in some regions. Leaves generally turn bronze by mid- to late-summer, but defoliation is variable. Don't try preventive spraying because hybrid rugosa roses are sensitive to foliar sprays and show their resentment by promptly dropping their leaves. Simply plant 'Agnes' in a border where perennials or shrubs will hide its ragged foliage from midsummer on.

Rosa rugosa and its hybrids are susceptible to rose stem girdler. Keep bushes free of deadwood and prune out canes that exhibit signs of the infection.

'Alba Semi-Plena'

Cultivar Name:	'Alba Semi-Plena'
Classification:	Alba
Parentage:	*Rosa alba* derivation
Introduced:	Cultivated before 1500 in Europe
USDA Plant Hardiness Zones:	3 to 8

DESCRIPTION: 'Alba Semi-Plena' is a very old alba rose that has been cultivated for centuries. It bears pure white flowers composed of eight to twelve petals, which open flat to reveal showy, golden stamens. Alba roses bloom in late spring to early summer with no repeat. The strongly perfumed, dainty flowers are followed by a fine crop of red hips in late summer. The shrub grows with a graceful habit reaching 6 feet tall and has upright, thorny canes and gray-green foliage. Fresh petals can be dried for use in potpourri.

LANDSCAPE USES: 'Alba Semi-Plena' is an extremely long-lived, stately old rose worthy of cultivation in modern gardens. Its size can be used to advantage as an espalier for a wall or fence, as a pillar rose, as a freestanding specimen shrub, and as an informal hedge. In mixed borders, wrap it up a pillar as an accent to contribute height, charming blooms, and effective hip display throughout autumn.

CULTURE: Plant 'Alba Semi-Plena' in well-drained soil in a sunny spot if you have one. However, alba roses tolerate some dappled afternoon shade better than most of the old roses. Top-dress with compost annually. Prune after flowering to keep the shrub in bounds and to maintain a graceful shape. Although a few alba roses can be grown in southern gardens, 'Alba Semi-Plena' is not recommended for the South (Zones 8 to 9).

DISEASE AND PEST PROBLEMS: 'Alba Semi-Plena' and its kin are extremely hardy and disease-free. Monitor for pest damage.

RELATED CULTIVARS: 'Maxima' (probably a sport of 'Alba Semi-Plena', to which it sometimes reverts; cultivated prior to 1500 in Europe) is a grand old rose, also known as 'Great Double White'. It bears very full double, soft blush flowers that change to creamy white and have an exquisite fragrance. Larger and more upright than 'Alba Semi-Plena', it makes a big bush, 6 to 8 feet tall and half as wide, with coarse, gray-green leaves. 'Maxima' can be trained the same way as 'Alba Semi-Plena' or grown as a freestanding shrub used to fill a position in the back of the shrub or mixed border.

'Suaveolens' (cultivated prior to 1750) produces extremely fragrant, pure white, semidouble flowers filled with a center of golden stamens. The floppy shrub reaches 5 to 6 feet tall and can be left to form a graceful arching bush or trained as a short climber or pillar rose. Flowers are harvested for attar of roses in the famous "Valley of the Roses" near Kazanlik, Bulgaria. 'Suaveolens' is worth growing for the intense perfume of its flowers, and it is a good choice for inclusion in an herb garden.

'Alchymist'

Cultivar Name:	**'Alchymist'**
Classification:	Shrub
Parentage:	'Golden Glow' × *Rosa eglanteria* hybrid
Introduced:	W. Kordes Söhne, Germany; 1956
USDA Plant Hardiness Zones:	5 to 9

DESCRIPTION: 'Alchymist' produces masses of very full double, old-fashioned, fragrant flowers that are a lovely blend of yellow and apricot. It blooms profusely in early summer with little or no repeat. This upright, vigorous shrub reaches 6 feet tall and wide; trained as a climber, it can be a bit taller. Heavy canes are very thorny; foliage is glossy, coppery, and clean.

LANDSCAPE USES: 'Alchymist' makes an excellent once-blooming climber or arching shrub. Very fragrant, apricot flowers look attractive with both antique and modern roses and perennials in the mixed border. Train 'Alchymist' on a wall, fence, or pillar at the back of the border so that it recedes from view when it is not in bloom. You can even grow a deep violet clematis woven through the rose as a color accent. Flower color, fragrance, old-fashioned charm, disease resistance, and better than average hardiness place this rose in a class by itself.

CULTURE: Plant 'Alchymist' in a sunny location in well-drained garden soil that has been amended with organic matter. If training as a climber, provide strong support for heavy canes. Top-dress with compost annually and fertilize in early spring with a complete organic fertilizer. Prune after flowering to keep in bounds and to encourage new growth.

DISEASE AND PEST PROBLEMS: 'Alchymist' has excellent resistance to black spot and mildew. However, black spot may show up during rainy periods. If so, apply a preventive spray of fungicidal soap or of garden sulfur combined with an antitranspirant to protect the foliage. Monitor plants for pest damage.

'Aloha'

Cultivar Name:	'Aloha'
Classification:	Climbing hybrid tea
Parentage:	'Mercedes Gallart' × 'New Dawn'
Introduced:	Boerner; Jackson & Perkins, United States; 1949
USDA Plant Hardiness Zones:	5 to 9

DESCRIPTION: Flowers of 'Aloha' are fragrant and medium pink; undersides of petals are darker. This climber is smothered in blooms in spring with excellent rebloom through summer and autumn. Arching canes reach 6 to 10 feet tall with glossy, clean leaves.

LANDSCAPE USES: 'Aloha' makes an excellent short climber or pillar rose. The large, cupped, very full blooms give an old-fashioned appearance that looks lovely in mixed borders with antique and modern roses and perennials. It can be pegged as a groundcover, and it looks especially striking spilling over a wall, where its beautiful, fragrant flowers can be shown to advantage.

CULTURE: Plant 'Aloha' in rich garden soil in full sun for best flower production. Top-dress with compost annually; fertilize in spring and again after flowering with a complete organic fertilizer. Prune in late winter to rid plants of dead, damaged, and older wood, and clip young sideshoots to four buds. Deadhead spent flowers to encourage repeat bloom.

DISEASE AND PEST PROBLEMS: Like its vigorous 'New Dawn' parent, 'Aloha' has excellent resistance to black spot and mildew. Monitor plants for pest damage.

Altissimo®

Cultivar Name:	Altissimo®
Classification:	Large-flowered climber
Parentage:	'Tenor' × seedling
Introduced:	Delbard-Chabert, France; 1966
USDA Plant Hardiness Zones:	5 to 9

DESCRIPTION: Altissimo®, an eye-catching climber, bears very large, single, cardinal red flowers with golden stamens. Its 5-inch, lightly scented, bright red blooms hold their color and are borne continuously. Vigorous, upright canes are covered with lustrous, dark green leaves and reach 8 to 10 feet tall.

LANDSCAPE USES: Use this climber as an accent plant to brighten a quiet, green corner of the garden, or as a freestanding shrub in a mixed border of hot colors. Altissimo® is suitable for use as a pillar rose, espaliered on a wall, and as a climber on a trellis or arch. You can also let it clamber into trees.

CULTURE: Plant Altissimo® in a sunny location in well-drained soil that has been amended with organic matter. Top-dress with compost annually. Prune while dormant to rid plants of dead and damaged wood. Leave healthy, robust, young canes, and cut back sideshoots to four buds. Fertilize in early spring and again after the first bloom with a complete organic fertilizer. Altissimo® is recommended for all regions.

DISEASE AND PEST PROBLEMS: Altissimo® is largely disease-resistant. However, you may need to protect new foliage in spring with fungicidal soap or with garden sulfur combined with an antitranspirant to prevent black spot. Reapply as needed to keep foliage clean. Monitor for insect damage.

'America'

Cultivar Name:	'America'
Classification:	Large-flowered climber
Parentage:	'Fragrant Cloud' × 'Tradition'
Introduced:	Warriner; Jackson & Perkins, United States; 1976 1976 All-America Rose Selection
USDA Plant Hardiness Zones:	5 to 9

DESCRIPTION: 'America' produces fragrant, salmon, hybrid tea–type flowers. One of the best short climbers for reliable repeat bloom, it has a bushy, upright habit, reaching 8 to 10 feet tall with glossy leaves. The single or clustered flowers hold their color and make good cut flowers. 'America' is one of the few climbing roses to be named as an All-America Rose Selection.

LANDSCAPE USES: 'America' makes an excellent pillar rose for perennial borders. Its salmon flowers blend easily with both cool pastels and hot sunset colors. It looks

particularly attractive with deep violet clematis woven through it. Try Jackman clematis (*Clematis* × *jackmanii*) for large, showy, violet flowers, or *Clematis viticella* 'Etoile Violette' for smaller blooms of the same color.

CULTURE: Plant 'America' in full sun in well-drained garden soil. Top-dress with compost annually; fertilize in spring and after the first flowering with a complete organic fertilizer. For the first two or three years, little pruning is required. Just tie the canes to their support and deadhead spent blooms. Prune mature plants in late winter each year, removing deadwood and crowded canes. Choose young, stocky canes to replace older ones, and reduce sideshoots to four buds. Deadhead spent blooms to encourage repeat bloom.

DISEASE AND PEST PROBLEMS: 'America' exhibits excellent disease resistance. However, black spot may strike under wet conditions. If you garden in a rainy area, protect foliage with fungicidal soap or with garden sulfur combined with an antitranspirant as soon as leaves emerge in early spring. Spray again if you see any signs of the disease. Monitor plants for insect damage.

'Apothecary's Rose'

Cultivar Name:	'Apothecary's Rose' (also called *Rosa gallica* var. *officinalis*)
Classification:	Gallica
Parentage:	Variety of *Rosa gallica*
Introduced:	Cultivated before 1600
USDA Plant Hardiness Zones:	3 to 8

DESCRIPTION: 'Apothecary's Rose' produces showy, semidouble flowers of light crimson that open flat to reveal golden yellow stamens. It produces a profusion of fragrant blooms in June with no repeat bloom; round red hips ripen in late summer. 'Apothecary's Rose' forms a small, twiggy, upright bush 3 feet tall and as wide. The foliage is rough and medium green. The flower petals are sometimes dried and used medicinally, so the plant is right at home in the medicinal or herb garden.

LANDSCAPE USES: One of the most beautiful antique roses for small gardens, 'Apothecary's Rose' also belongs in the herb garden, where its fragrant petals are appreciated. Consider growing this delightfully scented rose for use in potpourri. It combines particularly well with other antique roses and companion perennials such as foxglove and campanulas (bellflowers) in mixed borders. Underplant it with blue-leaved 'Bath's Pink' dianthus (*Dianthus* 'Bath's Pink') or the silver-leaved 'Big Ears' lamb's-ears (*Stachys* 'Big Ears') to create a handsome contrast to the rough, green leaves of 'Apothecary's Rose'. This rose's upright, twiggy growth also makes it an excellent candidate for use as a low, once-blooming hedge.

CULTURE: Like most gallicas, 'Apothecary's Rose' is easy to grow because it is vigorous and extremely hardy. Grow it in full sun or in a combination of full sun and very light afternoon shade from deciduous trees. Plant in well-drained organic soil and top-dress with compost annually. Fertilize in spring with a complete organic fertilizer. Prune after flowering to shape and reduce crowded stems. In spring, trim bushes lightly to remove old seed heads and deadwood and to maintain the hedge shape. 'Apothecary's Rose' is recommended for all regions.

DISEASE AND PEST PROBLEMS: 'Apothecary's Rose' exhibits good resistance to black spot, but mildew can be a problem in the autumn. At the first sign of this disease, spray foliage with fungicidal soap or with horticultural oil at a rate of 1 to 2 tablespoons per 1 gallon of water; reapply as necessary. Monitor plants for insect damage.

RELATED CULTIVARS: 'Rosa Mundi' (*Rosa gallica* var. *versicolor*; a sport of 'Apothecary's Rose') bears remarkable, semidouble flowers of deep pink to light crimson with various patterns of white stripes. Each flower looks hand painted. In all other respects, 'Rosa Mundi' is identical to 'Apothecary's Rose'. Double the fragrant blooms in your garden by growing both of these charming roses.

'Apricot Nectar'

Cultivar Name:	**'Apricot Nectar'**
Classification:	Floribunda
Parentage:	Seedling × 'Spartan'
Introduced:	Boerner; Jackson & Perkins, United States; 1965 1966 All-America Rose Selection
USDA Plant Hardiness Zones:	5 to 9

DESCRIPTION: 'Apricot Nectar' produces clusters of large, double, apricot-rose flowers with a fruity fragrance. Blooms are produced continuously on bushy, vigorous shrubs that are 3 feet tall, 2 feet wide, and covered with glossy, clean foliage.

LANDSCAPE USES: 'Apricot Nectar' is a choice floribunda suitable for use as a specimen or in a mass or foundation planting. In mixed borders, its pastel flowers mingle easily with perennials and other shrubs. Plant it in drifts of three or more bushes to make a mass of all-season bloom. The blossoms make excellent cut flowers.

CULTURE: Plant 'Apricot Nectar' in a sunny location in well-drained soil that has been amended with organic matter. Prune severely in late winter or early spring to rid plants of overwintering disease spores and to encourage vigorous new growth. Don't be afraid to cut canes back by about two-thirds of their length. Fertilize after pruning and again after the first bloom with a complete organic fertilizer. Top-dress with compost annually. Deadhead spent blooms through the season. Apply a mound of mulch to cover the graft union to protect it from winter injury in Zone 5. 'Apricot Nectar' is recommended for all regions.

DISEASE AND PEST PROBLEMS: 'Apricot Nectar' is moderately disease-resistant. Apply fungicidal soap or garden sulfur combined with an antitranspirant as soon as leaves emerge in spring to prevent black spot; monitor plants and reapply at least monthly thereafter. Monitor insect feeding, and apply insecticidal soap as needed to prevent damage to buds and leaves.

'Baby Faurax'

Cultivar Name:	'Baby Faurax'
Classification:	Polyantha
Parentage:	Not recorded
Introduced:	Lille, France; 1924
USDA Plant Hardiness Zones:	5 to 9

DESCRIPTION: One of the few purple-flowering modern roses, 'Baby Faurax' bears large sprays of fragrant blooms; each exquisite sweetheart blossom is small, double, and violet-mauve, opening flat to reveal a yellow center. The bushy plants are 18 inches tall and 12 inches wide. They are continuously covered with blooms.

LANDSCAPE USES: 'Baby Faurax' creates drifts of all-season color in the foreground of mixed borders. Plant in groups of three to five to form a small mass. To make a lovely garden picture, combine 'Baby Faurax' with red-leaved rose (*Rosa glauca*), the lavender globes of giant onion (*Allium giganteum*), spiky larkspur, and an underplanting of 'Butterfly Blue' scabiosa (*Scabiosa* 'Butterfly Blue'). The dwarf, bushy shrubs are also suitable for low edging and containers.

CULTURE: Plant in full sun in well-drained soil that has been amended with plenty of organic matter. Prune at bud break, removing about two-thirds of top growth. Shear the flowering stems after each bloom period to encourage successive flowering. Top-dress with well-rotted manure or compost annually. Fertilize after pruning and again after the first bloom with a complete organic fertilizer to stimulate continuous flower production. 'Baby Faurax' is highly recommended for all regions.

DISEASE AND PEST PROBLEMS: 'Baby Faurax' possesses excellent disease resistance. However, to be safe, apply fungicidal soap or garden sulfur combined with an antitranspirant (or an antitranspirant alone) when leaves emerge in spring; reapply as needed. Small-leaved roses are sometimes bothered by spider mites. If you spot these tiny pests, spray the undersides of leaves with a high-pressure burst of water to dislodge them. Monitor the plants, and apply insecticidal soap if water alone doesn't solve the problem.

'Ballerina'

Cultivar Name:	'Ballerina'
Classification:	Hybrid musk
Parentage:	Not recorded
Introduced:	Bentall, United Kingdom; 1937
USDA Plant Hardiness Zones:	5 to 9

DESCRIPTION: Treasured for its dainty flowers, 'Ballerina' is covered with large clusters of five-petaled, pink flowers. Each flower has a white center filled with deep yellow stamens. Abundant spring bloom is followed by scattered summer bloom and showy autumn repeat bloom. Multiflora rose influence is clearly evident in both the flower form and prickly, flexible canes. Shrubs left unpruned eventually mound to 5 feet tall and wide. With an annual hard pruning, 'Ballerina' forms a prostrate bush 3 feet tall and wide. Trained as a pillar rose or short climber, it stretches to 6 feet tall.

LANDSCAPE USES: This versatile rose makes a beautiful and effective display in mixed borders. It can be pruned hard and grown near the front of the border, underplanted with silver-leaved perennials such as santolina and lamb's-ears. Or 'Ballerina' can be pruned into an exquisite pillar rose and incorporated into the middle or back of mixed beds to conserve space and provide height. Try training a delicate purple *Clematis viticella* to grow up through it.

CULTURE: Plant in a sunny location in well-drained soil that has been amended with organic matter. Prune hard while dormant, cutting the plants back by about one-half to maintain compact growth. Prune lightly for big bushes. Prune climbers to remove older canes, and cut back the sideshoots to four buds. Fertilize after pruning and again after first bloom with a complete organic fertilizer. Top-dress with compost annually. 'Ballerina' is highly recommended for all regions.

DISEASE AND PEST PROBLEMS: 'Ballerina' is resistant to black spot and mildew. However, if either problem strikes, protect the foliage with an application of fungicidal soap or garden sulfur combined with an anti-transpirant. Monitor the plants for insect damage.

RELATED CULTIVARS: Marjorie Fair® ('Ballerina' × 'Baby Faurax'; Harkness, United Kingdom; 1977), also known as 'Red Ballerina', bears large clusters of single, crimson flowers, each with a distinctive white eye. Flowers are slightly fragrant and produced continuously. Vigorous bushes are covered with small, semiglossy foliage and grow 3 feet tall and wide.

Rush® (['Ballerina' × 'Britannia'] × *R. multiflora*; Lens, Belgium; 1983) is a handsome shrub with all the charm of 'Ballerina' but with larger, fragrant flowers. Massive clusters of dark pink buds open to five-petaled flowers that are pink with a white eye. There is a generous repeat bloom. Rush® makes an upright, bushy shrub 4 feet tall and 3 feet wide, covered with glossy leaves.

Sally Holmes® ('Ivory Fashion' × 'Ballerina'; Holmes, United Kingdom; 1976) combines the best traits of both of its famous parents. It produces large clusters of lightly scented, five-petaled, cream blooms with golden stamens throughout the season. Covered with dark green, glossy foliage, these vigorous shrubs grow 4 feet tall and 3 feet wide.

'Baronne Prévost'

Cultivar Name:	**'Baronne Prévost'**
Classification:	Hybrid perpetual
Parentage:	Not recorded
Introduced:	Desprez, France; 1842
USDA Plant Hardiness Zones:	4 to 8

DESCRIPTION: One of the early members of the hybrid perpetual class, 'Baronne Prévost' maintains some of the characteristics of its perpetual damask kin, including the rich damask perfume. Round, light crimson buds open to large, very full, quartered, rose-pink flowers with lilac shading. The heavy spring bloom is followed by scattered summer bloom and showy autumn repeat bloom. The plant itself has very prickly canes with plentiful coarse, dark green leaves, forming an upright, bushy shrub to 5 feet tall and 3 feet wide.

LANDSCAPE USES: 'Baronne Prévost' mingles nicely with other antique roses and companion perennials. In mixed borders, plant in a midground position where its perfumed flowers can be appreciated. 'Baronne Prévost' looks particularly fine combined with rich crimson-violet gallicas and blue-flowered perennials such as 'Dropmore' catmint (*Nepeta* × *faassenii* 'Dropmore') or 'Blue Hill' violet sage

(*Salvia* × *superba* 'Blue Hill'). An underplanting of silver-leaved lamb's-ears (*Stachys byzantina* 'Big Ears') sets off its rich pink blooms. 'Baronne Prévost' produces long canes that can be pegged to the ground, if space permits, to encourage abundant flower production. It can also be trained as a short pillar rose.

CULTURE: Plant in full sun in well-drained soil that has been liberally amended with organic matter. Prune while dormant: Remove older wood and prune remaining canes by one-half to two-thirds their length. Fertilize after ptunning and again after first flowering to encourage repeat bloom, and irrigate as needed. After the first bloom, deadhead spent flowers and reduce long shoots. Top-dress with compost or rotted manure annually. Recommended for all regions (and provide some winter protection in Zones 4 and 5).

DISEASE AND PEST PROBLEMS: Like most hybrid perpetual roses, 'Baronne Prévost' is susceptible to black spot and mildew. Apply fungicidal soap or garden sulfur combined with an antitranspirant as soon as leaves emerge in spring to prevent black spot. Monitor plants and reapply as needed thereafter. Check regularly for signs of insect feeding.

Cultivar Name:	**'Belle Poitevine'**
Classification:	Hybrid rugosa
Parentage:	Not recorded
Introduced:	Bruant, France; 1894
USDA Plant Hardiness Zones:	4 to 8

DESCRIPTION: 'Belle Poitevine' has abundant, large, semidouble, mauve-pink flowers, each with a center of showy, yellow stamens. The fragrant flowers repeat their bloom throughout summer and autumn but without fruit set. Bushes are dense and compact, growing 3 to 4 feet tall and wide. The medium green, deeply veined foliage changes to golden bronze in autumn.

LANDSCAPE USES: Use 'Belle Poitevine' as an effective low hedge, mass, or specimen shrub. Its massive spring bloom, followed by repeat bloom and autumn foliage color, make it an all-season shrub. In mixed borders, its cool flower color mingles easily with antique and modern roses, perennials, and herbs.

CULTURE: Plant 'Belle Poitevine' in a well-drained, sunny site. Top-dress with compost annually. Prune in late winter, removing deadwood and reducing canes by about one-third to shape the plant. Occasionally remove older canes to reduce crowding and to encourage new growth. 'Belle Poitevine' is recommended for all regions within Zones 4 to 8.

DISEASE AND PEST PROBLEMS: Rugosa hybrids, closely akin to the native species, are durable, disease-free shrubs. However, summer flowers sometimes attract Japanese beetles. If adults appear, pick them off and treat lawn areas with milky disease spores to control grubs. *Rosa rugosa* and its hybrids are susceptible to rose stem girdler. Keep plants free of deadwood, and prune out and destroy infected canes.

'Belle Poitevine'

'Betty Prior'

Cultivar Name:	**'Betty Prior'**
Classification:	Floribunda
Parentage:	'Kirsten Poulsen' × seedling
Introduced:	Prior, United Kingdom; 1935; Jackson & Perkins, United States; 1938
USDA Plant Hardiness Zones:	5 to 9

DESCRIPTION: 'Betty Prior' is one of the charming old-fashioned floribunda roses that are workhorses in modern gardens. Flowers are single, carmine-pink, slightly fragrant, and produced in clusters. Rarely out of bloom, the shrubs grow 4 feet tall and 3 feet wide.

LANDSCAPE USES: 'Betty Prior' shines in a mass or foundation planting or as a hedge or specimen. In mixed borders, its abundant flowers provide a colorful accent and combine well with perennials and other shrubs. Plant it in combination with 'The Fairy' rose, 'Blue Hill' salvia (*Salvia nemorosa* 'Blue Hill') and gray-leaved 'Huntingdon' artemisia (*Artemisia* 'Huntingdon') for all-season bloom.

CULTURE: Plant in a sunny location in well-drained soil that has been amended with organic matter. Prune hard while dormant to encourage vigorous new growth. To make a hedge, plant every 3 feet—the bushes will be touching in three years. Shape hedges of this rose by removing about one-third of the top growth; maintain the form by periodically cleaning out some of the older canes.

Fertilize after pruning and again after the first bloom with a complete organic fertilizer. Top-dress with compost annually. Deadhead spent blooms through the season. Don't fuss too much with maintenance, though. Forgotten 'Betty Prior' bushes are a common sight in older neighborhoods, blooming their heads off with little or no care. 'Betty Prior' is highly recommended for all regions.

DISEASE AND PEST PROBLEMS: 'Betty Prior' exhibits excellent resistance to black spot and mildew. As a preventive measure, apply fungicidal soap or garden sulfur combined with an antitranspirant to protect new foliage in spring; reapply as needed. Monitor for insect damage.

'Blanc Double de Coubert'

Cultivar Name:	**'Blanc Double de Coubert'**
Classification:	Hybrid rugosa
Parentage:	*Rosa rugosa* × 'Sombreuil'
Introduced:	Cochet-Cochet; 1892
USDA Plant Hardiness Zones:	3 to 8

DESCRIPTION: 'Blanc Double de Coubert' produces intensely fragrant, double, white flowers in late spring, scattered bloom in summer, and excellent autumn rebloom. It makes a dense, prickly shrub with deeply veined, dark green, leathery foliage that colors to a handsome bronze yellow in autumn. The arching to rounded shrubs reach a height of 4 to 5 feet tall and 4 feet across. The fragrant flower petals dry well for use in potpourri.

LANDSCAPE USES: A superb specimen shrub favored by English garden designer Gertrude Jekyll, 'Blanc Double de Coubert' integrates well with perennials and herbs and is a good candidate for mixed borders or herb gardens. The vigorous shrub also makes an excellent hedge, screen, or windbreak.

CULTURE: Plant 'Blanc Double de Coubert' in full sun in any well-drained soil. It will tolerate arid and poor soils as long as they have excellent drainage. To make a hedge, plant bushes 3½ feet apart—plants will be touching in three years. Prune mature specimens and hedges in late winter to shape them, taking off about one-third of top growth. Periodically remove older canes to keep plants growing vigorously. No other care is required.

DISEASE AND PEST PROBLEMS: Rugosa hybrids, like the species, are usually trouble-free plants. Summer flowers sometimes attract Japanese beetles. Pick off adult beetles and treat lawn areas with milky disease spores to control grubs. Rugosa hybrids are susceptible to rose stem girdler. Keep plants free of deadwood; prune out and destroy infected canes.

Cultivar Name:	**'Blaze'**
Classification:	Large-flowered climber
Parentage:	'Paul's Scarlet Climber' × 'Grus an Teplitz'
Introduced:	Kallay, Jackson & Perkins, United States; 1932
USDA Plant Hardiness Zones:	5 to 9

DESCRIPTION: North America's most popular red climber, 'Blaze' is noted for its large clusters of showy, scarlet flowers. Its blooms are cupped and semidouble, releasing a pleasing, light fragrance. Abundant spring bloom is followed by dependable repeat bloom. Upright, vigorous canes covered with lush, leathery, dark green leaves reach 10 to 12 feet tall.

LANDSCAPE USES: 'Blaze', like its popular parent 'Paul's Scarlet Climber', mixes nicely with both antique and modern roses. Use it to wrap a pillar, train it over arches, or espalier it on a fence. It is an excellent choice to brighten a quiet, green corner of the garden or cover an unsightly shed.

CULTURE: Plant 'Blaze' in full sun in well-drained soil that has been amended with organic matter. Top-dress with compost annually. Prune while dormant to rid plants of dead and damaged wood. Retain any healthy, robust, young canes; cut back sideshoots to four buds. Fertilize after pruning and again after the first bloom with a complete organic fertilizer.

DISEASE AND PEST PROBLEMS: 'Blaze' exhibits moderate disease resistance. Protect new foliage in spring with fungicidal soap or garden sulfur combined with an antitranspirant to prevent black spot; reapply if signs of the disease appear. Monitor for insect damage.

RELATED CULTIVARS: 'Red Fountain' ('Don Juan' × 'Blaze'; Williams, Conard-Pyle, United States; 1975) bears fragrant, double, cupped, scarlet blooms. June bloom is followed by generous repeat flowering. Upright canes are covered with leathery, dark green leaves and reach 8 to 10 feet tall.

'Blaze'

'Bonica'

Cultivar Name:	**'Bonica'** (also called 'MEIdomonac')
Classification:	Shrub
Parentage:	([*Rosa sempervirens* × 'Mlle. Marthe Caron'] × 'Picasso')
Introduced:	Meilland, France, 1981; Conard-Pyle, United States, 1987; 1987 All-America Rose Selection
USDA Plant Hardiness Zones:	4 to 9

DESCRIPTION: 'Bonica' is the first shrub rose ever to capture the prestigious All-America Rose Selections Award. It is covered with clusters of small, double, rose-pink flowers in spring. Scattered summer bloom is followed by dependable autumn repeat bloom. Vigorous, bushy shrubs grow 4 to 5 feet tall and 4 feet wide with small, dark, glossy leaves. The foliage and small, orange-red autumn hips persist into winter. 'Bonica' represents an important breakthrough in breeding for disease resistance.

LANDSCAPE USES: 'Bonica' is suitable for massing, foundation planting, and hedging. As a specimen in mixed borders, its pink flowers combine nicely with antique and modern roses, perennials, and shrubs. In meadows and wild gardens, you can count on it for repeat bloom and fruit that attracts birds.

CULTURE: Plant in full sun in well-drained soil. Top-dress with organic matter and fertilize annually with a complete organic fertilizer. Prune during the dormant period by thinning out older canes and reducing the remaining canes by one-third of their length. Prune hedges lightly to shape them; clean up old seed heads and periodically remove older canes. To make a hedge, plant bushes every 3½ feet—plants will be touching in three years. 'Bonica' is highly recommended for all regions, but apply winter protection in Zone 4.

DISEASE AND PEST PROBLEMS: 'Bonica' is resistant to black spot, mildew, and rust. This means that it will maintain about half of its foliage even without fungicide treatments. The Conard-Pyle Company, U.S. producer of the rose, recommends three preventive spray treatments if you want plants to keep their foliage through the season; apply fungicidal soap or garden sulfur combined with an antitranspirant as soon as leaves emerge in spring and twice thereafter.

'Bride's Dream'

Cultivar Name:	**'Bride's Dream'**
Classification:	Hybrid tea
Parentage:	'Royal Highness' × seedling
Introduced:	W. Kordes Söhne, Germany; 1984
USDA Plant Hardiness Zones:	5 to 9

DESCRIPTION: Elegant, urn-shaped buds open to pale pink, double flowers that have a light tea fragrance. Shrubs are upright, vigorous, and covered in deep green foliage. They grow to 5 feet tall and 2½ feet wide. 'Bride's Dream' is a classic exhibition rose that makes an excellent cut flower.

LANDSCAPE USES: Like other tall hybrid tea roses, 'Bride's Dream' has a somewhat stiff habit and looks best positioned near the back of mixed borders. There the beautiful flowers will be shown to advantage, while the leggy canes are camouflaged by foreground perennials and shrubs. Plant in groups of three for mass effect and enjoy blooms from spring through frost. They make a nice addition to the cutting garden.

CULTURE: Plant in a sunny location in well-drained soil that has been amended with organic matter. Prune hard while dormant to rid plants of damaged canes and overwintering disease spores. Fertilize after pruning and again after first bloom with a complete organic fertilizer. Top-dress with compost annually. Protect the graft union with a mound of mulch in Zone 5. 'Bride's Dream' is recommended for all regions.

DISEASE AND PEST PROBLEMS: Like most hybrid tea roses, 'Bride's Dream' is susceptible to diseases. Protect new foliage with an application of fungicidal soap or garden sulfur combined with an antitranspirant to prevent black spot; repeat at least monthly or as necessary thereafter to keep foliage healthy. Monitor the plants for insect damage.

'Buff Beauty'

Cultivar Name:	**'Buff Beauty'**
Classification:	Hybrid musk
Parentage:	'William Allen Richardson' × seedling
Introduced:	Bentall, United Kingdom; 1939
USDA Plant Hardiness Zones:	5 to 9

DESCRIPTION: One of the loveliest of the hybrid musks, 'Buff Beauty' is covered with clusters of very fragrant, double, yellow-buff flowers. It forms a floppy, spreading bush with coppery-tinted young leaves that change to crisp dark green. Shrubs mound to 5 feet tall and as wide. Trained as a pillar or along a fence, expect it to stretch to 7 feet. Shrubs in Zone 5 may be smaller due to winter dieback.

LANDSCAPE USES: 'Buff Beauty' makes a wonderful mounding specimen, espalier, or pillar and shines in a mass planting or hedge. At Wisley in England, it is trained on a fence to create an upright, hedgelike, flowering barrier. In mixed borders, enhance its soft lemon flowers with blue-flowered perennial companions.

CULTURE: Site 'Buff Beauty' in as much sun as you can give it, although it will readily accept some light shade from deciduous trees. Plant in well-drained soil that has been amended with organic matter. Prune while dormant to keep shrubs in bounds; remove about one-third of the top growth and periodically cut out older canes. Fertilize in spring and again after flowering with a complete organic fertilizer to encourage repeat bloom.

DISEASE AND PEST PROBLEMS: 'Buff Beauty' is resistant to black spot and mildew, but protect new foliage with fungicidal soap or garden sulfur combined with an antitranspirant; reapply thereafter as needed. Monitor plants for insect damage.

'Camaieux'

Cultivar Name:	**'Camaieux'**
Classification:	Gallica
Parentage:	Not recorded
Introduced:	1830
USDA Plant Hardiness Zones:	4 to 8

DESCRIPTION: 'Camaieux' is one of the most exquisite of the striped gallicas descended from 'Rosa Mundi'. Its fragrant, many-petaled flowers are creamy white with rose and purple stripes. Vigorous bushes grow 3 feet tall and 3 feet wide. They provide abundant spring bloom with no repeat.

LANDSCAPE USES: 'Camaieux' is an excellent compact shrub for small gardens. Use near the front of a bed or border where its fragrant striped blooms can be enjoyed. Combine with rich pink perpetual damasks and crimson gallica roses. Allow it to mingle with spikes of foxglove and underplant with 'Bath's Pink' dianthus (*Dianthus* 'Bath's Pink'), blood-red cranesbill (*Geranium sanguineum*), and 'Silver Brocade' artemisia (*Artemisia* 'Silver Brocade').

CULTURE: 'Camaieux' is easy to grow because it is robust and hardy. Site in full sun, plant in well-drained organic soil, and top-dress liberally with compost. Fertilize in spring with a complete organic fertilizer. Prune while dormant to thin out crowded stems and shape bushes.

DISEASE AND PEST PROBLEMS: 'Camaieux' is resistant to black spot. Mildew is sometimes a problem. At the first sign of the disease, spray foliage with fungicidal soap or with horticultural oil at a rate of 1 to 2 tablespoons per gallon of water to eradicate and prevent mildew infection and also discourage black spot; repeat as necessary. Monitor plants for insect damage.

RELATED CULTIVARS: 'Perle de Panachees' (Vibert, France; 1845) produces double, creamy white flowers that are striped with violet or rose. Dwarf bushes grow 2½ feet tall and wide. It flowers in spring with no repeat bloom.

'Tricolore de Flandre' (Van Houtte, Holland; 1846) bears small, double, fragrant flowers of a soft blush-striped pink that ages to mauve. Bushes are floppy and dense, reaching a height of 3 feet with similar width. This cultivar blooms profusely in spring with no repeat.

Cultivar Name:	'Cardinal de Richelieu'
Classification:	Gallica
Parentage:	Not recorded
Introduced:	Laffay, France; 1840
USDA Plant Hardiness Zones:	4 to 8

DESCRIPTION: 'Cardinal de Richelieu' produces masses of fragrant, many-petaled flowers that are loosely cupped, showing the China rose influence. Each bloom is exquisite: Mauve buds open to large flowers of crimson shaded with lilac and close into purple globes that fade to blue-black. The once-blooming, upright, bushy plants grow 3 to 4 feet tall and 2 to 3 feet wide. The canes bear dark green foliage and have few thorns.

LANDSCAPE USES: One of the darkest and most elegant of the purple gallicas, 'Cardinal de Richelieu' should always be surrounded with silver foliage plants such as lamb's-ears or artemisia. Use this handsome rose as an accent in mixed borders dominated by white- and pink-flowered perennials.

CULTURE: 'Cardinal de Richelieu' is a dependable bloomer, producing a good crop of flowers annually. It is vigorous and extremely hardy. Plant in full sun in well-drained soil that has been amended with organic matter. Top-dress liberally with compost every year. Fertilize in spring with a complete organic fertilizer. Prune annually after flowering to shape it and to reduce crowded stems.

DISEASE AND PEST PROBLEMS: 'Cardinal de Richelieu' is resistant to black spot. Mildew is sometimes a problem. At the first sign of the disease, spray foliage with fungicidal soap or with horticultural oil at a rate of 1 to 2 tablespoons per 1 gallon of water to control and prevent mildew infection and to discourage black spot; repeat as necessary. Monitor plants for insect damage.

'Cardinal de Richelieu'

Carefree Beauty™

Cultivar Name:	Carefree Beauty™
Classification:	Shrub
Parentage:	Seedling × 'Prairie Princess'
Introduced:	Buck; Conard-Pyle, United States; 1977
USDA Plant Hardiness Zones:	4 to 9

DESCRIPTION: Carefree Beauty™ produces large, loosely double, rose-pink blooms that repeat throughout the season. Plants are vigorous, upright bushes that reach 5 feet tall and 3 feet wide.

LANDSCAPE USES: Use Carefree Beauty™ as an attractive mass, hedge, or specimen. Its old-fashioned flowers combine well with both antique and modern roses. It produces orange-red hips that are attractive to birds.

CULTURE: Carefree Beauty™ is a robust, hardy shrub that's easy to grow in full sun in any well-drained soil. Top-dress with compost annually, and fertilize in spring with a complete organic fertilizer. Prune annually while dormant, removing older canes and one-third of the top growth and thinning out crowded stems. To make a hedge, plant bushes every 3 feet—plants will be touching in three years.

DISEASE AND PEST PROBLEMS: Carefree Beauty™ is resistant to black spot, mildew, and rust. Without any fungicide treatments, it will maintain about one-half of its foliage. The Conard-Pyle Company, U.S. producer of the rose, recommends three preventive spray treatments if you want plants to keep their foliage through the season. Apply fungicidal soap or garden sulfur combined with an antitranspirant as soon as leaves emerge in spring; spray again twice thereafter.

RELATED CULTIVARS: Carefree Wonder™ (Shrub; [('Prairie Princess' × 'Nirvana') × ('Eyepaint' × 'Rustica')] Selection; Meilland, France, 1978; Conard-Pyle, United States; 1991 All-America Rose Selection) is superior to Carefree Beauty™ in both flower production and disease resistance, but it does not produce hips. The double flowers are deep pink with cream on the back of the petals; they are carried in large clusters. Shrubs grow 5 feet tall and 3 feet wide, bloom continuously, and are disease-free. This cultivar is highly recommended for all regions.

'Cécile Brunner'

Cultivar Name:	'Cécile Brunner' (also called 'Mignon', 'Sweetheart Rose')
Classification:	Polyantha
Parentage:	Probably a double form of *Rosa multiflora* × 'Souvenir d'un Ami'
Introduced:	Pernet-Ducher, France; 1881
USDA Plant Hardiness Zones:	5 to 9

DESCRIPTION: The original and best known of the polyantha, or sweetheart, roses, 'Cécile Brunner' produces clusters of scented, double blooms. Small, perfectly formed, light pink roses cover the dwarf bushes through the growing season. The stems have few thorns and sparse foliage. Plants grow 18 to 24 inches tall and 12 inches wide.

LANDSCAPE USES: Polyantha roses are ideal for creating drifts of all-season color in the front of mixed borders. Plant in groups of three to five to form a small mass. The dwarf, bushy shrubs are also suitable for low edging and containers.

CULTURE: Plant in full sun in well-drained soil that has been amended with plenty of organic matter. Prune hard at bud break to reduce bushes by about two-thirds. Shear the bushes after each bloom period to encourage successive flowering. Top-dress with well-rotted manure or compost annually. Fertilize after pruning and again after the first bloom with a complete organic fertilizer to stimulate continuous flower production. 'Cécile Brunner' is recommended for all regions.

DISEASE AND PEST PROBLEMS: 'Cécile Brunner' has excellent disease resistance. To provide extra disease protection, apply fungicidal soap, garden sulfur combined with an antitranspirant, or an antitranspirant alone when leaves emerge in spring; reapply as needed. Small-leaved roses like these are sometimes bothered by mites. If any mites appear, spray the undersides of the leaves with a strong burst of water to dislodge them. Monitor the plants, and apply insecticidal soap if mites continue to be a problem.

RELATED CULTIVARS: 'Climbing Cécile Brunner' (Hosp, 1894) is a vigorous, once-blooming climber that is covered with clusters of light pink sweetheart roses in early summer. It climbs to 20 feet and is extremely disease-resistant and hardy. This cultivar is highly recommended for all regions.

'Spray Cécile Brunner' (Howard, 1941; often sold as 'Bloomfield Abundance') produces its sprays of light pink sweetheart roses atop awkward-looking bushes. The smooth, 4-foot stems have sparse foliage.

'Baby Cécile Brunner' (Miniature; 'Climbing Cécile Brunner' × 'Fairy Princess'; Moore, 1981) is a miniature version of 'Cécile Brunner' reaching only 10 to 12 inches tall and wide.

'Baby Betsy McCall' (Miniature; 'Cécile Brunner' × 'Rosy Jewel'; Morey, 1960) is a micro-miniature that bears tiny, double, scented, light pink flowers. The dwarf bushes are covered with leathery foliage and grow 8 to 10 inches tall and wide. It is highly recommended for all regions.

'Perle d'Or' (also called 'Yellow Cécile Brunner'; 'Polyantha' × 'Madame Falcot'; Rambaux, France; 1884) bears fragrant, golden pink, double blooms in clusters atop wiry bushes that are 3 feet tall and less wide.

'Celestial'

Cultivar Name:	'Celestial'
	(also called 'Celeste')
Classification:	Alba
Parentage:	*Rosa alba* hybrid
Introduced:	Before 1848
USDA Plant Hardiness Zones:	3 to 8

DESCRIPTION: 'Celestial' produces fragrant, loosely double, pink blush blooms that open to reveal golden stamens. Bushes are vigorous and upright, reaching 5 feet tall and 4 feet wide with blue-green foliage. Flowers appear in late spring with no repeat bloom.

LANDSCAPE USES: Use 'Celestial' as a specimen, shrub mass, hedge, or screen. Its characteristic bluish foliage provides a lovely backdrop for the soft pink flowers. Plant it in the back of a mixed border, where its handsome foliage and nodding flowers provide a backdrop for companion perennials. The soft pink flowers look beautiful with the spires of foxglove, lilac globes of star of Persia (*Allium christophii*), and purple spikes of 'May Night' violet sage (*Salvia* × *superba* 'May Night').

CULTURE: 'Celestial' is a robust, hardy shrub. It thrives in full sun but will also tolerate some high shade from deciduous trees. Plant 'Celestial' in any well-drained soil, top-dress with compost annually, and fertilize in spring with a complete organic fertilizer. Prune lightly to thin out crowded stems. To make a hedge, set plants every 3½ feet—plants will be touching in three years. 'Celestial' is highly recommended for all regions.

DISEASE AND PEST PROBLEMS: 'Celestial' is disease-free.

'Celsiana'

Cultivar Name:	**'Celsiana'**
Classification:	Damask
Parentage:	Not recorded
Introduced:	Before 1750
USDA Plant Hardiness Zones:	3 to 8

DESCRIPTION: The lovely, crinkled, late-spring flowers of 'Celsiana' have an exquisite damask fragrance. The large, semidouble, clear pink blooms are filled with distinctive golden stamens and are produced in clusters. The vigorous plants grow 4 to 5 feet tall and a little less wide, with prickly canes covered by smooth, gray-green, scented foliage. You'll find 'Celsiana' flowers pictured in paintings by Dutch Masters as well as by Redouté.

LANDSCAPE USES: Use 'Celsiana' as an attractive specimen or in groups of three or more. Plant it near the middle of mixed borders and enjoy its delicious scent. It's also at home in the herb garden, where it looks attractive with catmint, sage, cottage pinks, scented geraniums, and lady's-mantle. You may also harvest the flower petals for use in potpourri.

CULTURE: 'Celsiana' is easy to grow in full sun in any well-drained soil. Top-dress with compost annually, and fertilize in spring with a complete organic fertilizer. After flowering, cut back canes that bloomed to about one-third their length. That's also a good time to thin out crowded stems and remove older wood. If you have room, peg the arching canes to the ground to encourage greater flower production. This rose is recommended for all regions.

DISEASE AND PEST PROBLEMS: 'Celsiana' is disease-free.

'Centifolia'

Cultivar Name:	**'Centifolia'** (also called 'Rose des Peintres')
Classification:	Centifolia
Parentage:	Not recorded
Introduced:	Prior to 1600
USDA Plant Hardiness Zones:	4 to 8

DESCRIPTION: Hybridized in Holland prior to 1600 and often painted by Dutch Masters, 'Centifolia' produces large, globular, rose-pink flowers. The charming, richly perfumed blooms are typically composed of two hundred petals around a buttonlike center. The plant blooms abundantly for a few weeks in spring with no repeat bloom. It forms a vigorous shrub with an arching, open habit that is 5 feet tall and wide; thorny canes are covered in rough, green foliage.

LANDSCAPE USES: Use 'Centifolia' as an attractive specimen. Position it near the back of the border, where its old-fashioned flowers can nod above perennials and compact shrubs. Give its canes plenty of space to arch when laden with blooms. You may also mass a few plants in a tight group or train them up sturdy tripods or along a fence to manage the long canes.

CULTURE: 'Centifolia' is a robust, hardy shrub that's easy to grow in full sun in any well-drained soil. Top-dress it with compost annually, and fertilize in spring with a complete organic fertilizer. Prune after the bloom in summer, cutting back the canes that flowered to about one-third their length; also remove some older wood and thin out crowded stems. 'Centifolia' is recommended for all regions.

DISEASE AND PEST PROBLEMS: 'Centifolia' is moderately disease-resistant. Plant it near the back of the border to hide any diseased leaves that may appear. This rose is best left to fend for itself.

RELATED CULTIVARS: 'Centifolia Variegata' (also called *Rosa centifolia* var. *variegata*, 'Cottage Maid') bears abundant, full, fragrant blooms of creamy white with fine pink striping. It forms a bush 5 feet tall and slightly less wide, with a more upright habit than 'Centifolia'.

'Bullata' (introduced before 1815) produces globular, full, pink flowers on upright bushes to 4 feet tall and wide. Also known as the "lettuce-leaved rose," it is grown as a curiosity for its crinkled foliage that resembles lettuce leaves.

'La Noblesse' (1856) bears full, fragrant, light pink flowers on arching, thorny canes. Allow the open bush to sprawl, train it on a tripod or fence, or plant it in a tight group of three to create an upright mass.

'Rose de Meaux' (Sweet, United Kingdom; 1789) is a miniature centifolia that bears small, rose-pink, very full double, cupped blooms that resemble pompons. Twiggy bushes reach 3 feet tall and wide. A tiny version of the bigger centifolias, 'Rose de Meaux' is a good choice for small gardens and can be an effective once-blooming shrub in mixed borders.

'Champney's Pink Cluster'

Cultivar Name:	**'Champney's Pink Cluster'** (also called 'Champney's Rose')
Classification:	Noisette
Parentage:	*Rosa chinensis* ✕ *Rosa moschata*
Introduced:	Champney, United States; 1811
USDA Plant Hardiness Zones:	6 to 9

DESCRIPTION: The first rose hybridized in the United States, 'Champney's Pink Cluster' was the prototype for the entire Noisette class. It is a cross between the China rose 'Old Blush' and the musk rose, and it shares the best characteristics of each parent. Large clusters of small, double, pink, fragrant flowers bloom continuously on vigorous, upright shrubs. The smooth stems are covered with small, narrow-leaved, light green foliage. Pruned bushes may grow to 4 feet tall and less wide, while specimens trained as pillars stretch 6 to 10 feet tall.

LANDSCAPE USES: 'Champney's Pink Cluster' mixes beautifully with both antique and modern roses. Use it to wrap a pillar, train it over an arch or trellis, or espalier it on a fence. As a pruned shrub, it looks lovely in the middle of mixed borders, where its dainty, nonstop blooms nod above perennial companions.

CULTURE: Plant in full sun in well-drained soil that has been amended with organic matter. Top-dress with compost annually. Prune while dormant to rid plants of dead and damaged wood and to promote vigorous new basal buds. Fertilize with a complete organic fertilizer after pruning and again after the first bloom.

Noisettes and their China parents are among the best roses for southern gardens and are highly recommended for all regions in Zones 7 to 9. They may survive in Zone 6 if you plant them in a sheltered location and protect the crown from winter injury with a mound of mulch. Since canes are susceptible to winter injury, it also helps to prune the shrubs hard at bud break to form dainty, compact, see-through bushes 3 to 4 feet tall. Train climbers on a warm, sunny wall for protection.

DISEASE AND PEST PROBLEMS: All noisettes exhibit moderate disease resistance. Protect new foliage in spring with fungicidal soap or garden sulfur combined with an antitranspirant to prevent black spot; reapply as needed. Monitor for insect damage.

RELATED CULTIVARS: 'Blush Noisette' ('Champney's Pink Cluster' seedling; 1817) is a choice everblooming rose recommended for all regions in Zones 6 to 9. It bears clusters of deep pink buds opening to cupped, clear pink flowers that have a wonderful perfume. Pruned shrubs remain compact and bushy, growing to about 3 feet tall with a spread of 2 feet. Wrapped on a pillar or espaliered on a wall or fence, this cultivar stretches to about 6 feet.

'Alister Stella Gray' ('Golden Rambler'; Gray, United Kingdom; 1894) bears clusters of pointed, apricot buds that open to pale yellow flowers with apricot centers; older flowers fade to white. The fragrant blooms are produced continuously on vigorous, upright canes 8 to 10 feet tall. It makes an admirable everblooming pillar rose, and is highly recommended for all regions of Zones 7 to 9 and sheltered sites in Zone 6.

'Lamarque' ('Blush Noisette' × 'Park's Yellow Tea-scented China'; Maréchal, France; 1830) is an excellent everblooming climber for southern gardens (Zones 7 to 9 and sheltered situations in Zone 6). Clusters of pure white, pointed buds open to large, creamy white, double flowers with yellow centers and an exquisite perfume. The vigorous, trailing, smooth canes are covered with light green leaves and reach 12 to 15 feet or more to cover arches, pergolas, trellises, and trees.

'Jaune Desprez' ('Blush Noisette' × 'Park's Yellow Tea-scented China'; Desprez, France; 1830) bears pale yellow-

apricot, double flowers with rich perfume. Rarely out of bloom, it makes an extremely vigorous climber or scrambler, reaching 12 to 20 feet. This cultivar is highly recommended for all regions in Zones 7 to 9 and sheltered situations in Zone 6.

'Madame Alfred Carrière' (Schwartz, France; 1879) is one of the best known of the noisettes. Clusters of fragrant, white, double flowers bloom in spring and again through the season. Vigorous canes with semiglossy leaves and few prickles reach 10 to 15 feet or more. In 1900, it was recommended by garden writer Gertrude Jekyll as the best white repeat-blooming climber. Like its musk rose parent, it is hardier than other Noisettes and recommended for all regions in Zones 6 to 9. In Zone 6, plant it next to a warm wall with a southern or eastern exposure.

'Charles de Mills'

Cultivar Name:	'Charles de Mills'
Classification:	Gallica
Parentage:	Not recorded
Introduced:	Nineteenth century
USDA Plant Hardiness Zones:	4 to 8

DESCRIPTION: 'Charles de Mills' is the most showy of the gallicas. It bears large, full, rich crimson blooms that open flat and quartered, with a buttonlike center. The scented flowers appear in spring with no repeat bloom. The vigorous canes have few thorns but many tiny bristles. The upright plants reach 4 to 5 feet tall and 3 feet wide and are covered with rough, green foliage.

LANDSCAPE USES: 'Charles de Mills' is showy enough to use as a specimen. Its old-fashioned, crimson flowers provide a focal point in borders of white and pink flowers. It also looks attractive with other antique roses and companion perennials. Surround it with silver foliage plants to set off its rich flower color.

CULTURE: 'Charles de Mills' is a robust, hardy shrub that is easy to grow in full sun in any well-drained soil. Top-dress with compost annually, and fertilize in spring with a complete organic fertilizer. Prune during the dormant season to thin out crowded stems and to shape the plants.

DISEASE AND PEST PROBLEMS: 'Charles de Mills' is resistant to black spot. Mildew is sometimes a problem in late summer. At the first sign of the disease, spray foliage with horticultural oil at a rate of 1 to 2 table-spoons per 1 gallon of water or with fungicidal soap to control mildew infection. Repeat as necessary to prevent later mildew outbreaks and discourage black spot. Monitor plants for insect damage.

RELATED CULTIVARS: 'Belle de Crecy' (1848) bears fragrant, very full, mauve-pink flowers that change to violet and open to reveal a buttonlike center. Upright bushes covered with rough, green leaves are 4 feet tall and not quite as wide, with many small bristles but few thorns.

Cultivar Name:	'China Doll'
Classification:	Polyantha
Parentage:	'Mrs. Dudley Fulton' × 'Tom Thumb'
Introduced:	Lammerts; Armstrong Nursery, United States; 1946
USDA Plant Hardiness Zones:	5 to 9

DESCRIPTION: 'China Doll' is covered with clusters of small, double, clear pink sweetheart roses with a light scent. Rarely out of bloom, it forms a dwarf shrub 18 inches tall and 12 inches wide.

LANDSCAPE USES: Use 'China Doll' and other polyantha roses to create drifts of all-season color in the front of mixed borders. Plant in groups of three to five to form a small mass. 'China Doll' is also an excellent choice for edging and planting in containers.

CULTURE: Plant in full sun in well-drained soil that has been amended with organic matter. Prune hard at bud break to reduce bushes by about two-thirds. Shear after each bloom period to encourage successive flowering. Top-dress with well-rotted manure or compost annually. Fertilize after pruning and again after the first bloom with a complete organic fertilizer to stimulate continuous flower production. 'China Doll' is recommended for all regions.

DISEASE AND PEST PROBLEMS: 'China Doll' possesses excellent disease resistance. To prevent any damage, you could apply fungicidal soap, garden sulfur combined with an antitranspirant, or an antitranspirant alone when leaves emerge in spring; reapply as needed. Small-leaved roses such as 'China Doll' are sometimes bothered by mites. If you spot any of the tiny pests, spray the undersides of the leaves with a strong burst of water to dislodge them. Monitor the plants, and apply insecticidal soap if mite problems continue.

'China Doll'

'Chrysler Imperial'

Cultivar Name:	'Chrysler Imperial'
Classification:	Hybrid tea
Parentage:	'Charlotte Armstrong' × 'Mirandy'
Introduced:	Lammerts; Germain's, United States; 1952 1953 All-America Rose Selection
USDA Plant Hardiness Zones:	5 to 9

DESCRIPTION: 'Chrysler Imperial' is one of the most fragrant modern roses and is worth growing for this trait alone. Large buds open in the classic, high-center form. The full blooms are deep crimson red, gradually fading to magenta-blue. Flowers are produced in such abundance from early summer to frost that their bluing or fading effect is easily forgiven. Some say it's just part of their charm. 'Chrysler Imperial' makes a compact bush 3½ feet tall and 2½ feet wide, covered with matte-green leaves. The bush is covered with prickles and bristles right up to the neck of its flowers. Besides being chosen as an All-America Rose Selection in 1953, this popular cultivar also received the James Alexander Gamble Rose Fragrance Medal in 1965.

LANDSCAPE USES: 'Chrysler Imperial' is a knock-out in mixed borders. Its deep crimson flowers are enhanced by blending pink, blue, and violet perennial flowers with it. It is a must for the cutting garden, as an individual bloom can perfume an entire room.

CULTURE: Plant in a sunny location in well-drained soil that has been amended with organic matter. Like all hybrid tea roses, 'Chrysler Imperial' responds well to hard pruning in early spring to rid the bush of overwintering disease spores and to promote vigorous new growth. Fertilize after pruning in spring and after first flowering with a complete organic fertilizer to ensure repeat flowering. Deadhead spent flowers by cutting back to the second five-leaflet node. Top-dress with compost annually. In Zone 5, mound mulch or pine needles over the crown of the plants in late autumn as winter protection.

DISEASE AND PEST PROBLEMS: 'Chrysler Imperial' is susceptible to black spot and mildew. For best results, prune severely in early spring and apply fungicidal soap or garden sulfur combined with an antitranspirant as soon as leaves emerge; reapply at least monthly until frost. In wet weather, apply preventive sprays more frequently. Monitor bushes for pests, and apply insecticidal soap or neem extract if they appear.

'Cinderella'

Cultivar Name:	'Cinderella'
Classification:	Miniature
Parentage:	'Cécile Brunner' × 'Tom Thumb'
Introduced:	Devink, Holland; 1953
USDA Plant Hardiness Zones:	5 to 9

DESCRIPTION: One of the best micro-miniature roses, 'Cinderella' bears tiny, fragrant, shell pink sweetheart blooms nonstop through the season. Bushes are 10 inches tall and wide with tiny, glossy leaves.

LANDSCAPE USES: 'Cinderella' is an excellent choice for edging and using in a rock garden, rock wall, and container. Use a grouping of three to five plants to create drifts of all-season color in the foreground of mixed borders.

CULTURE: Plant in full sun in well-drained soil. Prune hard at bud break to reduce canes to two to three buds or about two-thirds of their length. Shear after each bloom period to encourage successive flowering. Top-dress with well-rotted manure or compost annually. Fertilize after pruning and again after the first bloom with a complete organic fertilizer to stimulate continuous flower production. 'Cinderella' is highly recommended for all regions.

DISEASE AND PEST PROBLEMS: 'Cinderella' is disease-free.

'City of York'

Cultivar Name:	**'City of York'**
Classification:	Large-flowered climber
Parentage:	'Professor Gnau' × 'Dorothy Perkins'
Introduced:	Tantau, Germany; 1945
USDA Plant Hardiness Zones:	5 to 9

DESCRIPTION: 'City of York' is one of the best white climbers. It bears clusters of large, semidouble, creamy white, cupped flowers that have a heady perfume. It covers itself with a profusion of blooms in early summer; there is some repeat bloom if it is deadheaded immediately after flowering. Vigorous canes covered with glossy foliage easily grow to 10 to 12 feet tall with a similar spread when fanned out on a trellis.

LANDSCAPE USES: This hardy, free-flowering climber can be used to cover a pillar, trellis, wall, arch, or fence. It looks particularly fine sharing a lattice with a large-flowered blue clematis, such as 'Will Goodwin', for interesting seasonal contrast. Train this rose's flexible canes to scramble into a crab apple tree. It also makes a useful groundcover to cascade down a sunny slope or over a wall.

CULTURE: Give 'City of York' a sunny location in well-drained soil that has been amended with organic matter. Top-dress with compost annually. Prune while dormant. Choose healthy canes to fit the space you have, tie them to their supports, and reduce the sideshoots to four buds. Deadhead spent flowers to neaten the plants and encourage repeat bloom. Fertilize after pruning and again after the first bloom with a complete organic fertilizer. This rose is highly recommended for all regions.

DISEASE AND PEST PROBLEMS: 'City of York' is not usually bothered by diseases.

Clair Matin®

Cultivar Name:	**Clair Matin®**
Classification:	Large-flowered climber
Parentage:	'Fashion' × [('Independence' × 'Orange Triumph') × 'Phyllis Bide']
Introduced:	Meilland, France; 1960; Conard-Pyle, United States; 1963
USDA Plant Hardiness Zones:	6 to 9

DESCRIPTION: Clair Matin® bears charming clusters of fragrant, pink, semidouble, cupped blooms that open flat. The abundant spring bloom is followed by dependable repeat bloom. Upright, vigorous canes are covered with leathery, dark green, glossy leaves. The bushes reach 8 to 10 feet tall.

LANDSCAPE USES: Clair Matin® easily wins the hearts of all who have enjoyed it in full bloom. It looks attractive with both antique and modern roses. Use it to wrap a pillar or tripod, train it over an arch, or espalier it on a fence. Clair Matin® is an excellent choice to brighten a quiet, green corner of the garden or cover an unsightly shed.

CULTURE: Plant in full sun in well-drained soil that has been amended with organic matter. Top-dress with compost annually. Prune while dormant to rid plants of dead and damaged wood. Leave healthy, robust young canes and cut back sideshoots to four buds. Fertilize after pruning and again after the first bloom with a complete organic fertilizer.

DISEASE AND PEST PROBLEMS: Clair Matin® has moderate disease resistance. Protect new foliage in spring with fungicidal soap or garden sulfur combined with an antitranspirant to prevent black spot; reapply if signs of the disease appear. Monitor plants for insect damage.

'Class Act'

Cultivar Name:	'Class Act'
	(also called 'First Class')
Classification:	Floribunda
Parentage:	'Sunflare' × seedling
Introduced:	Warriner; Jackson & Perkins, United States; 1988
	1989 All-America Rose Selection
USDA Plant Hardiness Zones:	5 to 9

DESCRIPTION: 'Class Act' is one of the best white floribunda roses on the market. It bears large clusters of pure white, semidouble flowers that open flat and have a soft perfume. Blooms are carried continuously on bushy, glossy-leaved, vigorous shrubs 2½ to 3 feet tall and 2 feet wide.

LANDSCAPE USES: Grow 'Class Act' as an everblooming shrub in a mass planting, in a foundation planting, or as a specimen. In mixed borders, its elegant blooms look attractive with perennials and other shrubs. Plant it in drifts of three or more bushes to make a mass of all-season bloom. 'Class Act' makes an excellent cut flower.

CULTURE: Plant 'Class Act' in a sunny location in well-drained soil amended with organic matter. Prune hard in late winter or early spring to rid plants of overwintering disease spores and to encourage vigorous new growth. Fertilize after pruning and again after the first bloom with a complete organic fertilizer. Top-dress with compost annually. Deadhead spent blooms through the season. Apply a mound of mulch to protect the graft union from winter injury in Zone 5. This cultivar is highly recommended for all regions.

DISEASE AND PEST PROBLEMS: 'Class Act' has excellent disease resistance. To provide extra protection against black spot, apply fungicidal soap or garden sulfur combined with an antitranspirant as soon as leaves emerge in spring; monitor plants and reapply as needed. Check for signs of insect feeding, and apply insecticidal soap as needed to prevent damage to buds and leaves.

'Clotilde Soupert'

Cultivar Name:	'Clotilde Soupert'
Classification:	Polyantha
Parentage:	Probably 'Mignonette' × 'Madame Damaizin'
Introduced:	Soupert & Notting, United Kingdom; 1890
USDA Plant Hardiness Zones:	5 to 9

DESCRIPTION: 'Clotilde Soupert' is continuously covered with clusters of large, fragrant, very full double, white sweetheart blooms. The stems of this dwarf shrub have few prickles and sparse, glossy foliage. Plants grow 18 inches tall and 12 inches wide.

LANDSCAPE USES: Grow 'Clotilde Soupert' in masses of three to five plants to create drifts of all-season color in the front of mixed borders. The dwarf, bushy shrubs are also suitable as a low edging and in containers. 'Clotilde Soupert' also makes an excellent low, ever-blooming hedge.

CULTURE: Plant in full sun in well-drained soil that has been amended with organic matter. Prune hard at bud break to reduce bushes by about two-thirds. Shear after each bloom period to encourage successive flowering. Top-dress with well-rotted manure or compost annually. Fertilize after pruning and again after the first bloom with a complete organic fertilizer to stimulate continuous flower production. 'Clotilde Soupert' is recommended for all regions.

DISEASE AND PEST PROBLEMS: 'Clotilde Soupert' has excellent disease resistance. For best results, apply fungicidal soap, garden sulfur combined with an antitranspirant, or an antitranspirant alone when leaves emerge in spring; reapply as needed. Small-leaved roses like 'Clotilde Soupert' are sometimes bothered by mites. If mites appear, spray the undersides of leaves with a strong burst of water to dislodge the pests. Monitor the plants, and apply insecticidal soap if mite problems continue.

Cultivar Name:	**'Common Moss'** (also called 'Communis', 'Centifolia Muscosa', 'Old Pink Moss')
Classification:	Moss
Parentage:	A sport of 'Centifolia'
Introduced:	Reported circa 1696 in southern France
USDA Plant Hardiness Zones:	4 to 8

DESCRIPTION: 'Common Moss' is one of the first and best of the moss roses. The buds are covered with sticky, mosslike, glandular bristles that exude a balsam fragrance when brushed. They open to globular and very full, rich pink blooms that are flat and quartered with a buttonlike center. The blooms are similar to 'Centifolia', although smaller, and have inherited its strong perfume. Bushes grow to 5 feet tall and 4 feet wide. The prickly, arching stems are covered with coarsely toothed, dark green foliage.

LANDSCAPE USES: 'Common Moss' is certainly a curiosity, but it is also an attractive garden shrub that bears profuse spring bloom. It is a large, open shrub, similar to 'Centifolia'. Plant a few bushes close together to make a thick mass, or support its arching canes on a fence, tripod, or pillar. Grow a repeat-flowering clematis over it to extend the season of bloom. 'Common Moss' has charming flowers that look lovely with other antique roses and companion perennials.

CULTURE: 'Common Moss' is a robust, hardy shrub that's easy to grow in full sun in any well-drained soil. Top-dress with compost annually, and fertilize in spring with a complete organic fertilizer. After flowering, thin out crowded stems and shape bushes by cutting back stems that have flowered by one-third their length.

DISEASE AND PEST PROBLEMS: 'Common Moss' has moderate disease resistance. At the first sign of fungal problems, spray foliage with horticultural oil at a rate of 1 to 2 tablespoons per 1 gallon of water or with fungicidal soap; repeat as necessary to control and prevent mildew infection and discourage black spot. Monitor plants for insect damage.

RELATED CULTIVARS: 'Comtesse de Murinais' (Vibert, France; 1843) bears mossy buds that open to perfumed, very full, quartered flowers with buttonlike centers. New flowers are flesh pink and fade to white. Arching, prickly bushes with rough, green leaves reach 6 feet tall and are best supported on a fence, tripod, or pillar. This cultivar has exceptional disease resistance.

'Common Moss'

'Complicata'

Cultivar Name:	'Complicata'
Classification:	Gallica
Parentage:	Probably a gallica parent and *Rosa micrantha*
Introduced:	Nineteenth century
USDA Plant Hardiness Zones:	4 to 8

Constance Spry®

Cultivar Name:	Constance Spry®
Classification:	English rose
Parentage:	'Belle Isis' × 'Dainty Main'
Introduced:	Austin, United Kingdom; 1961
USDA Plant Hardiness Zones:	4 to 9

DESCRIPTION: 'Complicata' may have a complex ancestry, but its flower is one of the most simple and lovely of the gallicas. Light crimson buds open to large, deep pink, single flowers filled with golden stamens. Its smooth, almost thornless stems are vigorous and upright, mounding 5 to 6 feet tall and wide. Plants are covered with light green foliage.

LANDSCAPE USES: 'Complicata' is a lovely specimen plant, especially when it is in full bloom. But if space is limited, the best way to manage 'Complicata' is to train it as a pillar or short climber or allow it to climb into a tree. To provide later bloom, train a clematis cultivar to climb through it.

CULTURE: 'Complicata' is a hardy shrub that's easy to grow in full sun, although it tolerates high shade from deciduous trees. Top-dress annually with compost. Prune the bush after flowering to keep it in bounds. Thin out crowded stems, cut out older canes, and clip back the stems that bore flowers to a pleasing shape.

DISEASE AND PEST PROBLEMS: 'Complicata' is moderately disease-resistant. This rose is best left to fend for itself.

DESCRIPTION: Constance Spry® is the original English rose bred by David Austin. Clusters of fragrant, pink, very full double, cupped blooms with antique charm are produced abundantly in spring, with no repeat bloom. Upright, vigorous canes, covered with leathery, dark green leaves, reach 6 feet tall and wide to form a large shrub. It is commonly trained as a climber and stretches to 15 feet.

LANDSCAPE USES: Constance Spry® is a stunning sight in full bloom, especially when trained on a wall. It mixes beautifully with both antique and modern roses. Use it to drape arches, fences and walls, or allow it to scramble into a tree. It's a good choice to brighten a quiet green corner or cover an unsightly shed. Train a repeat-flowering clematis over it to extend the season of bloom. It can also be grown as a freestanding shrub.

CULTURE: Plant this rose in full sun in well-drained soil that has been amended with organic matter. Top-dress with compost annually. Prune after flowering to thin out crowded stems, and cut back flowering shoots by one-third their length. Fertilize in early spring with a complete organic fertilizer.

DISEASE AND PEST PROBLEMS: Constance Spry® has exceptional disease resistance and seldom needs spraying.

RELATED CULTIVARS: Chaucer® (Constance Spry® × 'Duchesse de Montebello'; Austin, United Kingdom; 1970) produces large, cupped, fragrant, light pink blooms. It flowers abundantly in spring with some autumn repeat bloom. Suitable for small gardens, the upright shrubs grow to 3½ feet tall and less wide. The bushes have gallica-type bristles but few thorns; the foliage is medium green. Austin roses exhibit variable resistance to diseases; application of preventive spray (such as fungicidal soap) is recommended by the breeder.

Cultivar Name:	'Cornelia'
Classification:	Hybrid musk
Parentage:	Not recorded
Introduced:	Pemberton, United Kingdom; 1925
USDA Plant Hardiness Zones:	5 to 9

DESCRIPTION: One of the loveliest of the hybrid musks, 'Cornelia' is blanketed in clusters of very fragrant, loosely double flowers of apricot-pink. They open to reveal golden stamens and then fade to creamy blush. Flowers are held in flat sprays. An abundant spring bloom is followed by excellent repeat bloom. 'Cornelia' makes an upright, spreading, relatively thornless bush with coppery-tinted young leaves that change to glossy, crisp dark green. Pruned shrubs mound to 5 feet tall and wide. Trained as a climber it stretches to 8 feet. In Zone 5 shrubs are smaller due to winter dieback.

LANDSCAPE USES: 'Cornelia' makes a lovely specimen, mass, and informal hedge. Create a beautiful garden scene by massing the shrubs with the floppy spikes of blue catmint (*Nepeta* × *faassenii* 'Dropmore'). In mixed borders, its soft pastel flowers and coppery leaves are complemented by purple smokebush (*Cotinus coggygria*), blue-flowered perennials, and silver-leaved plants. 'Cornelia' can also be trained as a pillar rose or climber.

CULTURE: Site 'Cornelia' in as much sun as you can give it, although it will take some light shade from deciduous trees. Plant in well-drained soil that has been amended with organic matter. Prune while dormant to keep shrubs

in bounds, removing about one-third of its top growth and periodically cutting out older canes. Fertilize in spring and again after spring flowering with a complete organic fertilizer to encourage repeat bloom. To make a hedge, plant bushes every 4 feet—they will be touching in three years.

DISEASE AND PEST PROBLEMS: 'Cornelia' is resistant to black spot and mildew. To protect the new foliage, spray with fungicidal soap or garden sulfur combined with an antitranspirant; reapply as needed.

RELATED CULTIVARS: 'Felicia' ('Trier' × 'Ophelia'; Pemberton, United Kingdom; 1928) bears large clusters of fragrant, apricot-blush buds that open to blush pink, semidouble flowers. Repeat bloom is reliable. Shrubs grow upright and spreading to 5 feet tall and wide. 'Felicia' is suitable as a hedge, specimen, mass, and pillar rose.

'Cornelia'

'Dainty Bess'

Cultivar Name:	'Dainty Bess'
Classification:	Hybrid tea
Parentage:	'Ophelia' × 'King of Kings'
Introduced:	Archer, United Kingdom; 1925
USDA Plant Hardiness Zones:	5 to 9

DESCRIPTION: Elegant 'Dainty Bess' is one of the best old-fashioned, single-flowered hybrid tea roses. Deep pink, urn-shaped buds open to large, fragrant, rose-pink flowers, each with five fringed petals and distinctive burgundy stamens. These lovely blooms are borne singly or in clusters on an upright shrub to 4 feet tall and 2 feet wide. The stems are covered with leathery leaves.

LANDSCAPE USES: Few hybrid tea roses look so well with perennials and antique roses in mixed borders. Use 'Dainty Bess' to fill a position in the middle of the border, where its stiff hybrid tea stems will be hidden by foreground plantings. Plant drifts of three or more bushes for effective floral displays, and surround them with perennials that will bloom in sequence through the season. A good combination would be the deep pink plumes of Japanese meadowsweet (*Filipendula purpurea*) in late spring, followed by white-flowered garden phlox 'Miss Lingard' in summer, the blue flowers of 'Dark Knight' bluebeard (*Caryopteris* 'Dark Knight') and asters in late summer, and white anemone (*Anemone* 'Honorine Jobert') in autumn.

CULTURE: Plant in a sunny location in well-drained soil that has been amended with organic matter. Prune hard in late winter or early spring to rid plants of damaged canes and overwintering disease spores. Fertilize after pruning and again after first bloom with a complete organic fertilizer. Top-dress with compost annually.

DISEASE AND PEST PROBLEMS: 'Dainty Bess' has fair disease resistance. Protect new foliage with an application of fungicidal soap or garden sulfur combined with an antitranspirant to prevent black spot; repeat as necessary. Monitor the plants for insect damage.

'Dapple Dawn'

Cultivar Name:	'Dapple Dawn'
Classification:	English rose
Parentage:	Sport of 'Red Coat'
Introduced:	Austin, United Kingdom; 1983
USDA Plant Hardiness Zones:	5 to 9

DESCRIPTION: Single-flowered 'Dapple Dawn' bears sprays of bright pink blooms veined with deeper pink. Each bloom opens to reveal golden stamens. The scented flowers repeat their bloom. Pruned bushes reach 4 feet tall and wide.

LANDSCAPE USES: Use 'Dapple Dawn' as a specimen or in a mass or hedge. Its delicate flowers look attractive with both antique and modern roses.

CULTURE: Plant in full sun in well-drained soil that has been amended with organic matter. Top-dress with compost annually. Prune while dormant to remove deadwood, thin out crowded stems, and reduce the canes by one-half to two-thirds their length. Fertilize after pruning and again after flowering with a complete organic fertilizer.

DISEASE AND PEST PROBLEMS: Although 'Dapple Dawn' has good disease resistance, the breeder recommends applying preventive sprays for best results. Spray with fungicidal soap or garden sulfur combined with an antitranspirant as soon as leaves emerge in spring to prevent black spot; reapply as needed.

'Don Juan'

Cultivar Name:	'Don Juan'
Classification:	Large-flowered climber
Parentage:	'New Dawn' seedling × 'New Yorker'
Introduced:	Malandrone, France; Jackson & Perkins, United States; 1958
USDA Plant Hardiness Zones:	6 to 9

DESCRIPTION: 'Don Juan' produces fragrant, classic hybrid tea–type flowers of burgundy red. It blooms profusely in spring, with stingy repeat bloom. The bushy, upright plants reach 8 feet tall and are covered with glossy foliage. The flowers are borne singly or in clusters. They keep their color and make good cut flowers.

LANDSCAPE USES: 'Don Juan' is worth growing for its lovely, fragrant flowers. It can be grown on a pillar, espaliered on a wall, or trained on an arch or trellis. It looks well with cool pastel color schemes and looks particularly fine with blue or pink flowers and silver-leaved perennials.

CULTURE: This is a rose for mild climates. In Zone 6, it grows best on a warm wall. Plant 'Don Juan' in full sun in well-drained soil that has been amended with organic matter. Top-dress with compost annually and fertilize in spring and after first flowering with a complete organic fertilizer. For the first two or three years, little pruning is required. Just tie in the canes to their support and deadhead spent blooms. Prune the mature plants in late winter each year, removing deadwood and crowded canes and choosing young, stocky canes to replace older ones. Reduce sideshoots to four buds.

DISEASE AND PEST PROBLEMS: 'Don Juan' has good disease resistance. For extra protection, apply fungicidal soap, garden sulfur combined with an antitranspirant, or an antitranspirant alone when leaves emerge in spring; reapply as needed.

Dortmund®

Cultivar Name:	Dortmund®
Classification:	Kordesii
Parentage:	Seedling × *Rosa kordesii*
Introduced:	W. Kordes Söhne, Germany; 1955
USDA Plant Hardiness Zones:	5 to 9

DESCRIPTION: One of the best known Kordesii climbers, Dortmund® features huge clusters of large, single, red flowers, each with a prominent white eye. The massive spring bloom is not duplicated in autumn, but repeat bloom is good if you remove the spent flowers. If not deadheaded, the plant forms large, orange-red hips but few autumn flowers. The blooms have a light, fruity fragrance. The vigorous, thorny canes are covered with dark green, glossy leaves. Trained as a climber, the canes reach 8 to 10 feet. When grown as a shrub, the plant forms a mounding mass 5 to 6 feet tall and wide.

LANDSCAPE USES: Dortmund® is one of the showiest red climbers. It is wonderful when grown on a fence, espaliered on a wall, or trained on an arch or trellis. Its scarlet bloom combines nicely with pastel color schemes and looks particularly fine with blue-flowered and silver-leaved perennials. Its prostrate canes make it a good choice for a mounding groundcover; it also looks lovely cascading over a wall.

CULTURE: This is a hardy rose for tough situations in full sun. Plant in well-drained soil, top-dress with compost annually, and fertilize in spring with a complete organic fertilizer. A second application of fertilizer after the spring bloom encourages repeat bloom. For the first two or three years, little pruning is required. Just tie in the canes to their support and deadhead spent blooms. Prune mature plants while dormant, removing deadwood and crowded canes. At that time, also choose young, stocky canes to replace older ones and cut back sideshoots to four buds.

DISEASE AND PEST PROBLEMS: Dortmund® is exceptionally resistant to diseases. For extra protection, make one application of fungicidal soap, garden sulfur combined with an antitranspirant, or an antitranspirant alone when leaves emerge in spring; reapply if needed.

RELATED CULTIVARS: In 1952, Wilhelm Kordes originated *Rosa kordesii* from spontaneous chromosome doubling in a 'Max Graf' (*Rosa rugosa* × *Rosa wichuraiana*) seedling. It was never introduced commercially, but Kordes used it to breed a new class known as Kordesii roses. All are hardy, disease-resistant, reblooming roses with long canes. They are usually trained as pillars and climbers but occasionally are grown as freestanding, mounding shrubs.

'Hamburger Phoenix' (Kordesii; *Rosa kordesii* × seedling; Kordes, Germany; 1954) produces fragrant, semidouble, red flowers in large clusters, followed by orange-red hips and repeat bloom. It makes a robust pillar or climber to about 9 feet tall.

'Heidelberg' (Kordesii; Kordes, Germany; 1959) bears large, double, crimson flowers with lighter red on the back of the petals. It makes a vigorous pillar rose to 8 feet tall.

'Illusion' (Kordesii; Kordes, Germany; 1961) is covered in fragrant, scarlet, double blooms in spring with repeat bloom in autumn. It makes a robust, disease-free climber 8 to 10 feet tall.

Ilse Krohn Superior® (Kordesii; Kordes, Germany; 1964) produces fragrant, double, pure white flowers in spring with repeat bloom in summer; strong canes grow 8 to 10 feet tall.

'Leverkusen' (Kordesii; *Rosa kordesii* × 'Golden Glow'; Kordes, Germany; 1954) is a hardy, yellow climber. It produces fragrant, double, high-centered, creamy yellow flowers in sprays in spring with some repeat bloom in summer. Glossy foliage covers long canes that make a choice, 10-foot pillar rose or large, mounding shrub.

Parkdirektor Riggers® (Kordesii; *Rosa kordesii* × 'Our Princess'; Kordes, Germany; 1957) is reminiscent of Dortmund® and produces fragrant, semidouble, crimson flowers in huge clusters in spring with abundant repeat bloom in summer. Vigorous canes clothed in dark, glossy foliage make a climber or pillar rose that grows 10 to 12 feet tall.

'Raymond Chenault' (Kordesii; *Rosa kordesii* × 'Montezuma'; Kordes, Germany; 1960) is a showy climber blanketed with fragrant, large, cardinal red, single flowers in spring with summer rebloom. It bears huge floral clusters on vigorous canes that grow 9 to 12 feet tall with glossy, leathery leaves. It is suitable for training on an arch, pergola, or trellis, or you can let it climb into a tree.

Rosarium Uetersen® (Kordesii; Kordes, Germany; 1977) bears double, deep pink, fragrant blooms in spring with summer rebloom. It makes a lovely pillar rose with 8- to 10-foot stems covered in dark, glossy foliage.

'Eden Climber'

Cultivar Name:	**'Eden Climber'** (also called 'Eden', 'Eden Rose 88', Pierre de Ronsard®)
Classification:	Large-flowered climber
Parentage:	('Danse des Sylphes' × 'Haender') × 'Climbing Pink Wonder'
Introduced:	Meilland, France; 1985; Conard-Pyle, United States; 1988
USDA Plant Hardiness Zones:	5 to 9

DESCRIPTION: 'Eden Climber', sometimes sold simply as 'Eden', is an excellent, hardy climbing rose. Clusters of fat, round, creamy buds open to large, cupped, very full double flowers. Each has a swirl of soft pink petals in the center surrounded by creamy outer petals that are tinted with lemon-yellow. The charming, fragrant, old-fashioned flowers are produced with abandon for several weeks in early summer with only a few later blooms in most regions. Even with little or no rebloom, 'Eden Climber' is worth growing for its massive annual display of well-scented flowers. Vigorous canes easily scale an 8- to 10-foot trellis and fan out to fill a similar spread. The robust canes are armed with large prickles and covered with glossy, large leaves that form a flattering dark background for the soft pink flowers.

LANDSCAPE USES: This vigorous, hardy, free-flowering climber can be used to cover a trellis, wall, arch, or fence. It looks particularly fine sharing a lattice with the repeat-blooming deep pink climber 'Parade'. Weave a large-flowered clematis through it for later-season blooms. 'Eden Climber' can also serve as a freestanding shrub or impenetrable mass.

CULTURE: Give 'Eden Climber' a sunny location in well-drained soil that has been amended with organic matter. Top-dress with compost annually. Prune while dormant: Choose healthy canes to fit the space you have, tie them to their supports, and reduce sideshoots to four buds. Deadhead spent flowers to neaten plants and encourage repeat bloom. Fertilize after pruning and again after the first bloom with a complete organic fertilizer. This rose is highly recommended for all regions.

DISEASE AND PEST PROBLEMS: 'Eden Climber' has excellent disease resistance.

Cultivar Name:	Electron®
Classification:	Hybrid tea
Parentage:	'Paddy McGredy' × 'Prima Ballerina'
Introduced:	McGredy, New Zealand; 1970
	1973 All-America Rose Selection
USDA Plant Hardiness Zones:	5 to 9

DESCRIPTION: Rarely out of bloom, Electron® bears deep pink, fragrant flowers. Shapely buds open to large, high-centered, double blooms carried singly or in sprays. Vigorous, compact bushes reach 4 feet tall and 3 feet wide. The very thorny stems are covered with leathery, dark green foliage. Electron® makes an excellent cut flower.

LANDSCAPE USES: Electron® is a dependable bloomer, producing flowers nonstop through the season. Use it as a handsome specimen or in masses in shrub borders. In mixed borders, its continuous flower production provides a bright spot of color throughout the season. Its fragrant, long-lasting blooms make it a must for the cutting garden.

CULTURE: Plant Electron® in a sunny location in well-drained soil that has been amended with organic matter. Prune hard in late winter or early spring to rid plants of damaged canes and overwintering disease spores. Fertilize after pruning and again after first bloom with a complete organic fertilizer. Top-dress with compost annually. Deadhead spent blooms to encourage repeat bloom. Apply a mound of mulch as winter protection in Zones 5 and 6. Electron® is highly recommended for all regions.

DISEASE AND PEST PROBLEMS: Like other hybrid teas, Electron® is susceptible to diseases. Protect new foliage with an application of fungicidal soap or garden sulfur combined with an antitranspirant to prevent black spot; reapply monthly. Monitor the plants for insect damage.

Electron®

Escapade®

Cultivar Name:	Escapade®
Classification:	Floribunda
Parentage:	'Pink Parfait' × 'Baby Faurax'
Introduced:	Harkness, United Kingdom; 1967
USDA Plant Hardiness Zones:	5 to 9

DESCRIPTION: Escapade® is an excellent everblooming floribunda that produces large clusters of mauve-pink, semidouble flowers that open to reveal a white eye. It forms a dense, rounded shrub to 3 feet tall and 2 feet wide with glossy foliage.

LANDSCAPE USES: Escapade® is suitable for use as an everblooming shrub mass, foundation planting, low hedge, specimen, or container plant. In mixed borders, the elegant, old-fashioned blooms combine well with perennials and other shrubs. Plant it in drifts of three or more bushes to make a mass of all-season bloom.

CULTURE: Plant Escapade® in a sunny location in well-drained soil that has been amended with organic matter. Prune hard in late winter or early spring to rid plants of overwintering disease spores and to encourage vigorous new growth. Fertilize after pruning and again after the first bloom with a complete organic fertilizer. Top-dress with compost annually. Deadhead spent blooms through the season. Apply a mound of mulch to protect the graft union from winter injury in Zone 5. This rose is highly recommended for all regions.

DISEASE AND PEST PROBLEMS: Escapade® exhibits excellent disease resistance. For extra protection, apply fungicidal soap or garden sulfur combined with an antitranspirant as soon as leaves emerge in spring to

prevent black spot. Monitor plants and reapply as needed. Monitor insect feeding, and apply insecticidal soap as needed to prevent damage to buds and leaves.

Europeana®

Cultivar Name:	Europeana®
Classification:	Floribunda
Parentage:	'Ruth Leuwerik' × 'Rosemary Rose'
Introduced:	deRuiter, Holland; 1963 1968 All-America Rose Selection
USDA Plant Hardiness Zones:	5 to 9

DESCRIPTION: Europeana® is one of the best of the dark red, everblooming floribunda roses. It produces large clusters of double, deep red flowers. It makes a dense, rounded shrub to 3 feet tall and 2 feet wide, covered with glossy foliage.

LANDSCAPE USES: Europeana® is wonderful as an everblooming shrub mass, foundation planting, low hedge, specimen, or container plant. In mixed borders, the elegant, old-fashioned blooms mingle easily with perennials and other shrubs. Plant it in drifts of three or more bushes to make a mass of all-season bloom.

CULTURE: Plant Europeana® in a sunny location in well-drained soil that has been amended with organic matter. Prune hard in late winter or early spring to rid plants of overwintering disease spores and to encourage vigorous new growth. Fertilize after pruning and again after the first bloom with a complete organic fertilizer. Top-dress with compost annually. Deadhead spent blooms through the season. Apply a mound of mulch to protect the graft union from winter injury in Zone 5. This rose is highly recommended for all regions.

DISEASE AND PEST PROBLEMS: Europeana® exhibits moderate disease resistance. Apply fungicidal soap or garden sulfur combined with an antitranspirant as soon as leaves emerge in spring to prevent black spot; monitor plants and reapply as needed. Check for insect feeding, and apply insecticidal soap as needed to prevent damage to buds and leaves.

Fair Bianca®

Cultivar Name:	Fair Bianca®
Classification:	English rose
Parentage:	Includes 'Belle Isis'
Introduced:	Austin, United Kingdom; 1982
USDA Plant Hardiness Zones:	5 to 9

DESCRIPTION: Deep pink buds open to very full, quartered, pure white flowers, that often reveal a button-like center. Flowers are similar to those of the damask rose 'Madame Hardy' but with the added benefit of repeat bloom. Clusters of myrrh-scented flowers are borne on compact bushes that grow 3 feet tall and wide. The stems are armed with bristles, but few thorns, and covered with small, light green, semiglossy leaves.

LANDSCAPE USES: Fair Bianca® has a habit similar to a floribunda rose and makes an attractive mass, low hedge, specimen, and container plant. In mixed borders, plant a group of three bushes in a drift near the front so you can enjoy its fragrance. Underplant with perennial companions like 'Johnson's Blue' cranesbill (*Geranium* 'Johnson's Blue'), 'Bath's Pink' dianthus (*Dianthus* 'Bath's Pink'), and 'Blue Hill' salvia (*Salvia* 'Blue Hill'). One of

the most compact of the English roses, Fair Bianca® is an excellent choice for small gardens, herb gardens, and borders of all-white flowers. It looks attractive with both antique and modern roses.

CULTURE: Plant Fair Bianca® in full sun in well-drained soil that has been amended with organic matter. Top-dress with compost annually. Prune dormant plants to clear the centers and reduce canes to about 12 inches. Fertilize after pruning and again after spring bloom with a complete organic fertilizer. This rose is recommended for all regions, but protect the crown with a hill of mulch to prevent winter damage in Zone 5.

DISEASE AND PEST PROBLEMS: Fair Bianca® exhibits moderate disease resistance, but protect new foliage with an application of fungicidal soap or garden sulfur combined with an antitranspirant to prevent black spot. Repeat if a problem develops. Monitor the plants for insect damage.

'The Fairy'

Cultivar Name:	'The Fairy'
Classification:	Polyantha
Parentage:	'Paul Crampel' × 'Lady Gay'
Introduced:	Bentall, United Kingdom; 1932
USDA Plant Hardiness Zones:	4 to 9

DESCRIPTION: One of the best and most versatile of the polyanthas, 'The Fairy' is an international favorite. Sprays of dainty, clear pink double flowers are produced continuously from spring through frost. The compact, spreading, dense shrub reaches 2 feet tall and 3 feet wide and is covered with small, glossy leaves.

LANDSCAPE USES: Use this everblooming shrub as a groundcover, low hedge, mass, or container specimen. In mixed borders, its old-fashioned, rosette flowers mix beautifully with antique and modern roses and perennials. Plant it in drifts of three or more bushes to make a mass of all-season bloom.

CULTURE: Grow 'The Fairy' in a sunny location, although it does accept light shade. Plant in well-drained soil that has been amended with organic matter. Prune while dormant to thin out crowded stems, shape bushes, and encourage new growth. To keep plants compact, prune stems hard (as you would on a floribunda). Fertilize after pruning and again after the first bloom with a complete organic fertilizer. Top-dress with compost annually. This rose is highly recommended for all regions. Provide winter protection in Zone 4.

DISEASE AND PEST PROBLEMS: 'The Fairy' is generally disease-free. For extra protection, you may apply fungicidal soap or garden sulfur combined with an antitranspirant as soon as leaves emerge in spring to prevent black spot. Treat mildew with an application of fungicidal soap or horticultural oil.

Cultivar Name:	**'Fantin-Latour'**
Classification:	Centifolia hybrid
Parentage:	Not recorded
Introduced:	Nineteenth century
USDA Plant Hardiness Zones:	4 to 8

DESCRIPTION: Little is known about the origins of this rose, except that it combines centifolia and China rose characteristics. 'Fantin-Latour' bears deep pink buds that open to large, cupped, very full, pale pink flowers. The charming, richly perfumed, quartered blooms are typically composed of two hundred petals and open to reveal a buttonlike center. 'Fantin-Latour' blooms abundantly for a few weeks in spring with no repeat bloom. The canes have few prickles and are covered with dark green, round, semiglossy leaves. In cool climates, this hardy, upright, well-branched shrub grows 5 to 6 feet tall and less wide. In

warm climates, it tends to make a smaller bush about 4 feet tall and wide.

LANDSCAPE USES: Use 'Fantin-Latour' as a specimen positioned near the back of a mixed border, where its old-fashioned flowers will nod above perennial companions and lower shrubs. Give it plenty of room, or support the canes on a sturdy tripod or pillar to conserve space. Its soft blush flowers blend easily with other roses. It looks particularly handsome planted with the tall spires of foxgloves and surrounded by rich crimson blooms of gallica or English roses.

CULTURE: This vigorous shrub is easy to grow in full sun in any well-drained soil. Top-dress with compost annually, and fertilize in spring with a complete organic fertilizer. Prune after the bloom in summer, cutting back canes that flowered to about one-third their length. Also remove some older wood and thin out crowded stems. This rose is recommended for all regions.

DISEASE AND PEST PROBLEMS: 'Fantin-Latour' is moderately disease-resistant. If desired, protect new foliage with an application of fungicidal soap or garden sulfur combined with an antitranspirant to prevent black spot.

'Fantin-Latour'

'Félicité Parmentier'

Cultivar Name:	'Félicité Parmentier'
Classification:	Alba
Parentage:	Not recorded
Introduced:	1834
USDA Plant Hardiness Zones:	3 to 8

DESCRIPTION: Unusual ivory buds, tinged pale green, open to very full, flesh pink flowers. The quartered blooms open flat and fade to creamy white. The fragrant flowers are produced in profusion in spring with no repeat bloom. Compact, vigorous bushes grow 4 feet tall and wide. The upright, thorny stems are covered in gray-green leaves.

LANDSCAPE USES: The compact size of 'Félicité Parmentier' makes it a very versatile garden rose. Use it as a specimen, or group a few to make a shrub mass or infor-mal hedge. Its characteristic gray-green foliage provides a lovely backdrop for the flesh pink flowers. In the middle of mixed borders, its blush flowers look beautiful with spires of foxgloves, globes of star of Persia (*Allium christophii*), and spikes of violet sage (*Salvia* × *superba*).

CULTURE: 'Félicité Parmentier' is a robust, hardy shrub that's easy to grow in full sun in any well-drained soil. Top-dress with compost annually, and fertilize in spring with a complete organic fertilizer. Prune lightly to

thin out crowded stems. To make a hedge, set plants every 3 feet—plants will be touching in three years. This rose is highly recommended for all regions.

DISEASE AND PEST PROBLEMS: 'Félicité Parmentier' is generally disease-free, but mildew sometimes affects the foliage. At the first sign of fungal problems, spray with fungicidal soap or horticultural oil at a rate of 1 to 2 tablespoons per 1 gallon of water.

'Ferdinand Pichard'

Cultivar Name:	'Ferdinand Pichard'
Classification:	Hybrid perpetual
Parentage:	Not recorded
Introduced:	Tanne, France; 1921
USDA Plant Hardiness Zones:	4 to 9

DESCRIPTION: A superb striped rose, 'Ferdinand Pichard' produces double, cupped blooms of pale blush pink streaked with crimson. A heavy spring crop of fragrant flowers is followed by scattered summer repeat bloom. Vigorous bushes grow 4 to 5 feet tall and less wide with relatively smooth stems covered with light green leaves.

LANDSCAPE USES: This rose deserves a special place where you can easily appreciate its beautifully striped, fragrant flowers. You might use it as an accent in a mixed planting with shorter shrub roses of rich crimson and add a few plants of blue-spiked catmint (such as *Nepeta sibirica* 'Souvenir d'André Chaudron'). It can also be pegged or trained along a fence.

CULTURE: Plant 'Ferdinand Pichard' in a sunny location in well-drained soil that has been amended with organic matter. Prune bushes while dormant to rid plants of damaged canes, reducing canes by one-half their length. Fertilize after pruning and again after first bloom with a complete organic fertilizer. Top-dress with compost annually, and deadhead spent blooms to encourage repeat bloom. Apply a mound of mulch as winter protection in Zones 4 to 5.

DISEASE AND PEST PROBLEMS: Like most hybrid perpetual roses, 'Ferdinand Pichard' is susceptible to diseases. Protect the new foliage with an application of fungicidal soap or garden sulfur combined with an anti-transpirant to prevent black spot; repeat as needed. Monitor the plants for insect damage.

'F. J. Grootendorst'

Cultivar Name:	**'F. J. Grootendorst'**
Classification:	Hybrid rugosa
Parentage:	*Rosa rugosa* var. *rubra* × 'Madame Norbert Lavavasseur'
Introduced:	Degoey; F. J. Grootendorst, Holland; 1918
USDA Plant Hardiness Zones:	4 to 8

DESCRIPTION: 'F. J. Grootendorst' is unusual among hybrid rugosa roses because it bears odd fringed, bright red flowers that resemble carnations. The small, very full dou-

ble blooms with pinked or serrated edges are carried in sprays of about two dozen flowers. There is little or no scent. Abundant spring bloom is followed by plentiful repeat bloom. Dense, mounded shrubs grow 4 to 5 feet tall and wide. The leathery, semiglossy leaves, less wrinkled than those of *Rosa rugosa*, turn orange-red and purple in autumn. This is an odd rose that gardeners either love or hate.

LANDSCAPE USES: Grow 'F. J. Grootendorst' as a hedge, mass, screen, or specimen. Its unusual blooms, repeat flowering habit, and autumn color make this an ideal all-season shrub. This tough, hardy shrub thrives with little attention.

CULTURE: Plant 'F. J. Grootendorst' in full sun in any well-drained soil. To make a hedge, plant bushes every 4 feet—plants will be touching in three years. Prune specimens and hedges while they are dormant. Reduce shrubs by about one-third to shape and neaten, while periodically removing older canes to encourage vigorous new growth. 'F. J. Grootendorst' is not recommended for Zones 4 or 5 in the Midwest, where winter injury often occurs.

DISEASE AND PEST PROBLEMS: 'F. J. Grootendorst' generally develops some black spot by the end of the season, but the disease does not cause bushes to defoliate, so control is seldom needed.

RELATED CULTIVARS: 'Grootendorst Supreme' ('F. J. Grootendorst' sport; Grootendorst, Holland; 1936) bears deep crimson flowers but is otherwise similar to the parent.

'Pink Grootendorst' ('F. J. Grootendorst' sport; Grootendorst, Holland; 1923) bears flowers in clear pink but is otherwise similar to the parent.

'Fimbriata' (*Rosa rugosa* × 'Madame Alfred Carrière'; Morlet, France, 1891) is a fringed rose with a little more refinement and a lot more scent than the 'Grootendorst' crowd. Small, starlike, blush-white flowers with fringed petals are produced lavishly in spring followed by a crop of red hips and respectable repeat bloom. Dense, mounding bushes grow 4 feet tall and wide and are covered with medium green, leathery foliage. An excellent specimen shrub for mixed borders, 'Fimbriata' looks particularly fine underplanted with blue-flowered catmints (*Nepeta* spp.), and surrounded by graceful spires of foxglove (*Digitalis purpurea*). Place it near the front of the border and enjoy its clusters of fragrant flowers all season. This charming rose is fragrant, disease-free, and hardy to Zone 4.

'Four Seasons'

Cultivar Name:	'Four Seasons' (also called 'Rose des Quartre Saisons d'Italie')
Classification:	Damask perpetual
Parentage:	Not recorded
Introduced:	Not recorded
USDA Plant Hardiness Zones:	4 to 8

DESCRIPTION: The round, light crimson buds of 'Four Seasons' open to full flowers of deep magenta-pink held among the foliage on short, bristly stems. The quartered flowers have a sweet damask perfume and are produced abundantly in spring with liberal autumn rebloom. Vigorous, compact shrubs grow 3½ to 4 feet tall and 2½ feet wide and are armed with bristles but few prickles. The stems are covered with light green leaves.

LANDSCAPE USES: 'Four Seasons' and its damask perpetual relatives are the hardiest of the repeat-flowering old roses and make excellent compact shrubs for small gardens. For best effect, plant a grouping of three shrubs to create a drift of seasonal color in the border or herb garden. Use it near the front of the border, underplanted with artemisia and a group of polyantha roses.

CULTURE: Plant 'Four Seasons' in a sunny location in a well-drained soil that has been amended with organic matter. Prune while dormant to thin out crowded stems and to reduce canes by one-third their length. Fertilize after pruning and again after the first bloom with a complete organic fertilizer. Top-dress with compost annually. Deadhead to encourage late blooms. This rose is highly recommended for all regions. Provide winter protection in Zone 4.

DISEASE AND PEST PROBLEMS: 'Four Seasons' is moderately resistant to black spot and mildew. For extra protection, apply fungicidal soap or garden sulfur combined with an antitranspirant as soon as leaves emerge in spring and again in midsummer to prevent black spot. When plants are left unsprayed, the foliage turns bronze from black spot by autumn, but is not unsightly.

'Fragrant Cloud'

Cultivar Name:	'Fragrant Cloud'
Classification:	Hybrid tea
Parentage:	Seedling × 'Prima Ballerina'
Introduced:	Tantau, Germany; 1963; Jackson & Perkins, United States; 1968 1969 James Alexander Gamble Rose Fragrance Medal
USDA Plant Hardiness Zones:	5 to 9

DESCRIPTION: Elegant urn-shaped buds open to large, high-centered, double blooms. The orange-red flowers have an intense fruity perfume. The everblooming, midsized shrubs are upright, bushy, 4 to 5 feet tall and 2½ feet wide, and covered with dark green foliage. 'Fragrant Cloud' makes a superb cut flower.

LANDSCAPE USES: Use a grouping of 'Fragrant Cloud' for an accent of all-season bloom in flower borders with hot color schemes. Camouflage its stiff hybrid tea habit by combining it with informal perennials such as 'Coronation Gold' yarrow (*Achillea* × 'Coronation Gold'), 'Moonbeam' coreopsis (*Coreopsis verticillata* 'Moonbeam'), and silver-leaved artemisias. Accent it with background spires of Carolina lupine (*Thermopsis caroliniana*) and mulleins (*Verbascum* spp.). It is a must for the cutting garden for its fragrant, long-lasting blooms.

CULTURE: Plant 'Fragrant Cloud' in a sunny location in well-drained soil that has been amended with organic matter. Prune hard in late winter or early spring to rid plants of damaged canes and overwintering disease spores. Fertilize after pruning and again after the first bloom with a complete organic fertilizer. Top-dress with compost annually. Deadhead the spent blooms to encourage repeat bloom. Apply a mound of mulch as winter protection in Zone 5.

DISEASE AND PEST PROBLEMS: Like other hybrid teas, 'Fragrant Cloud' is susceptible to diseases. Protect the new foliage with an application of fungicidal soap or garden sulfur combined with an antitranspirant to prevent black spot; repeat monthly. Monitor the plants for insect damage.

LANDSCAPE USES: A fine hedge, groundcover, or specimen, 'Frau Dagmar Hartopp' is the best overall performer and most useful compact landscape plant of the rugosa hybrids. The nearly continuous bloom creates a bright spot in the mixed border when interplanted with perennials and herbs—especially those of a deeper pastel color. The tough, hardy shrub is tolerant of seaside conditions and urban landscapes. Few shrubs are better adapted to sidewalk, driveway, or parking lot plantings.

CULTURE: Plant 'Frau Dagmar Hartopp' in full sun in any well-drained soil. Like other rugosa hybrids, it tolerates hot spots characterized by reflected heat from paving. To make a hedge, plant bushes every 2½ feet—plants will be touching in three years. Prune mature specimens and hedges in late winter. Remove about one-third of the top growth to shape the plants, and remove older canes every year or two to encourage vigorous new growth. No other care is required.

DISEASE AND PEST PROBLEMS: Rugosa hybrids are tough plants typically not bothered by diseases or pests. The summer flowers sometimes attract Japanese beetles; pick off adult beetles, and treat lawn areas with milky disease spores to control grubs. Rugosa hybrids are susceptible to rose stem girdler. Keep plants free of deadwood; prune out and destroy infected canes.

Cultivar Name:	**'Frau Dagmar Hartopp'** (also called 'Fru Dagmar Hastrup')
Classification:	Hybrid rugosa
Parentage:	*Rosa rugosa* seedling
Introduced:	Hastrup, Holland; 1914
USDA Plant Hardiness Zones:	3 to 8

DESCRIPTION: 'Frau Dagmar Hartopp' forms a dense, bushy, compact shrub about 3½ feet tall and 3 feet wide. Buds are deep pink, opening to large, silver-pink, single flowers with golden yellow stamens. Masses of the fragrant flowers are produced almost continuously throughout the season. Large tomato red hips ripen in late summer. The autumn foliage color is an attractive golden bronze typical of the species. To ensure good development of the hips, plant a companion such as *Rosa rugosa* var. *alba*, or var. *rubra* for cross-pollination. Harvest fresh hips to make an excellent jam, or dry them for use as an herbal tea rich in vitamin C.

'Frau Dagmar Hartopp'

'Frau Karl Druschki'

Cultivar Name:	**'Frau Karl Druschki'** (also called 'Snow Queen')
Classification:	Hybrid perpetual
Parentage:	'Merveille de Lyon' × 'Madame Caroline Testout'
Introduced:	Lambert, Germany; 1901
USDA Plant Hardiness Zones:	4 to 9

DESCRIPTION: 'Frau Karl Druschki' is one of the last great hybrid perpetual roses produced before the line was abandoned in favor of hybrid teas. It produces elegant, long, pointed buds that are touched with deep pink. The buds open to large, high-centered flowers of snow white. The lovely, double, hybrid tea–type blooms are carried singly or in clusters on vigorous bushes reaching 5 to 7 feet tall by 3 feet wide. It blooms profusely in spring with good repeat bloom. The blooms have no scent but make excellent cut flowers.

LANDSCAPE USES: Grow 'Frau Karl Druschki' as a freestanding, upright shrub or train it as a pillar rose. It makes a handsome specimen at the back of mixed borders, where its large, pure white blooms will show above lower plants and blend easily with both modern and antique roses. It looks wonderful surrounded by spires of foxgloves and the tall, graceful plumes of lavender mist (*Thalictrum rochebrunianum*).

CULTURE: Plant this rose in a sunny location in well-drained soil that has been amended with organic matter. Prune hard while the plants are dormant to rid them of damaged canes and overwintering disease spores. Fertilize after pruning and again after the first bloom with a complete organic fertilizer. Top-dress with compost annually. Deadhead spent blooms to encourage repeat bloom. Prune pillars by removing older canes and shortening sideshoots to four buds. Apply a mound of mulch as winter protection in Zones 4 and 5.

DISEASE AND PEST PROBLEMS: Like other hybrid perpetuals, 'Frau Karl Druschki' is susceptible to diseases. Protect new foliage with an application of fungicidal soap or garden sulfur combined with an antitranspirant to prevent black spot; reapply monthly. Monitor the plants for insect damage.

'Fruhlingsmorgen'

Cultivar Name:	**'Fruhlingsmorgen'** (also called 'Spring Morning')
Classification:	Hybrid spinosissima
Parentage:	('E. G. Hill' × 'Catherine Kordes') × *Rosa spinosissima* var. *altaica*
Introduced:	W. Kordes Söhne, Germany; 1942
USDA Plant Hardiness Zones:	4 to 9

DESCRIPTION: In full bloom, 'Fruhlingsmorgen' makes a magnificent late-spring show. Although there is no rebloom, it is worth growing for its stunning spring performance. At that time, vigorous bushes are blanketed with huge, cherry pink blossoms. Each bloom is flushed amber in the center and filled with maroon stamens. The dense shrubs grow 5 to 6 feet tall with a similar spread. The tall, arching canes are modestly armed with prickles and covered with soft gray-green foliage.

LANDSCAPE USES: Use 'Fruhlingsmorgen' as a seasonal accent in mixed borders, where it can fade into a green background mass when not in bloom. It is also suitable for massing, screening, and edging.

CULTURE: Plant in a sunny location in well-drained soil that has been amended with organic matter. To make a hedge, plant bushes every 4 feet—the plants will be touching in three years. Prune while dormant to thin out crowded stems and keep plants in bounds. Prune hedges to shape and neaten. Fertilize after pruning with a complete organic fertilizer. Top-dress with compost annually. This rose is highly recommended for all regions.

DISEASE AND PEST PROBLEMS: 'Fruhlingsmorgen' has good disease resistance. Black spot occurs in some regions but does not defoliate plants.

RELATED CULTIVARS: Fruhlingsgold® ('Joanna Hill' × *Rosa spinosissima* var. *hispida*; W. Kordes Söhne, Germany; 1937) is a hardy yellow rose for northern gardens. Pointed, orange buds open to large, pale yellow, fragrant flowers. Otherwise it is similar to 'Fruhlingsmorgen'.

Cultivar Name:	'Gene Boerner'
Classification:	Floribunda
Parentage:	'Ma Perkins' × 'Garnette Supreme'
Introduced:	Boerner; Jackson & Perkins, United States; 1968 1969 All-America Rose Selection
USDA Plant Hardiness Zones:	5 to 9

DESCRIPTION: Rarely out of bloom, 'Gene Boerner' bears huge clusters of full-petaled, star-shaped, clear pink flowers. It makes a tall, upright shrub that is 3½ to 4 feet tall and 2 feet wide and covered with semiglossy foliage. It is named for the American hybridizer who created many great roses, including 'Apricot Nectar' and 'Aloha'.

LANDSCAPE USES: 'Gene Boerner' is a dependable bloomer, suitable for use as a shrub mass, foundation planting, medium hedge, or specimen. In mixed borders, its old-fashioned blooms look attractive with perennials and other shrubs. Plant it in drifts of three or more bushes to make a mass of all-season bloom.

CULTURE: Plant in a sunny location in well-drained soil that has been amended with organic matter. Prune hard in late winter or early spring to rid plants of over-wintering disease spores and to encourage vigorous new growth. Fertilize after pruning and again after the first bloom with a complete organic fertilizer. Top-dress with compost annually. Deadhead spent blooms through the season. Apply a mound of mulch to protect the graft union from winter injury in Zone 5. This floribunda is highly recommended for all regions.

DISEASE AND PEST PROBLEMS: 'Gene Boerner' has moderate disease resistance. For extra protection, apply fungicidal soap or garden sulfur combined with an antitranspirant as soon as leaves emerge in spring to prevent black spot. Monitor plants and reapply as needed. Monitor insect feeding, and apply insecticidal soap as needed to prevent damage to buds and leaves.

'Gene Boerner'

'Gloire de Dijon'

'Gloire de France'

Cultivar Name:	'Gloire de Dijon'
Classification:	Climbing tea
Parentage:	Tea rose × 'Souvenir de la Malmaison'
Introduced:	Jacotot, France; 1853
USDA Plant Hardiness Zones:	6 to 9

Cultivar Name:	'Gloire de France' (also called 'Fanny Bias')
Classification:	Gallica
Parentage:	Not recorded
Introduced:	Cultivated before 1819
USDA Plant Hardiness Zones:	4 to 8

DESCRIPTION: A free-flowering climber, 'Gloire de Dijon' bears large, full, high-centered blooms of rich buff. They open flat and sometimes quartered to display an orange center. Abundant spring bloom is followed by reliable repeat bloom. Vigorous, upright canes 10 to 12 feet tall are covered with glossy, leathery leaves. The blooms make excellent cut flowers.

LANDSCAPE USES: 'Gloire de Dijon' makes a superb climber on a pillar, wall, arch, or trellis. It blends well with perennials in mixed borders, providing some height, while the perennials hide its leggy lower stems. Try weaving dainty violet *Clematis viticella* up through it to provide interesting contrast.

CULTURE: Plant in well-drained soil in full sun. Prune out older canes to encourage vigorous new growth, while shortening sideshoots to four buds. Top-dress with compost in autumn. Fertilize in spring and again after flowering with a complete organic fertilizer to encourage repeat bloom. Deadhead spent blooms through the season. In Zone 6, provide a shelter site such as a south-facing wall.

DISEASE AND PEST PROBLEMS: 'Gloire de Dijon' has good disease resistance. For extra protection, apply fungicidal soap or garden sulfur combined with an antitranspirant as soon as leaves emerge in spring to prevent black spot; repeat as necessary.

DESCRIPTION: 'Gloire de France' is one of the few gallicas noted for soft lilac-pink flowers and low, spreading growth. Its full, sweetly-scented flowers are composed of many petals that form a ball when fully opened. The vigorous, spreading bushes grow 2½ to 3 feet tall and wide with bristly canes covered with rough, gray-green foliage.

LANDSCAPE USES: This is an excellent once-blooming shrub rose for small gardens. Use it near the front of a border, where you can appreciate its fragrant, shapely blooms. Try grouping it with rich crimson gallicas and underplanting it with pinks (*Dianthus* spp.), cranesbills (*Geranium* spp.), and 'Big Ears' lamb's-ears (*Stachys byzantina* 'Big Ears').

CULTURE: 'Gloire de France' is easy to grow in any sunny location. Plant it in well-drained soil that has been amended with organic matter. Top-dress with compost annually. Fertilize in spring with a complete organic fertilizer. Prune while dormant to thin out crowded stems and to shape bushes. This rose is recommended for all regions.

DISEASE AND PEST PROBLEMS: 'Gloire de France' is usually resistant to black spot, but mildew is often a problem. At the first sign of the disease, spray foliage with fungicidal soap or with horiticultural oil at a rate of 1 to 2 tablespoons per 1 gallon of water to control and prevent mildew and to discourage black spot. Reapply as necessary.

Gold Medal®

Golden Showers®

Cultivar Name:	Gold Medal®
Classification:	Grandiflora
Parentage:	'Yellow Pages' × 'Shirley Langhorn'
Introduced:	Christensen; Armstrong Nursery, United States; 1982
USDA Plant Hardiness Zones:	5 to 9

Cultivar Name:	Golden Showers®
Classification:	Large-flowered climber
Parentage:	'Charlotte Armstrong' × 'Captain Thomas'
Introduced:	Lammerts, United States; 1956 1957 All-America Rose Selection
USDA Plant Hardiness Zones:	6 to 9

DESCRIPTION: The best yellow in its class, Gold Medal® starts its bloom cycle with elegant, orange-tinged buds. These buds open to large, high-centered, double, golden yellow flowers that fade to pale yellow. Blooms are produced singly or in sprays over dark green leaves and have a light tea scent. The everblooming shrubs are upright and bushy, reaching 5 to 6 feet tall and 2½ feet wide. The blooms make excellent cut flowers.

LANDSCAPE USES: Use a grouping of Gold Medal® as an accent of all-season bloom in borders where hot colors dominate. Position it near the back of the border, and camouflage its stiff hybrid tea habit by planting informal shrub roses and perennials in front of it.

CULTURE: Plant Gold Medal® in a sunny location in a well-drained soil that has been amended with organic matter. Prune hard in late winter or early spring to rid plants of damaged canes and overwintering disease spores. Fertilize after pruning and again after first bloom with a complete organic fertilizer. Top-dress with compost annually. Deadhead spent blooms to encourage repeat bloom. Apply a mound of mulch as winter protection in Zone 5.

DISEASE AND PEST PROBLEMS: Gold Medal® is susceptible to diseases. Apply fungicidal soap or garden sulfur combined with an antitranspirant to prevent black spot; repeat monthly. Monitor the plants for insect damage.

DESCRIPTION: Golden Showers® is a showy pillar rose that is especially lovely during its peak bloom in late May and June. The large, loosely double flowers are clear yellow and open flat to reveal distinctive golden bronze stamens. The major complaint about this rose is that the lightly scented blooms drop their petals quickly. However, when it covers itself with a profusion of flowers, it is a glorious sight. It can always be counted on to produce a few blooms through the season, with a good show in autumn. The canes are covered with glossy foliage and grow 6 to 10 feet tall. They make a good display when wrapped on a pillar.

LANDSCAPE USES: Use this free-flowering climber to cover a pillar, trellis, arch, or fence. It looks particularly fine sharing a pillar with a large-flowered blue clematis, such as 'Will Goodwin'. Position Golden Showers® on a pillar at the back of a border to create a dramatic seasonal accent of bright yellow blooms.

CULTURE: Give Golden Showers® a sunny location in well-drained soil that has been amended with organic matter. Top-dress with compost annually. The pliable canes are easy to train, especially around a pillar. Prune while dormant: Choose healthy canes to fit the space you have, tie them to their supports, and reduce sideshoots to four buds. Deadhead spent flowers to neaten plants and encourage repeat bloom. Fertilize after pruning and again after first bloom with a complete organic fertilizer. In Zone 6, it often suffers winterkill; grow it on a warm wall. Damaged canes are usually replaced quickly each spring, and the new canes bloom the first season. This rose is recommended for all regions in Zones 6 to 9.

DISEASE AND PEST PROBLEMS: Golden Showers® is susceptible to black spot. For best results, apply fungicidal soap or garden sulfur combined with an antitranspirant as leaves emerge; reapply as needed.

'Golden Wings'

Cultivar Name:	'Golden Wings'
Classification:	Shrub
Parentage:	'Soeur Therese' × (*Rosa spinosissima* var. *altaica* × 'Ormiston Roy'
Introduced:	Sheperd, United States; 1956
USDA Plant Hardiness Zones:	4 to 9

DESCRIPTION: 'Golden Wings' is one of the most admired of the single roses. Throughout most of the season, it is covered with clusters of large, yellow, five-petaled flowers that are filled with golden stamens. The flowers

are lightly fragrant. Bushes are vigorous and upright, reaching 4 to 5 feet tall and 3 feet wide. The thorny canes are covered with light green foliage.

LANDSCAPE USES: Grow 'Golden Wings' as an attractive mass, hedge, or specimen. Its old-fashioned flowers look attractive with both antique and modern roses and combine well with perennials.

CULTURE: 'Golden Wings' is a robust, hardy shrub that is easy to grow in full sun and well-drained soil. Top-dress with compost annually, and fertilize in spring with a complete organic fertilizer. Prune annually while dormant, removing older canes and one-third of the growth and thinning out crowded stems. To make a hedge, plant bushes every 3 feet—plants will be touching in three years.

DISEASE AND PEST PROBLEMS: 'Golden Wings' is noted for its disease resistance, but it is susceptible to black spot in some regions. For best results, apply fungicidal soap or garden sulfur combined with an antitranspirant as soon as the leaves emerge in spring and twice thereafter. This rose is highly recommended for all regions.

RELATED CULTIVARS: Windrush® (seedling × ['Canterbury' × 'Golden Wings']; Austin, United Kingdom; 1984) produces fragrant, large, nearly single blooms of pale lemon with distinctive golden stamens. The repeat-flowering bushes are vigorous and grow to 4 feet tall and wide and are covered with pale green foliage.

Cultivar Name:	Graham Thomas™
Classification:	English rose
Parentage:	'Charles Austin' × ('Iceberg' × an English rose)
Introduced:	Austin, United Kingdom; 1983
USDA Plant Hardiness Zones:	5 to 9

DESCRIPTION: The large, cupped, deep yellow, old-fashioned blooms of Graham Thomas™ are celebrated for their rich perfume. The late-spring bloom is wonderful and abundant. Unfortunately, any later-season blooms are carried atop awkward, upright stems that often reach 6 to 8 feet. Like other roses bred in northern Europe, Graham Thomas™ responds to our hot summers by sending up incredibly long shoots but setting few flower buds. Hard pruning can moderate growth to about 5 feet tall and 2 to 3 feet wide.

LANDSCAPE USES: If you must have Graham Thomas™ for its lovely flowers, plant a group of the bushes to provide some mass. Use it in the back of mixed borders, where it can fade into the background when not in bloom (which is most of the time). Some gardeners manage the long canes by training them along a fence, but there are a wealth of rose cultivars better suited to this purpose.

CULTURE: Give Graham Thomas™ a sunny location in well-drained soil that has been amended with organic matter. Top-dress with compost annually. Treat this cultivar like a tall hybrid tea. Prune it hard while dormant and again after bloom to manage the long canes while encouraging repeat bloom. Fertilize with a complete organic fertilizer. Apply winter protection in Zone 5.

DISEASE AND PEST PROBLEMS: Graham Thomas™, like other English roses, has variable disease resistance. The breeder recommends preventive sprays for best results. Apply fungicidal soap or garden sulfur combined with an antitranspirant as soon as leaves emerge in spring to prevent black spot; reapply as needed.

RELATED CULTIVARS: 'Othello' ('Lilian Austin' × 'The Squire'; Austin, United Kingdom; 1986) bears very large, full, cupped, crimson flowers with intense perfume. Upright bushes reach 5 feet tall and less wide and are covered with dark green foliage.

'Green Ice'

Cultivar Name:	**'Green Ice'**
Classification:	Miniature
Parentage:	(*Rosa wichuraiana* × 'Floradora') × 'Jet Trail'
Introduced:	Moore, United States; 1971
USDA Plant Hardiness Zones:	5 to 9

DESCRIPTION: 'Green Ice' is a lovely, unique miniature. The lightly fragrant double flowers are a white-tinged soft green in rosette form. This bushy shrub grows 12 to 15 inches tall and wide, and is covered with small, glossy leaves.

LANDSCAPE USES: Miniature roses are suitable for edging, massing, rock gardens, and containers. Plant it in drifts of three or more bushes for season-long bloom.

CULTURE: Plant 'Green Ice' in a sunny location in well-drained soil that has been amended with organic matter. Prune hard in late winter or early spring to rid plants of overwintering disease spores and encourage new growth. Fertilize after pruning and again after the first bloom with a complete fertilizer. Top-dress with compost annually. Deadhead spent blooms through the season. 'Green Ice' is highly recommended for all regions.

DISEASE AND PEST PROBLEMS: 'Green Ice' is typically disease-free. If mites appear, wash leaves with a spray of water, and if feeding persists, apply insecticidal soap.

RELATED CULTIVARS: 'Simplex' ([*Rosa wichuraiana* × 'Floradora'] × seedling; Moore, United States; 1961) has apricot buds open to small, five-petaled, white flowers held in clusters. Bushes grow 12 to 15 inches tall and wide, and are clothed in small, glossy leaves. 'Simplex' is highly recommended for all regions.

Graham Thomas™

'Gruss an Aachen'

Cultivar Name:	**'Gruss an Aachen'**
Classification:	Floribunda
Parentage:	'Frau Karl Druschki' × 'Franz Deegen'
Introduced:	Geduldig, Germany; 1909
USDA Plant Hardiness Zones:	5 to 9

DESCRIPTION: Rarely out of bloom, 'Gruss an Aachen' bears clusters of red-tinged buds that open to blush white, double flowers that age to creamy white. The flowers are lightly fragrant. The dwarf bushes grow 2 to 3 feet tall and 2 feet wide and are covered with leathery, dark green foliage. Although this little gem was in the trade for a quarter of a century before the introduction of the floribunda class, it seems to fit best here.

LANDSCAPE USES: 'Gruss an Aachen' is a dependable bloomer suitable for use as a shrub mass, foundation planting, low hedge, or specimen. In mixed borders, its old-fashioned blooms combine well with perennials and other shrubs. Plant it in drifts of three or more bushes to make a mass of all-season bloom. Underplant with white perennials such as 'Aqua' Allwood pinks (*Dianthus* × *allwoodii* 'Aqua') and white-flowered blood-red cranesbill (*Geranium sanguineum* 'Album'). It also looks wonderful with 'Silver King' artemisia (*Artemisia ludoviciana* 'Silver King').

CULTURE: Plant in a sunny location in well-drained soil that has been amended with organic matter. Prune hard in late winter or early spring to rid plants of overwintering disease spores and to encourage vigorous new growth. Fertilize after pruning and again after the first bloom with a complete organic fertilizer. Top-dress with compost annually. Deadhead spent blooms through the season. Apply a mound of mulch to protect the graft union from winter injury in Zones 5 and 6. This rose is highly recommended for all regions.

DISEASE AND PEST PROBLEMS: 'Gruss an Aachen' is moderately disease-resistant. To prevent black spot, apply fungicidal soap or garden sulfur combined with an antitranspirant as soon as leaves emerge in spring; monitor plants and reapply as needed. Monitor insect feeding, and apply insecticidal soap to prevent damage to buds and leaves.

'Hansa'

Cultivar Name:	**'Hansa'**
Classification:	Hybrid rugosa
Parentage:	Not recorded
Introduced:	Schaum & Van Tol, Hansa Nursery, Holland; 1905
USDA Plant Hardiness Zones:	3 to 8

DESCRIPTION: 'Hansa' makes an aristocratic, architectural shrub that is almost without rival among the superior hybrid rugosa roses. It produces plentiful, intensely fragrant, large, semidouble flowers of purple-red in late spring and has excellent repeat bloom. It makes a dense, prickly, arching shrub reaching 6 to 7 feet tall and wide. The dark green, wrinkled, leathery leaves change to a handsome bronze yellow in autumn. Orange-red hips ripen in late summer. You can dry the fragrant flower petals for use in potpourri.

LANDSCAPE USES: This superb shrub looks wonderful with perennials and herbs in mixed borders or herb gardens. In mixed borders, an underplanting of lady's-mantle (*Alchemilla mollis*) and 'Palace Purple' heuchera (*Heuchera* 'Palace Purple') is particularly attractive. This shrub also makes an excellent hedge, screen, or windbreak.

CULTURE: Plant 'Hansa' in full sun in any well-drained soil. It will tolerate arid and poor soils as long as they are well drained. To make a hedge, plant bushes every 4 feet—the plants will be touching in three years. Prune mature specimens and hedges in late winter to shape them, taking off about one-third of the top growth. Periodically remove older canes to keep the plants growing vigorously. No other care is required. 'Hansa' is recommended for all regions.

DISEASE AND PEST PROBLEMS: Like other rugosa hybrids, 'Hansa' is usually trouble-free. However, the summer flowers sometimes attract Japanese beetles; pick off the adults and treat lawn areas with milky disease spores to control grubs. Rugosa hybrids are also susceptible to rose stem girdler. Keep the plants free of deadwood; prune out and destroy infected canes.

RELATED CULTIVARS: 'Dart's Dash' (Darthuis Nursery, Holland) resembles a compact 'Hansa' with large, purple-red, semidouble, perfumed blooms followed by orange-red hips. The dense bush grows 4 feet tall and wide. Plants are covered with healthy, wrinkled leaves and bloom from spring through frost.

'Harison's Yellow'

Cultivar Name:	**'Harison's Yellow'**
Classification:	Hybrid foetida
Parentage:	Probably *Rosa foetida* 'Persian Yellow' × *Rosa spinosissima*
Introduced:	Circa 1830
USDA Plant Hardiness Zones:	3 to 8

DESCRIPTION: 'Harison's Yellow' has long been a garden favorite valued for its flower color. The semidouble, cupped flowers are deep yellow with golden yellow stamens. This once-blooming shrub has an upright, arching habit to about 5 feet tall and 3 to 4 feet wide. The stems are covered with attractive, fernlike leaves.

LANDSCAPE USES: 'Harison's Yellow' looks attractive with other antique roses and with perennials and shrubs in informal plantings. One of the earliest of the old roses to bloom, it typically produces its golden flowers about the same time as species roses and rugosa hybrids. It is striking when planted with deep blue 'Persimmon' Siberian iris (*Iris sibirica* 'Persimmon') and a skirt of blue pansies.

CULTURE: 'Harison's Yellow' is a bit of a slow starter. Some claim that it thrives in poor soils and lags in rich soils. It is somewhat less vigorous than most hybrids of wild roses and probably resents being moved around in the garden. Find a permanent location that is well drained and relatively sunny. Like many once-blooming roses, 'Harison's Yellow' does not require full sun and will tolerate some dappled shade from deciduous trees. Spare the pruners and allow the bush to attain its graceful, upright to arching form. Prune out damaged canes, and periodically remove older canes to encourage new growth. Fertilize in spring with a complete organic fertilizer. No other care is required.

DISEASE AND PEST PROBLEMS: 'Harison's Yellow' is not severely bothered by diseases and pests, and is generally left unsprayed.

'Henri Martin'

Cultivar Name:	**'Henri Martin'** (also called 'Red Moss')
Classification:	Moss
Parentage:	Not recorded
Introduced:	Laffay, France; 1863
USDA Plant Hardiness Zones:	4 to 8

DESCRIPTION: The mossy, crimson buds of 'Henri Martin' open to rich, crimson-purple, loosely double flowers with heavy perfume. The generous spring bloom is followed by small, red hips. Vigorous, upright, prickly bushes, 5 feet tall and less wide, are covered with rough, dark foliage. Harvest the petals for use in potpourri.

LANDSCAPE USES: 'Henri Martin' makes a striking mass, accent, or specimen. Use a group of several plants in the middle of a mixed border, surrounded by shrub roses and companion perennials. A mass of this moss rose surrounded by the cerise-pink plumes of Japanese meadowsweet (*Filipendula purpurea*) is a classic combination in the rose garden at Sissinghurst Castle in England. This simple, bold planting provides an interesting textural contrast of two similar tones of red.

CULTURE: 'Henri Martin' is a workhorse in the garden, producing a good single crop of blooms annually. It is vigorous and extremely hardy. Site in full sun in well-drained soil that has been amended with organic matter. Top-dress liberally with compost. Fertilize in spring with a complete organic fertilizer. Prune annually after flowering to shape plants; also thin crowded stems and reduce stems that flowered by one-half their length.

DISEASE AND PEST PROBLEMS: 'Henri Martin' is disease-resistant. For extra protection, you could apply fungicidal soap, garden sulfur combined with an antitranspirant, or an antitranspirant alone when leaves emerge in spring to prevent black spot.

RELATED CULTIVARS: 'Nuits de Young' (also called 'Old Black'; Laffay, France; 1845) forms an upright bush reaching 4 feet tall and less wide. The stems are covered with dark green leaves highlighted with tones of sable brown. Its velvety, fragrant, maroon-purple flowers contrast beautifully with the yellow stamens.

Cultivar Name:	'Hermosa'
Classification:	China
Parentage:	Not recorded
Introduced:	Marcheseau, France; before 1837
USDA Plant Hardiness Zones:	6 to 9

DESCRIPTION: Rarely out of bloom, 'Hermosa' bears cluster of double, cupped, clear pink flowers from June through frost. Its flowers age to darker tones of light crimson. This compact shrub normally grows 2 to 3 feet tall and less wide; it makes a bigger bush in warm climates. The smooth stems are covered with small, blue-green, semiglossy leaves and few thorns.

LANDSCAPE USES: 'Hermosa' is suitable for use as a mass, low hedge, edging, or container plant. In mixed borders, its elegant blooms look attractive with perennials and other shrubs. Plant it in the front of a border in drifts of three or more bushes to make a mass of all-season bloom. For a striking combination, plant it with blood-red cranesbill (*Geranium sanguineum*), violet sage (*Salvia × superba*), and 'Angel's Blush' rose campion (*Lychnis coronaria* 'Angel's Blush').

CULTURE: Plant 'Hermosa' in a sunny location in well-drained soil that has been amended with organic matter. Prune hard at bud break in spring to rid plants of overwintering disease spores and to encourage vigorous new growth. Fertilize after pruning and again after the first bloom with a complete organic fertilizer. Top-dress with compost annually. Deadhead spent blooms through the season. Apply a mound of mulch to protect the graft union from winter injury in Zone 6. This rose is highly recommended for all regions.

DISEASE AND PEST PROBLEMS: 'Hermosa' is moderately disease-resistant. Apply fungicidal soap or garden sulfur combined with an antitranspirant as soon as leaves emerge in spring to prevent black spot; monitor plants and reapply as needed.

'Hermosa'

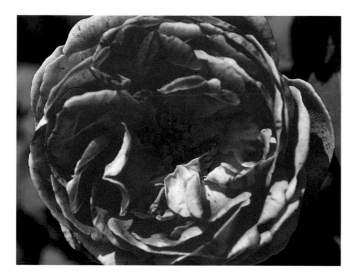

'Honorine de Brabant'

Cultivar Name:	'Honorine de Brabant'
Classification:	Bourbon
Parentage:	Not recorded
Introduced:	France; mid-nineteenth century
USDA Plant Hardiness Zones:	6 to 9

'Iceberg'

Cultivar Name:	'Iceberg' (also called 'Schneewittchen')
Classification:	Floribunda
Parentage:	'Robin Hood' × 'Virgo'
Introduced:	W. Kordes Söhne, Germany; 1958
USDA Plant Hardiness Zones:	5 to 9

DESCRIPTION: A free-flowering shrub, 'Honorine de Brabant' produces cupped, double, pale lilac flowers that are striped and spotted with violet and crimson. Masses of the charming, fragrant blooms are produced in spring, with some autumn rebloom. The vigorous, upright plants grow to 6 feet tall and are covered with medium green foliage.

LANDSCAPE USES: 'Honorine de Brabant' has a loose habit that makes it suitable for use as a pillar or short climber. It looks attractive with perennials in mixed borders. Weave pink or violet clematis up through it to provide interesting contrast.

CULTURE: Plant this rose in well-drained soil in full sun. Prune out older canes to encourage vigorous new growth, while shortening sideshoots to four buds. Top-dress with compost in autumn. Fertilize in spring and again after flowering with a complete organic fertilizer.

DISEASE AND PEST PROBLEMS: 'Honorine de Brabant' exhibits above-average disease resistance for a Bourbon rose. For extra protection, apply fungicidal soap or garden sulfur combined with an antitranspirant as soon as leaves emerge in spring to prevent black spot; reapply if needed.

DESCRIPTION: The best white floribunda, 'Iceberg' is grown and enjoyed around the world. Its fragrant, double, pure white flowers are produced continuously in large clusters. The bushy, vigorous shrubs grow 3 to 4 feet tall and 2 to 3 feet wide.

LANDSCAPE USES: Grow 'Iceberg' as a mass, foundation planting, hedge, or container specimen. In mixed borders, its elegant, pure white blooms look lovely with antique and modern roses and companion perennials. Plant it in drifts of three or more bushes to make a dramatic show of all-season bloom.

CULTURE: Plant this rose in a sunny location in well-drained soil that has been amended with organic matter. Prune hard in late winter or early spring to rid plants of overwintering disease spores and to encourage vigorous new growth. Fertilize after pruning and again after the first bloom with a complete organic fertilizer. Top-dress with compost annually. Deadhead spent blooms through the season. Apply a mound of mulch to protect the graft union from winter injury in Zones 5 and 6. 'Iceberg' is highly recommended for all regions.

DISEASE AND PEST PROBLEMS: 'Iceberg' is moderately disease-resistant. Apply fungicidal soap or garden sulfur combined with an antitranspirant as soon as leaves emerge in spring to prevent black spot; monitor plants and reapply monthly or as needed. Monitor insect feeding, and apply insecticidal soap as needed to prevent damage to buds and leaves.

RELATED CULTIVARS: 'Climbing Iceberg' (sport of 'Iceberg'; Cant, United Kingdom; 1968) produces the same wonderful pure white flowers in large clusters on upright stems reaching 10 to 12 feet tall. Repeat bloom increases as plants get older.

'Impatient'

Cultivar Name:	'Impatient'
Classification:	Floribunda
Parentage:	'America' × seedling
Introduced:	Warriner, United States; 1982; Jackson & Perkins 1984 All-America Rose Selection
USDA Plant Hardiness Zones:	5 to 9

DESCRIPTION: Rarely out of bloom, 'Impatient' is one of the best orange floribunda roses. The semidouble, orange-red flowers are held in large, showy clusters. The lightly scented blooms are produced continuously from late spring until frost. The bushy shrubs grow 3½ feet tall and 2 feet wide and are covered with glossy leaves.

LANDSCAPE USES: 'Impatient' is a workhorse suitable for use as an everblooming shrub mass, foundation planting, or specimen. It is a great addition to mixed borders dominated by hot colors. Plant 'Impatient' in drifts of three or more bushes to make a mass of all-season bloom.

CULTURE: Give 'Impatient' a sunny location in well-drained soil that has been amended with organic matter. Top-dress with compost annually. Prune hard in late winter or early spring to rid plants of overwintering disease spores and to encourage vigorous new growth. Fertilize after pruning and again after the first bloom with a complete organic fertilizer. Deadhead spent blooms through the season. Apply a mound of mulch to protect the graft union from winter injury in Zones 5 and 6. This rose is highly recommended for all regions.

DISEASE AND PEST PROBLEMS: 'Impatient' is moderately disease-resistant. For best results, apply fungicidal soap or garden sulfur combined with an antitranspirant as leaves emerge; reapply as needed. Monitor insect feeding, and apply insecticidal soap if pests begin to damage leaves and buds.

'Ispahan'

Cultivar Name:	'Ispahan'
Classification:	Damask
Parentage:	Not recorded
Introduced:	Cultivated before 1832
USDA Plant Hardiness Zones:	3 to 8

DESCRIPTION: 'Ispahan' has long been grown for its intense damask fragrance. The rich pink, semidouble flowers open flat. Bushes grow 5 feet tall and 3 feet wide and are covered in handsome gray-green foliage.

LANDSCAPE USES: 'Ispahan' is attractive as a specimen, in a mass, or on a pillar. The best way to grow it is in a tight group of three plants in the middle of a mixed border. Its blooms look beautiful nodding above dark-flowered gallicas, foxgloves (*Digitalis* spp.), giant allium (*Allium giganteum*), and gray-leaved perennials.

CULTURE: 'Ispahan' is a vigorous shrub that's easy to grow in full sun in any well-drained soil. Top-dress with compost annually, and fertilize in spring with a complete organic fertilizer. Prune after the June bloom, thinning out crowded stems and reducing canes by one-third their length. This rose is recommended for all regions.

DISEASE AND PEST PROBLEMS: 'Ispahan' is diseases-resistant. For extra protection, apply fungicidal soap or garden sulfur combined with an antitranspirant as soon as leaves emerge in spring.

Cultivar Name:	**'Jacques Cartier'** (also called 'Marchesa Boccella')
Classification:	Portland (damask perpetual)
Parentage:	Not recorded
Introduced:	1860
USDA Plant Hardiness Zones:	4 to 9

DESCRIPTION: Portland, or damask perpetual, roses are the unsung heros of the rose world, and 'Jacques Cartier' is one of the best of these hardy, repeat-flowering old roses. It bears clear pink, full-petaled flowers that are quartered with a buttonlike center. The blooms are held on short bristly stems with leaves right up to the base of the flower. These fragrant flowers are produced abundantly in late spring with good repeat bloom. Vigorous, compact bushes grow 3 to 4 feet tall and less wide. They are covered with the light green foliage typical of damask roses.

LANDSCAPE USES: 'Jacques Cartier' is an excellent compact shrub for small gardens. Use it near the front of a border, where you can appreciate its fragrant blooms. Group it with rich crimson gallicas and spires of foxgloves (*Digitalis* spp.), underplanted with a carpet of pinks (*Dianthus* spp.), cranesbills (*Geranium* spp.), lady's-mantle (*Alchemilla mollis*), or any of your favorite silver-leaved plants.

CULTURE: Robust and hardy, 'Jacques Cartier' is easy to grow in a sunny location in well-drained soil that has been amended with organic matter. Top-dress liberally with compost. Where summers are hot, water regularly. Fertilize in spring and after the first bloom with a complete organic fertilizer to encourage repeat bloom. Prune while dormant to thin out crowded stems and to shape bushes. This rose is highly recommended for all regions.

DISEASE AND PEST PROBLEMS: 'Jacques Cartier' has good disease resistance. One preventive application of fungicide in spring goes a long way toward warding off a black spot problem. For best results, apply fungicidal soap or garden sulfur combined with an antitranspirant as soon as leaves emerge in spring; reapply in midsummer.

RELATED CULTIVARS: 'Comte de Chambord' (Moreau-Robert, France; 1860) bears lovely, double, medium pink flowers that are quartered with a buttonlike center. It is similar to 'Jacques Cartier' and often described as superior because of more continuous bloom. The trade-off is that it is more susceptible to black spot so it will need a few more preventive treatments to keep its foliage through the season.

'Jacques Cartier'

Jean Kenneally™

Cultivar Name:	Jean Kenneally™
Classification:	Miniature
Parentage:	'Futura' × 'Party Girl'
Introduced:	Bennett, United States; Tiny Petals; 1984 1986 Award of Excellence
USDA Plant Hardiness Zones:	5 to 9

DESCRIPTION: The apricot, double, high-centered flowers of this miniature rose are held singly or in clusters. Rarely out of bloom Jean Kenneally™ forms an upright, bushy shrub, 24 to 30 inches tall and 12 inches across, covered with semiglossy leaves. The lightly scented blooms make excellent cut flowers.

LANDSCAPE USES: Try Jean Kenneally™ for edging or massing. It also looks wonderful as a low hedge and makes a charming container plant. Plant it in drifts of three or more bushes to make a mass of all-season bloom.

CULTURE: Plant in a sunny location in well-drained soil that has been amended with organic matter. Prune hard in late winter or early spring to rid plants of overwintering disease spores and to encourage vigorous new growth. Fertilize after pruning and again after the first bloom with a complete organic fertilizer. Top-dress with compost annually. Deadhead or shear spent blooms through the season to encourage repeat bloom and maintain a compact habit. This miniature is highly recommended for all regions.

DISEASE AND PEST PROBLEMS: Jean Kenneally™ has good disease resistance. For extra protection, apply fungicidal soap or garden sulfur combined with

an antitranspirant as soon as leaves emerge in spring; reapply as needed. Mites sometimes bother this small-leaved rose. Wash leaves with a strong spray of water to knock off the pests. If mites continue to be a problem, apply insecticidal soap.

'Jeanne Lajoie'

Cultivar Name:	'Jeanne Lajoie'
Classification:	Climbing miniature
Parentage:	('Casa Blanca' × 'Independence') × 'Midget'
Introduced:	Sima, United States; Mini-Roses; 1975 1977 Award of Excellence
USDA Plant Hardiness Zones:	5 to 9

DESCRIPTION: The fragrant, double, medium pink flowers of 'Jeanne Lajoie' are produced nonstop through the season. Vigorous, spreading bushes grow 4 to 8 feet tall and are covered with small, glossy, dark foliage.

LANDSCAPE USES: Use 'Jeanne Lajoie' as a short climber to cover a trellis, fence, or pillar. Or grow it in a container, where the trailing stems will cascade gracefully over the edge of the planter. It also makes an excellent trailing groundcover and looks great spilling over a wall.

CULTURE: Plant 'Jeanne Lajoie' in a sunny location in well-drained soil that has been amended with organic matter. Prune climbers while dormant; remove deadwood and crowded canes, choosing young, stocky canes to replace older ones, and reduce laterals to four buds.

Fertilize after pruning and again after the first bloom with a complete organic fertilizer. Top-dress with compost annually. Deadhead or shear spent blooms through the season. This rose is highly recommended for all regions.

DISEASE AND PEST PROBLEMS: 'Jeanne Lajoie' has good disease resistance. For extra protection, apply fungicidal soap or garden sulfur combined with an antitranspirant as soon as leaves emerge in spring; reapply monthly or as needed. Mites sometimes bother this small-leaved plant. Wash leaves with a strong spray of water to knock off the pests. If mites continue to be a problem, apply insecticidal soap.

'John Cabot'

Cultivar Name:	'John Cabot'
Classification:	Kordesii
Parentage:	*Rosa kordesii* × ('Masquerade' × *Rosa laxa*)
Introduced:	Svejda, Canada Department of Agriculture; 1978
USDA Plant Hardiness Zones:	3 to 9

DESCRIPTION: The Canadian Explorer rose 'John Cabot' is almost too good to be true. A versatile, hardy, and disease-free rose, it bears fragrant, double, light crimson-magenta flowers in late spring with good repeat bloom. Its prickly, arching stems are covered with light green foliage. It makes a vigorous, mounding 6-foot shrub. When grown as a climber, it stretches 8 to 10 feet tall.

LANDSCAPE USES: Grow 'John Cabot' to brighten a dull corner of the garden. This repeat-flowering climber looks wonderful covering a pillar, fence, arch, or trellis or even scampering into a small tree. 'John Cabot' blends beautifully with both hot and cool color schemes and looks particularly fine with blue flowers. Train a delicate clematis to grow up through it for an interesting color contrast.

CULTURE: Plant 'John Cabot' in a sunny location in well-drained soil that has been amended with organic matter. Top-dress with compost annually. For the first two or three years, little pruning is required: Tie canes to their support and deadhead spent blooms. Prune mature plants while dormant, removing deadwood and crowded canes, choosing young, stocky canes to replace older ones, and reducing sideshoots to four buds. This rose is highly recommended for all regions.

DISEASE AND PEST PROBLEMS: 'John Cabot' is disease-free. If rose slugs skeletonize leaves early in the season, spray with insecticidal soap.

RELATED CULTIVARS: The Canadian Explorer roses are an important collection of hardy, repeat-flowering, disease-free Kordesii shrubs and climbers for northern gardens. They were bred by Felicitas Svejda at the Canada Department of Agriculture in Ottawa.

'Champlain' ([*Rosa kordesii* × seedling] × ['Red Dawn' × 'Suzanne']; 1982) produces double, deep red blooms that are lightly fragrant. It makes a bushy, compact, everblooming shrub to 3 feet tall and wide. It is typically pest-free and hardy to Zone 4.

'John Davis' ([*Rosa kordesii* × seedling] × seedling; 1986) bears large clusters of fragrant, double, deep pink flowers that age to medium pink. The everblooming, trailing canes are covered with leathery, glossy foliage reaching 6 feet tall. 'John Davis' can be trained as a short climber or pillar rose. It is hardy to Zone 3.

'Henry Kelsey' (*Rosa kordesii* hybrid × seedling; 1984) is a vigorous climber that bears clusters of fragrant, scarlet crimson, loosely double blooms that open to reveal golden stamens. Trailing canes covered with glossy foliage reach 8 to 10 feet tall. The most cold-tolerant red climber, it is hardy to Zone 4. Replace your winter-killed 'Don Juan' with 'Henry Kelsey'.

'William Baffin' (*Rosa kordesii* seedling; 1983) is a vigorous climber that produces deep strawberry pink, loosely double blooms in huge clusters. Arching, prickly canes grow 8 to 10 feet tall and are covered with glossy foliage. Rarely out of bloom, this climber also makes an excellent arching shrub mass or hedge that grows to 6 feet tall. It is hardy to Zone 3.

'Kardinal'

Cultivar Name:	'Kardinal'
Classification:	Hybrid tea
Parentage:	Seedling × 'Flamingo'
Introduced:	W. Kordes Söhne, Germany; 1986
USDA Plant Hardiness Zones:	5 to 9

DESCRIPTION: 'Kardinal' produces elegant, urn-shaped buds that open to high-centered, double, red flowers. The lightly tea-scented blooms are carried on long stems. The everblooming, medium shrubs have semiglossy, dark green leaves and are upright and bushy, reaching 4 to 5 feet tall and 2½ feet wide. Originally bred as a florist flower, 'Kardinal' makes an excellent cut flower.

LANDSCAPE USES: Use a grouping of 'Kardinal' as an accent of all-season bloom in flower borders where hot colors dominate. Position it near the back of the border, and camouflage its stiff hybrid tea habit by planting informal shrub roses and perennials in front of it. It is a must for the cutting garden for its long-lasting blooms.

CULTURE: Plant 'Kardinal' in a sunny location in well-drained soil that has been amended with organic matter. Prune hard in late winter or early spring to rid plants of damaged canes and overwintering disease spores. Fertilize after pruning and again after the first bloom with a complete organic fertilizer. Top-dress with compost annually. Deadhead spent blooms to encourage repeat bloom. Apply a mound of mulch as winter protection in Zone 5.

DISEASE AND PEST PROBLEMS: Like other hybrid teas, 'Kardinal' is susceptible to diseases. Protect new

foliage with an application of fungicidal soap or garden sulfur combined with an antitranspirant to prevent black spot; repeat monthly. Monitor the plants for insect damage.

'Konigin von Danemark'

Cultivar Name:	'Konigin von Danemark' (also called 'Queen of Denmark')
Classification:	Alba
Parentage:	Probably *Rosa alba* × damask hybrid
Hybridizer:	Not recorded
Introduced:	1826
USDA Plant Hardiness Zones:	3 to 8

DESCRIPTION: An aristocratic rose, 'Konigin von Danemark' covers itself with showy, soft pink, full flowers in midsummer. The quartered blooms open to reveal a charming buttonlike center and have a heavy yet delightful perfume. The upright, prickly canes are covered with rough, blue-green leaves and form a mounded shrub 4 to 5 feet tall and wide.

LANDSCAPE USES: Use this rose as an attractive specimen, shrub mass, hedge, or screen. Its characteristic blue-green foliage provides a lovely contrast to the soft pink flowers. Plant it in the middle of a mixed border, where its foliage forms a handsome background through the season. Its soft pink flowers look beautiful with spires of foxgloves (*Digitalis* spp.), globes of star of Persia (*Allium christophii*), and spikes of violet sage (*Salvia* × *superba*).

CULTURE: 'Konigin von Danemark' is a robust, hardy shrub that's easy to grow in full sun. It also tolerates some high shade from deciduous trees better than most of the old roses. Plant in any well-drained soil. Top-dress with compost annually, and fertilize in spring with a complete organic fertilizer. Prune lightly to thin out crowded stems. To form a hedge, set plants every 4 feet—plants will be touching in three years. This rose is highly recommended for all regions.

DISEASE AND PEST PROBLEMS: 'Konigin von Danemark' is disease-free.

'La Sevillana'

Cultivar Name:	'La Sevillana'
Classification:	Floribunda
Parentage:	Complex hybrid from crosses between 'Zambra', 'Tropicana', and 'Rusticana'
Introduced:	Meilland, France; 1978
USDA Plant Hardiness Zones:	6 to 9

DESCRIPTION: Rarely out of bloom, 'La Sevillana' produces large clusters of flame-red, semidouble flowers. The bushy, compact, vigorous shrub reaches 3 feet tall and is covered with dark, bronzy, leathery foliage.

LANDSCAPE USES: Use this flamboyant floribunda to add color to a sunny spot in the garden. It makes an excellent everblooming mass, foundation planting, low hedge, or container plant. In mixed borders dominated by yellow, red, and orange, its vermilion blooms are a welcome addition. Plant it in drifts of three or more bushes for a mass of all-season bloom.

CULTURE: Plant 'La Sevillana' in a sunny location in well-drained soil that has been amended with organic matter. Prune hard in late winter or early spring to rid plants of overwintering disease spores and to encourage vigorous new growth. Fertilize after pruning and again after the first bloom with a complete organic fertilizer. Top-dress with compost annually. Deadhead spent blooms through the season. Apply a mound of mulch to protect the graft union from winter injury in Zones 5 and 6. This rose is highly recommended for all regions.

DISEASE AND PEST PROBLEMS: 'La Sevillana' is moderately disease-resistant. For extra protection, apply fungicidal soap or garden sulfur combined with an antitranspirant as soon as leaves emerge in spring; reapply monthly or as needed. Monitor insect feeding, and apply insecticidal soap as needed to prevent damage to buds and leaves.

'Lavender Dream'

Cultivar Name:	'Lavender Dream'
Classification:	Shrub
Parentage:	'Yesterday' × 'Nastarana'
Introduced:	Interplant, Holland; 1985
USDA Plant Hardiness Zones:	5 to 9

DESCRIPTION: Sprays of dainty, lilac-pink, semidouble flowers are produced continuously on this mounding shrub. The slender, smooth stems are covered with small, semiglossy leaves. Pruned shrubs remain compact at 3 feet tall and wide; left unpruned, bushes grow to about 4 feet tall and wide.

LANDSCAPE USES: Use this everblooming shrub as a groundcover, low hedge, or container plant. In mixed borders, the old-fashioned flowers look beautiful with antique and modern roses and perennials. Plant in drifts of three or more bushes to make a mass of all-season bloom.

CULTURE: Plant in a sunny or lightly shaded location, in well-drained soil that has been amended with organic matter. Prune while dormant to thin out crowded stems, shape bushes, and encourage new growth. To keep plants compact, prune hard as you would a floribunda. Fertilize after pruning and again after the first bloom with a complete organic fertilizer. Top-dress with compost annually. This rose is highly recommended for all regions.

DISEASE AND PEST PROBLEMS: 'Lavender Dream' has excellent disease resistance. For extra protection, you could apply fungicidal soap or garden sulfur combined with an antitranspirant as soon as leaves emerge in spring.

CULTURE: Site 'Lavender Lassie' in as much sun as you can give it, although it will readily accept some light shade from deciduous trees. Plant in well-drained soil that has been amended with organic matter. Prune while dormant to keep shrubs in bounds, removing about one-third of the top growth, and periodically cut out older canes. Fertilize in spring and again after spring flowering with a complete organic fertilizer to encourage repeat bloom. To form a hedge, plant bushes every 4 feet—plants will be touching in three years.

DISEASE AND PEST PROBLEMS: 'Lavender Lassie' is resistant to black spot and mildew. For extra protection, spray new foliage with fungicidal soap or garden sulfur combined with an antitranspirant; reapply if needed.

'Lavender Lassie'

'Leda'

Cultivar Name:	'Lavender Lassie'
Classification:	Hybrid musk
Parentage:	'Hamburg' × 'Madame Norbert Levavasseur'
Introduced:	W. Kordes Söhne, Germany; 1960
USDA Plant Hardiness Zones:	5 to 9

Cultivar Name:	'Leda' (also called 'Painted Damask')
Classification:	Damask
Parentage:	Not recorded
Introduced:	Cultivated before 1827
USDA Plant Hardiness Zones:	3 to 8

DESCRIPTION: Large clusters of perfumed, lilac-pink, semidouble powder puff flowers blanket this shrub in late spring, followed by good repeat bloom. 'Lavender Lassie' makes a tall, upright, well-branched bush with light green leaves and few thorns. The vigorous shrubs grow 5 feet tall and nearly as wide. Trained as a pillar or climber, this rose stretches 7 to 8 feet.

LANDSCAPE USES: 'Lavender Lassie' makes a lovely specimen, mass, climber, and informal hedge. In mixed borders, enhance the soft pastel flowers with the burgundy foliage of purple smokebush (*Cotinus coggygria*), blue-flowered perennials, and plants with silver foliage.

DESCRIPTION: 'Leda' produces red buds that unfold to ivory flowers edged in crimson. The fragrant, very full double blooms open to reveal a buttonlike center. This plant makes a floppy shrub 3 feet tall and wide, with prickly canes and gray-green leaves.

LANDSCAPE USES: 'Leda' mixes beautifully with other antique roses and perennials. It's at its best near the front of the border, climbing a low fence, or cascading over a wall. It also makes a good subject for pegging.

CULTURE: Plant 'Leda' in well-drained soil in full sun. Prune after bloom to shape and tidy bushes, shortening the stems that bloomed. Top-dress with compost annually, and fertilize in spring with a complete organic fertilizer.

DISEASE AND PEST PROBLEMS: 'Leda' is disease-free and usually not bothered by pests.

'Lilian Austin'

Cultivar Name:	**'Lilian Austin'**
Classification:	English rose
Parentage:	'Aloha' × 'Yeoman'
Introduced:	Austin, United Kingdom; 1973
USDA Plant Hardiness Zones:	5 to 9

DESCRIPTION: The semidouble, cupped, salmon-pink blooms of 'Lilian Austin' are produced in profusion in late spring followed by reliable repeat bloom. It makes a vigorous, arching, spreading shrub to 4 feet tall and wide and is covered with dark, glossy foliage.

LANDSCAPE USES: Grow this free-flowering shrub as a mass, hedge, foundation planting, or specimen. Plant a group of a few bushes in the middle of a mixed border, where its handsome flowers look beautiful with perennials.

CULTURE: Give 'Lilian Austin' a sunny location in well-drained soil that has been amended with organic matter. Top-dress with compost annually. Prune hard while dormant and again after the bloom to shape and to encourage repeat bloom. Fertilize with a complete organic fertilizer. Apply winter protection in Zone 5.

DISEASE AND PEST PROBLEMS: The English roses have variable disease resistance. The breeder recommends an application of preventive sprays for best results. Apply fungicidal soap or garden sulfur combined with an antitranspirant as soon as leaves emerge in spring to prevent black spot; reapply as needed.

RELATED CULTIVARS: 'English Garden' (['Lilian Austin' × seedling] × ['Iceberg' × 'Wife of Bath']; 1986) bears pale yellow, double blooms on upright bushes to 3 feet tall and less wide.

'The Reeve' ('Lilian Austin' × 'Chaucer'; 1977) forms a floppy shrub 3 feet tall and wide and has prickly stems covered with dark green foliage. Flowers are soft pink, very full, and chalice-shaped.

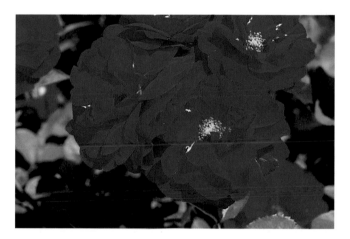

'Lili Marlene'

Cultivar Name:	**'Lili Marlene'**
Classification:	Floribunda
Parentage:	('Our Princess' × 'Rudolph Timm') × 'Ama'
Introduced:	W. Kordes Söhne, Germany; 1959
USDA Plant Hardiness Zones:	5 to 9

DESCRIPTION: The large, cupped, bright scarlet flowers of this rose are fragrant, loosely double, and carried in sprays. Rarely out of bloom, 'Lili Marlene' makes a bushy, compact, vigorous shrub reaching 2½ to 3 feet tall and covered with copper-tinged, leathery foliage.

LANDSCAPE USES: This bold, everblooming floribunda makes an excellent everblooming mass, foundation planting, edging, or container plant. Grow it in drifts of three or more bushes for a mass of all-season bloom. Its red blooms are a welcome addition to mixed borders dominated by hot colors. Create an eye-catching combination by grouping 'Lili Marlene' with drifts of lemon yellow 'Moonshine' yarrow (*Achillea* × 'Moonshine').

CULTURE: Plant this rose in a sunny location in well-drained soil that has been amended with organic matter. Prune hard in late winter or early spring to rid plants of overwintering disease spores and to encourage vigorous new growth. Fertilize after pruning and again after the first bloom with a complete organic fertilizer. Top-dress with compost annually. Deadhead spent blooms through the season. Apply a mound of mulch to protect the graft union from winter injury in Zone 5. This cultivar is highly recommended for all regions.

DISEASE AND PEST PROBLEMS: 'Lili Marlene' is moderately disease-resistant. Apply fungicidal soap or garden sulfur combined with an antitranspirant as soon as leaves emerge in spring to prevent black spot. Monitor plants and reapply as needed.

LANDSCAPE USES: Use 'Louise Odier' in the middle of mixed borders, surrounded by antique rose neighbors and companion perennials. It also makes a good subject for pegging.

CULTURE: Plant this rose in well-drained soil in full sun. Prune while dormant to shape bushes and to encourage vigorous growth, reducing canes by one-third their length. Deadhead after the first bloom. Top-dress with compost annually. Fertilize in spring and again after flowering with a complete organic fertilizer to encourage repeat bloom.

DISEASE AND PEST PROBLEMS: 'Louise Odier' is susceptible to black spot. Apply fungicidal soap or garden sulfur combined with an antitranspirant as soon as leaves emerge in spring; reapply as needed.

'Love'

'Louise Odier'

Cultivar Name:	'Louise Odier'
Classification:	Bourbon
Parentage:	Not recorded
Introduced:	France; 1851
USDA Plant Hardiness Zones:	5 to 9

Cultivar Name:	'Love'
Classification:	Grandiflora
Parentage:	Seedling × 'Redgold'
Introduced:	Warriner, United States; Jackson & Perkins, United States; 1980 1980 All-America Rose Selection
USDA Plant Hardiness Zones:	5 to 9

DESCRIPTION: 'Louise Odier' is worth growing for its wonderfully perfumed, full, shapely, soft pink flowers. The hardy, repeat-blooming bushes are vigorous and strongly upright, reaching 5 feet tall and less wide. The smooth stems are covered with light green foliage.

DESCRIPTION: Rarely out of bloom, 'Love' produces pointed buds that open to high-centered, hybrid tea–type, crimson red flowers that are white on the back. The blooms are carried in long-stemmed sprays continuously from June through frost. The upright, bushy shrubs are 4 to 5 feet tall and 2½ feet wide. Reddish maroon canes are well armed with large, red prickles and covered with semiglossy, copper-tinged leaves. The blooms make excellent cut flowers.

LANDSCAPE USES: 'Love' blooms dependably and is one of the best grandifloras. Use a grouping of 'Love' as an accent of all-season bloom in flower borders. Position it in the middle of the border, and camouflage its stiff, upright habit by planting informal shrub roses and perennials in front of it. It's a must for the cutting garden for its long-lasting blooms.

CULTURE: Plant 'Love' in a sunny location in well-drained soil that has been amended with organic matter. Prune hard in late winter or early spring to rid plants of damaged canes and overwintering disease spores. Fertilize after pruning and again after the first bloom with a complete organic fertilizer. Top-dress with compost annually. Deadhead spent blooms to encourage repeat bloom. Apply a mound of mulch as winter protection in Zone 5.

DISEASE AND PEST PROBLEMS: 'Love' has above-average disease resistance. For best results, protect new foliage with an application of fungicidal soap or garden sulfur combined with an antitranspirant to prevent black spot; repeat monthly or as needed. Monitor the plants for insect damage.

Cultivar Name:	**'Madame Hardy'**
Classification:	Damask
Parentage:	Not recorded
Introduced:	Hardy, France; 1832
USDA Plant Hardiness Zones:	4 to 8

DESCRIPTION: 'Madame Hardy' is well known for its fragrant, pure white, very full, quartered flowers that open flat to reveal a distinctive, green, buttonlike eye. Its perfect form is considered superior among old roses. The annual bloom is produced in abundance in late spring. The plant forms an upright, loose shrub reaching 5 to 6 feet tall and less wide, with prickly canes and gray-green foliage.

LANDSCAPE USES: 'Madame Hardy' makes an excellent pillar rose. Plant a large-flowered clematis to grow up through it and give some late-season color. Use this rose to provide height in mixed borders, where it looks beautiful with other antique roses and perennials.

CULTURE: Plant in well-drained soil in full sun. Prune after bloom to shape and tidy bushes, shortening the stems that bloomed by one-third their length. Top-dress with compost annually, and fertilize in spring with a complete organic fertilizer.

DISEASE AND PEST PROBLEMS: By late summer, the leaves take on a bronze appearance because of black spot. If you want to prevent this, apply fungicidal soap or garden sulfur combined with an antitranspirant as soon as the leaves emerge in spring; reapply as needed.

RELATED CULTIVARS: 'Madame Zoetmans' (Marest, France; 1830) bears fragrant, pure white blossoms flushed with pink. The full flowers open to reveal a buttonlike center. The bushy upright plants reach 4 feet tall, with prickly canes covered in gray-green foliage.

'Madame Hardy'

'Madame Isaac Pereire'

Cultivar Name:	'Madame Isaac Pereire'
Classification:	Bourbon
Parentage:	Not recorded
Introduced:	Garcon, France; 1881
USDA Plant Hardiness Zones:	5 to 9

DESCRIPTION: 'Madame Isaac Pereire' is one of the most fragrant roses and is worth growing for its intense perfume. The deep pink flowers are large, cupped, very full, and quartered. Lavish late-spring bloom is followed by respectable autumn rebloom. The upright, bushy plant grows 5 to 6 feet tall and nearly as wide. Its prickly canes are covered with dark, semiglossy leaves.

LANDSCAPE USES: This rose has a tall, upright habit that makes it suitable for use as a pillar or short climber. It looks attractive with perennials in mixed borders and provides some height when trained up. Weave pink or violet clematis up through it to provide interesting contrast. It also responds well to pegging.

CULTURE: Plant in well-drained soil in full sun. Prune while dormant to shape bushes, reducing the canes to one-third their length. Deadhead hard after spring bloom. Top-dress with compost in autumn. Fertilize in spring and after flowering with a complete organic fertilizer to encourage repeat bloom. It occasionally suffers some winter injury in Zones 5 and 6, but after pruning, it will quickly cover its support again in one season.

DISEASE AND PEST PROBLEMS: Like all Bourbons, 'Madame Isaac Pereire' is susceptible to black spot. Apply fungicidal soap or garden sulfur combined with an antitranspirant as soon as leaves emerge in spring; reapply monthly to keep leaves on the plant.

RELATED CULTIVARS: 'Madame Ernst Calvat' (sport of 'Madame Isaac Pereire'; Schwartz, France; 1888) is identical to its renowned parent except for its medium pink flowers.

'Madame Plantier'

Cultivar Name:	'Madame Plantier'
Classification:	Hybrid alba
Parentage:	Probably *Rosa alba* × *Rosa moschata*
Introduced:	Plantier, France; 1835
USDA Plant Hardiness Zones:	4 to 8

DESCRIPTION: 'Madame Plantier' has round, crimson-tinged buds that open into fragrant, very full, pure white flowers with a buttonlike center. The bushes are vigorous and upright, reaching 5 to 6 feet tall and nearly as wide, with smooth stems covered in blue-green foliage. The flowers are displayed abundantly in late spring with no repeat bloom.

LANDSCAPE USES: 'Madame Plantier' makes an excellent subject for training as a pillar or short climber. It looks especially charming scrambling into a small crab apple tree. 'Madame Plantier' also responds well to pegging. Use it as an attractive specimen, shrub mass, hedge, or screen. Plant it in the back of mixed borders to provide a background of handsome foliage for colorful perennials.

CULTURE: 'Madame Plantier' is a robust, hardy shrub that is easy to grow in full sun or high shade from deciduous trees. Plant in any well-drained soil, top-dress with compost annually, and fertilize in spring with a complete organic fertilizer. Prune lightly to thin out crowded stems and periodically remove older canes to encourage new growth. To form a hedge, set plants every 4 feet—plants will be touching in three years. This rose is highly recommended for all regions.

DISEASE AND PEST PROBLEMS: 'Madame Plantier' is disease-free and usually not bothered by pests.

RELATED CULTIVARS: 'Blush Hip' (hybrid alba; before 1846) produces well-scented, flesh pink, double flowers that are quartered with a buttonlike center. The smooth stems reach 5 to 6 feet tall and are suitable for wrapping up a pillar and for pegging.

'Madame Legras de St. Germain' (alba; 1846) is noted for its pure white, very full flowers with a hint of creamy yellow in the center. Smooth, upright canes are 6 to 7 feet tall.

'Magic Carrousel'

Cultivar Name:	**'Magic Carrousel'**
Classification:	Miniature
Parentage:	'Little Darling' × 'Westmont'
Introduced:	Moore, United States; Sequoia Nursery; 1972 1975 Award of Excellence
USDA Plant Hardiness Zones:	5 to 9

DESCRIPTION: 'Magic Carrousel' is a superb, eye-catching, bicolored miniature. Cupped, semidouble, lightly scented flowers are cream colored with crimson edges and cover the plant all season. Vigorous, bushy shrubs, 2 feet tall or more and 1 foot wide, are covered with small, semiglossy foliage.

LANDSCAPE USES: 'Magic Carrousel' is a versatile rose suitable for use as an edging, dwarf hedge, or container plant. It also looks great in rock gardens and flower beds. 'Magic Carrousel' is particularly attractive in raised planters, and its dwarf size makes it a good candidate for indoor culture under lights.

CULTURE: Plant in a sunny location in well-drained soil that has been amended with organic matter. Prune hard in late winter or early spring to rid plants of over-wintering disease spores and to encourage vigorous new growth. Fertilize after pruning and again after the first bloom with a complete organic fertilizer. Top-dress with compost annually. Shear after each bloom period through the season to avoid a leggy appearance. This rose is recommended for all regions.

DISEASE AND PEST PROBLEMS: 'Magic Carrousel' is moderately disease-resistant. Apply fungicidal soap or garden sulfur combined with an antitranspirant as soon as leaves emerge in spring to prevent black spot; reapply monthly or as needed. If mites bother the plants, wash the leaves with a strong spray of water to knock off the pests. If mites continue to be a problem, apply insecticidal soap.

RELATED CULTIVARS: 'Circus Clown' ('Pink Petticoat' × 'Make Believe'; Moore, United States; 1992) produces flowers similar to 'Magic Carrousel' on more compact bushes to 18 inches tall and 12 inches wide. The flowers are white with red edges and red backs.

'Maiden's Blush'

Cultivar Name:	**'Maiden's Blush'** (also called 'Small Maiden's Blush')
Classification:	Alba
Parentage:	Probably a sport of 'Great Maiden's Blush'
Introduced:	Kew Gardens, United Kingdom; 1797
USDA Plant Hardiness Zones:	3 to 8

DESCRIPTION: 'Maiden's Blush' produces fragrant, blush pink, very full, double blooms with swirled centers. The bushes are vigorous and upright, reaching 4 feet tall and nearly as wide, with prickly canes and blue-green foliage. The plant flowers heavily in late spring with no repeat bloom.

LANDSCAPE USES: Use 'Maiden's Blush' as an attractive specimen, shrub mass, hedge, or screen. Plant it in the back of mixed borders, where its pale pink flowers look attractive with foxgloves, star of Persia (*Allium christophii*), and violet sage (*Salvia* × *superba*).

CULTURE: This robust, hardy shrub is easy to grow in full sun or high shade from deciduous trees. Plant in any well-drained soil. Top-dress with compost annually, and fertilize in spring with a complete organic fertilizer. Prune lightly to thin out crowded stems. To make a hedge, set plants every 4 feet—plants will be touching in three years. This rose is highly recommended for all regions.

DISEASE AND PEST PROBLEMS: 'Maiden's Blush' is usually disease-free.

RELATED CULTIVARS: 'Great Maiden's Blush' (also called 'Cuisse de Nymphe'; prior to 1738) is a larger version of 'Maiden's Blush', growing 5 to 6 feet tall and nearly as wide.

extremely fragrant but do not repeat bloom. Grown as a shrub, it has a bushy, upright habit to 5 feet tall and wide, very prickly canes, and glossy foliage. Grown as a pillar or climber, it stretches 8 to 12 feet.

LANDSCAPE USES: 'Maigold' is worth growing for its lovely, fragrant flowers, abundant late-spring bloom, and reliable hardiness. It's a good choice for training on a pillar, wall, arch, or trellis. It is beautiful with modern and antique roses and perennials. 'Maigold' looks particularly fine combined with blue flowers. Train a large-flowered clematis, such as sky blue 'Will Goodwin', to weave through it and provide late-season blooms.

CULTURE: Plant in full sun in well-drained soil that has been amended with organic matter. Top-dress with compost annually, and fertilize with a complete organic fertilizer. For the first two or three years, little pruning is required: Just tie the canes to their support and deadhead spent blooms. Prune mature plants while dormant, removing crowded canes, choosing young stocky canes to replace older ones, and reducing sideshoots to four buds. Deadheading immediately after late-spring bloom may encourage a few later blooms. This rose is highly recommended for all regions.

DISEASE AND PEST PROBLEMS: 'Maigold' exhibits excellent disease resistance. For extra protection, apply fungicidal soap, garden sulfur combined with an antitranspirant, or an antitranspirant alone when leaves emerge in spring.

'Maigold'

Cultivar Name:	'Maigold'
Classification:	Shrub
Parentage:	'Poulsen's Pink' × 'Frühlingstag'
Introduced:	W. Kordes Söhne, Germany; 1953
USDA Plant Hardiness Zones:	5 to 9

Cultivar Name:	'Marijke Koopman'
Classification:	Hybrid tea
Parentage:	Not recorded
Introduced:	Fryer, United Kingdom; Fryer's Nursery Ltd.; 1979
USDA Plant Hardiness Zones:	5 to 9

DESCRIPTION: One of the hardiest gold climbers, 'Maigold' produces clusters of fat, red-tinged buds that open to large, semidouble blooms of bronze gold. Its flowers are

DESCRIPTION: Noted for its intense fragrance and reliable bloom, 'Marijke Koopman' bears long, pointed, deep pink buds that open to high-centered, double flowers of rich rose-pink swirled with deep pink. These elegant blooms are carried above dark green leaves on vigorous, upright shrubs reaching 5 to 6 feet tall and 2½ feet wide. The long-stemmed blooms make excellent cut flowers.

LANDSCAPE USES: Use a group of 'Marijke Koopman' as an accent for all-season bloom. Position it near the back of a border and camouflage the stiff hybrid tea habit by planting informal shrub roses and perennials in front of it. The rose is a must for the cutting garden for its long-lasting, fragrant blooms.

CULTURE: Plant 'Marijke Koopman' in a sunny location in well-drained soil that has been amended with organic matter. Prune hard in late winter or early spring to rid plants of damaged canes and overwintering disease spores. Fertilize after pruning and again after the first bloom with a complete organic fertilizer. Top-dress with compost annually. Deadhead spent blooms to encourage repeat bloom. Apply a mound of mulch as winter protection in Zone 5.

DISEASE AND PEST PROBLEMS: Like other hybrid teas, this cultivar is susceptible to diseases. Protect new foliage with an application of fungicidal soap or garden sulfur combined with an antitranspirant to prevent black spot; repeat monthly. Monitor the plants for insect damage.

'Mary Rose'

Cultivar Name:	**'Mary Rose'**
Classification:	English rose
Parentage:	Seedling × 'The Friar'
Introduced:	Austin, United Kingdom; 1983
USDA Plant Hardiness Zones:	5 to 9

DESCRIPTION: 'Mary Rose' is a shrub rose that looks much like an old rose. It produces abundant full, cupped, rose-pink blooms with a swirled center and soft fragrance. Generous late-spring bloom is followed by a respectable autumn rebloom. Vigorous, well-branched, twiggy bushes reach 4 to 5 feet tall and 4 feet wide and have prickly canes and matte green leaves. Pruning will keep the bushes more compact.

LANDSCAPE USES: This free-flowering shrub can be used as a mass, hedge, foundation planting, or specimen. Plant a group of three bushes in the middle of a mixed border, where the handsome flowers look wonderful with antique roses and perennials.

CULTURE: Give 'Mary Rose' a sunny location in well-drained soil that has been amended with organic matter. Top-dress with compost annually. Prune hard while dormant to keep bushes compact, reducing the canes by one-half their length. Deadhead hard after the bloom to encourage repeat bloom. Fertilize in spring and again after the first bloom with a complete organic fertilizer. This rose is recommended for all regions.

DISEASE AND PEST PROBLEMS: The English roses have variable disease resistance. The breeder recommends an application of preventive sprays for best results. Apply fungicidal soap or garden sulfur combined

'Marijke Koopman'

with an antitranspirant as soon as leaves emerge in spring to prevent black spot; reapply as needed.

RELATED CULTIVARS: 'Winchester Cathedral' (sport of 'Mary Rose'; Austin, United Kingdom; 1988) is identical to its parent except that it bears pure white flowers tinged with buff.

'Redoute' (sport of 'Mary Rose'; Austin, United Kingdom; 1992) is identical to its parent except for its flesh pink flowers.

'L. D. Braithwaite' ('Mary Rose' × 'The Squire'; Austin, United Kingdom; 1990) is the best of the deep crimson English roses. Flowers are well scented and loosely double with a swirled center. 'L. D. Braithwaite' has a bushy habit, spreading 3 to 4 feet tall and wide. It blooms profusely in late spring with respectable repeat bloom.

'Max Graf'

Cultivar Name:	**'Max Graf'**
Classification:	Hybrid rugosa
Parentage:	*Rosa rugosa* × *Rosa wichuraiana*
Introduced:	Bowditch, United States; 1919
USDA Plant Hardiness Zones:	4 to 8

DESCRIPTION: 'Max Graf' bears single, clear pink, fragrant flowers in clusters on a prostrate creeping shrub. It makes a trailing, once-blooming groundcover to 2 feet tall and 8 feet wide; the foliage is dark green and glossy. This humble rose has lent its hardy, disease-free characteristics to a new race of roses. It is renowned as the parent from which German hybridizer Kordes derived *Rosa kordesii*, which occurred through a genetic mutation.

LANDSCAPE USES: 'Max Graf' makes an excellent low-maintenance groundcover. Plant it on sunny slopes as a colorful alternative to juniper. It is a tough, useful plant for difficult situations, including seaside gardens, parking lot beds, highways, and industrial landscapes. It looks especially good spilling over a wall. To cover a slope or bed, plant bushes every 4 feet—plants will be touching in three years.

CULTURE: Plant in a sunny location in well-drained soil. Prune occasionally to remove deadwood. Shear the plant to keep it in bounds if it begins to creep out of its bed. No other care is required. This rose is highly recommended for all regions.

DISEASE AND PEST PROBLEMS: 'Max Graf' is disease-free.

'Mermaid'

Cultivar Name:	**'Mermaid'**
Classification:	Hybrid bracteata
Parentage:	*Rosa bracteata* × a double yellow tea rose
Introduced:	Paul, United Kingdom; 1918
USDA Plant Hardiness Zones:	6 to 9

DESCRIPTION: 'Mermaid' has been cherished for nearly a century, and it will continue to draw admirers wherever it is grown. It's simply a knockout. The bush bears huge, 5-inch, fragrant, single flowers of rich creamy yellow with gold stamens. Late-spring bloom is followed by autumn rebloom. Exuberant, trailing canes reaching 10 to 20 feet tall are well armed with prickles and covered with dark, glossy foliage. It is usually trained as a climber or scrambler that easily stretches to 20 feet in warm climates.

LANDSCAPE USES: Use 'Mermaid' to brighten a dull corner of the garden with sunny, fragrant flowers. It makes an excellent climber to cover a pillar, wall, arch, or trellis. It's also well suited to scramble into medium-sized trees and cover unsightly structures. It blends beautifully with antique roses and companion perennials.

CULTURE: Plant in full sun in well-drained soil that has been amended with organic matter. When planting to grow into a tree, guide it along a bamboo stake to the trunk and simply allow it to scramble into the branches. Occasionally remove deadwood (be sure to wear gloves). Try growing it on a warm wall in Zone 6; it will suffer winterkill but will typically shoot up vigorously and produce some blooms. This rose is highly recommended for all regions.

DISEASE AND PEST PROBLEMS: 'Mermaid' is disease-free.

RELATED CULTIVARS: 'Pearl Drift' ('Mermaid' × 'New Dawn'; LeGrice, United Kingdom; 1981) makes a repeat-flowering, mounding groundcover to 3 feet tall and 4 feet wide. The stems are well armed with prickles and covered with glossy, dark foliage. The semidouble, white-and-pink flowers are large, slightly fragrant, and produced in clusters. It is hardy in Zones 6 to 9.

Cultivar Name:	'Mister Lincoln'
Classification:	Hybrid tea
Parentage:	'Chrysler Imperial' × 'Charles Mallerin'
Introduced:	Swim & Weeks, United States; Conard-Pyle, United States; 1964 1965 All-America Rose Selection
USDA Plant Hardiness Zones:	5 to 9

DESCRIPTION: 'Mister Lincoln' is a noble hybrid tea rose. Its urn-shaped buds open to large, double, high-centered, crimson red flowers that have an intense perfume. The bushes are upright, reaching 5 to 6 feet tall and

2½ feet wide with matte green foliage. The elegant, long-stemmed blooms make excellent cut flowers.

LANDSCAPE USES: Use a group of 'Mister Lincoln' as an accent of all-season bloom. Position it near the back of a mixed border, where its lovely flowers will nod above companion shrubs and perennials and the lower plants will hide its stiff hybrid tea habit. 'Mister Lincoln' is a must for the cutting garden for its long-lasting, fragrant blooms.

CULTURE: Plant in a sunny location in well-drained soil that has been amended with organic matter. Prune hard while dormant to open centers to air and light and to rid plants of damaged canes and overwintering disease spores. Fertilize after pruning and again after the first bloom with a complete organic fertilizer. Top-dress with compost annually. Deadhead spent blooms to encourage repeat bloom. Apply a mound of mulch as winter protection in Zone 5. This rose is highly recommended for all regions.

DISEASE AND PEST PROBLEMS: Like other hybrid teas, 'Mister Lincoln' is susceptible to diseases. Protect new foliage with an application of fungicidal soap or garden sulfur combined with an antitranspirant to prevent black spot; reapply monthly. Monitor the plants for insect damage.

'Mister Lincoln'

'Morden Centennial'

Cultivar Name:	**'Morden Centennial'**
Classification:	Shrub
Parentage:	Complex hybrid developed from crosses between *Rosa arkansana* and floribunda roses
Introduced:	Marshall, Canada; Agriculture Canada; 1980
USDA Plant Hardiness Zones:	3 to 9

DESCRIPTION: 'Morden Centennial' is a hardy, everblooming compact shrub rose raised at the Morden Research Station in Manitoba, Canada. Rarely out of bloom, it is covered with clusters of double, clear pink blooms that have a light scent. Bushes are vigorous and bushy, reaching 3 to 4 feet tall and wide, with prickly canes, semiglossy, dark green foliage, and attractive hips.

LANDSCAPE USES: 'Morden Centennial' is a dependable bloomer that looks great as a shrub mass, foundation planting, hedge, or specimen. In mixed borders, its rich blooms combine beautifully with antique and modern roses and perennials. Plant it in drifts of three or more bushes to make a mass of all-season bloom.

CULTURE: This rose is a rugged, hardy shrub that's easy to grow in full sun in any well-drained soil. Top-dress with compost annually, and fertilize in spring with a complete organic fertilizer. Prune annually while dormant, removing damaged canes, thinning out crowded stems, and reducing canes by one-half their length to encourage vigorous new shoots. To form a hedge, plant bushes every 3 feet—plants will be touching in three years. This rose is highly recommended for all regions; because of its excellent cold hardiness, 'Morden Centennial' is particularily useful in northern gardens.

DISEASE AND PEST PROBLEMS: 'Morden Centennial' is disease-resistant. Apply fungicidal soap or garden sulfur combined with an antitranspirant as soon as leaves emerge in spring to prevent black spot; reapply as needed. Monitor insect feeding, and apply insecticidal soap as needed to prevent damage to buds and leaves.

RELATED CULTIVARS: The Morden series of compact, everblooming, hardy, floribunda-type shrub roses was developed at the Morden Research Station in Manitoba, Canada, from complex crosses between Arkansas rose and floribunda roses.

'Morden Amorette' (Marshall, Canada; 1977) produces rose-pink blooms in clusters from June to frost. Vigorous bushes reach 2 feet tall and wide.

'Morden Blush' (Marshall, Canada; 1988) bears sprays of small, double blooms of light pink fading to ivory that open flat. The compact shrubs are 24 inches tall and wide with matte green foliage.

'Morden Cardinette' (Marshall, Canada; 1980) bears cardinal red, double flowers produced continuously on compact shrubs reaching 24 to 30 inches tall and wide, with brown stems and smooth yellow-green foliage.

'Morden Fireglow' (seedling × 'Morden Cardinette'; Marshall, Canada; 1991) bears sprays of cupped, double flowers that are orange-red on the inside and red on the back. The compact bushes grow 24 to 30 inches tall and wide and are covered with matte green foliage.

Cultivar Name:	**'Mutabilis'** (also called *Rosa chinensis* var. *mutabilis*, 'Tipo Ideale')
Classification:	China
Parentage:	Variety of *Rosa chinensis*
Introduced:	Rehder; prior to 1894
USDA Plant Hardiness Zones:	6 to 9

DESCRIPTION: 'Mutabilis' is a real knockout. It always attracts attention because of its unique flowers— single, elegant blossoms that resemble butterflies! Pointed, copper buds open to dainty, single, apricot-orange flowers that change to pink and crimson. Bushes are wiry with smooth stems and shiny, pointed leaves. In cool climates, they normally grow 3 to 4 feet tall and wide. In mild climates and protected locations, plants are more vigorous, reaching 7 to 8 feet tall. 'Mutabilis' deserves a place in any garden where winters are not too severe.

LANDSCAPE USES: Use 'Mutabilis' as an attractive mass or specimen. The best place to grow 'Mutabilis' is in mixed borders, surrounded by perennials, herbs, other larger roses, and flowering shrubs. It lends an air of sprightly enchantment throughout the season with its butterfly flowers, and it can always be counted on to give a bit of color to the autumn garden.

CULTURE: 'Mutabilis' is a vigorous shrub that's easy to grow in full sun in any well-drained soil. Top-dress with compost annually, and fertilize in spring with a complete organic fertilizer. Prune while dormant, removing damaged canes, thinning out crowded stems, and reducing canes by one-half their length. This rose is highly recommended for all regions in Zones 7 to 9. It's also worth a try in a protected location in Zone 6.

DISEASE AND PEST PROBLEMS: 'Mutabilis' is noted for its disease resistance. For best results, apply fungicidal soap or garden sulfur combined with an antitranspirant as soon as leaves emerge in spring; monitor thereafter and reapply if needed.

'Nearly Wild'

Cultivar Name:	**'Nearly Wild'**
Classification:	Floribunda
Parentage:	'Dr. W. Van Fleet' × 'Leuchtstern'
Introduced:	Brownell, United States; 1941
USDA Plant Hardiness Zones:	4 to 9

DESCRIPTION: 'Nearly Wild' resembles a species rose with its sprays of clear pink, single flowers filled with yellow stamens. It is extremely hardy, and one of the best floribundas for continuous bloom. Shrubs are upright and rounded, growing 3 to 4 feet tall and wide, with small, light green, semiglossy leaves.

LANDSCAPE USES: 'Nearly Wild' is a dependable, easy-care rose for use as a shrub mass, foundation planting, medium hedge, or specimen. In mixed borders, its old-fashioned blooms mingle easily with perennials and other shrubs. Plant it in drifts of three or more bushes to make a mass of all-season bloom.

CULTURE: Plant this rose in a sunny location in well-drained soil that has been amended with organic matter. Prune hard while dormant to rid plants of overwintering disease spores and to encourage vigorous new growth. Fertilize after pruning and again after the first bloom with a complete organic fertilizer. Top-dress with compost

'Mutabilis'

annually. Deadhead spent blooms through the season. A rose no garden should be without, 'Nearly Wild' is highly recommended for all regions.

DISEASE AND PEST PROBLEMS: 'Nearly Wild' has excellent disease resistance. Apply an antitranspirant as soon as leaves emerge in spring to prevent disease problems, or allow plants to fend for themselves. If mildew shows up, spray with fungicidal soap or horticultural oil to eradicate it.

'New Dawn'

Cultivar Name:	**'New Dawn'**
Classification:	Large-flowered climber
Parentage:	'Dr. W. Van Fleet' sport
Introduced:	Dreer, United States; Somerset Rose Nursery; 1930
USDA Plant Hardiness Zones:	5 to 9

DESCRIPTION: Only nature could have improved upon the exceptional once-blooming memorial rose climber, 'Dr. W. Van Fleet'. And it did in 'New Dawn', its repeat-blooming sport. 'New Dawn' is a lovely and influential rose that has contributed its noble genes to create some of the best repeat-blooming, large-flowered climbing roses. The fragrant, loosely double, cupped blooms are pearly pink to white, opening flat to reveal golden stamens. They are produced with abandon in large sprays in early summer, followed by respectable late-summer repeat bloom. 'New Dawn' has an extremely vigorous, bushy, upright habit and easily reaches 10 to 12 feet or more. The foliage is glossy.

LANDSCAPE USES: 'New Dawn' makes an excellent climber to cover a pillar, wall, arch, fence, or trellis. It's extremely vigorous and needs sturdy support. It is easy to blend with pastel color schemes and looks particularly fine with blue-flowered or silver-leaved perennials. Grow your favorite large-flowered clematis over it to add colorful seasonal interest. It can also be grown as a mounding shrub.

CULTURE: Plant 'New Dawn' in full sun in well-drained soil that has been amended with organic matter. Top-dress with compost annually. Fertilize in spring and after the first flowering with a complete organic fertilizer. For the first two or three years, little pruning is required: Just tie the canes to their support and deadhead spent blooms. Prune mature plants in late winter each year, removing deadwood and crowded canes, choosing young stocky canes to replace older ones, and reducing lateral shoots to four buds. This rose is highly recommended for all regions.

DISEASE AND PEST PROBLEMS: Like its parent, 'New Dawn' is disease-free. Sometimes rose slugs attack the new foliage; spray with insecticidal soap.

RELATED CULTIVARS: 'White Dawn' ('New Dawn' × 'Lily Pons'; Longley, United States; 1949) is a reliable repeat-blooming white climber. It bears sprays of double, cupped, pure white, fragrant flowers in early summer, followed by exceptional repeat bloom in late summer. It grows 10 to 12 feet tall and has glossy leaves.

'Coral Dawn' (['New Dawn' seedling × yellow hybrid tea] × orange-red polyantha; Boerner, United States; 1952) produces clusters of fragrant rose-pink, double, cupped flowers in early summer followed by respectable late-summer repeat bloom. It grows 10 feet tall and has leathery, glossy leaves.

'Awakening' ('New Dawn' sport; Beales, United Kingdom; 1992) exhibits all of the excellent qualities of its parent and is noted for its full, old-fashioned, quartered flowers. For additional related cultivars, see the entries 'Aloha', 'Don Juan', 'Parade', 'Rhonda', and 'White Cockade'.

'Nozomi'

'Old Blush'

Cultivar Name:	**'Nozomi'**
Classification:	Climbing miniature
Parentage:	'Fairy Princess' × 'Sweet Fairy'
Introduced:	Onodera, Japan; 1968
USDA Plant Hardiness Zones:	5 to 9

Cultivar Name:	**'Old Blush'** (also called 'Common Monthly', 'Parson's Pink China', 'Old Pink Monthly')
Classification:	China
Parentage:	Not recorded
Introduced:	Introduced into Sweden in 1752; England, 1759
USDA Plant Hardiness Zones:	6 to 9

DESCRIPTION: 'Nozomi' produces abundant clusters of charming, tiny, pearly pink, single blooms in early summer with scattered repeat bloom. When grown as a groundcover, the trailing canes mound to 2 feet with a spread of 6 feet. The prickly stems bear small, glossy leaves.

LANDSCAPE USES: Dainty 'Nozomi' is delightful as a groundcover or as a short climber to cover a trellis, fence, or pillar. It also looks wonderful cascading gracefully over the top of a wall.

CULTURE: Plant in a sunny location in well-drained soil that has been amended with organic matter. Little pruning is required except to remove deadwood and to keep plants in bounds. Fertilize after pruning, and topdress with compost annually. This rose is recommended for all regions.

DISEASE AND PEST PROBLEMS: 'Nozomi' is typically disease-free. However, mites sometimes bother the plants. If the bugs appear, wash the leaves with a strong spray of water to knock off the pests. If feeding persists, apply insecticidal soap.

DESCRIPTION: Among the famous quartet of China roses that contributed their repeat-blooming character to modern roses, 'Old Blush' is still a favorite of gardeners. The cupped, lavender-pink, semidouble flowers are held in loose clusters atop wiry bushes that normally reach 3 to 5 feet tall and less wide and are covered with pointed, semiglossy leaves. They bloom continuously. In warm climates, the bushes grow considerably larger, although pruning keeps them more compact.

LANDSCAPE USES: Use 'Old Blush' as an attractive mass, drift, or container specimen. In warm climates, it also makes an excellent everblooming hedge. The best way to grow 'Old Blush' is in a drift in mixed borders, surrounded by perennials, herbs, other larger roses, and flowering shrubs. In Zone 6, you can grow it near the front of the border, since it must be pruned hard to get rid of winterkilled canes. A favorite combination at the Morris Arboretum blends 'Old Blush' with an underplanting of violet sage (*Salvia* × *superba*), Lancaster cranesbill (*Geranium sanguineum* var. *striatum*), and 'Angel's Blush' rose campion (*Lychnis coronaria* 'Angel's Blush') set against a dense background of the alba rose 'Félicité Parmentier'.

CULTURE: This vigorous shrub is easy to grow in full sun in any well-drained soil. Top-dress with compost annually, and fertilize in spring with a complete organic fertilizer. Prune while dormant, removing damaged canes, thinning out crowded stems, and reducing canes by one-half their length. This rose is highly recommended for all regions.

DISEASE AND PEST PROBLEMS: 'Old Blush' is moderately resistant to diseases. For best results, apply fungicidal soap or garden sulfur combined with an anti-transpirant as soon as leaves emerge in spring; reapply if needed.

'Parade'

Cultivar Name:	'Parade'
Classification:	Large-flowered climber
Parentage:	'New Dawn' seedling × 'World's Fair Climbing'
Introduced:	Boerner, United States; Jackson & Perkins, United States; 1953
USDA Plant Hardiness Zones:	5 to 9

DESCRIPTION: 'Parade' is one of the choice 'New Dawn' offspring and simply the best climber in its color range. Light crimson buds open to large, deep rose-pink, double flowers with a cupped, old-fashioned form. They

are very fragrant and produced with abandon in nodding sprays in early summer, followed by intermittent summer bloom and excellent autumn repeat bloom. It has an extremely vigorous, bushy, upright habit and easily reaches 10 feet tall. It has glossy leaves.

LANDSCAPE USES: 'Parade' makes an excellent climber to cover a pillar, wall, arch, fence, or trellis. It's extremely vigorous and needs sturdy support. It blends well with pastel color schemes, and looks particularly fine with blue flowers and silver-leaved perennials. Grow a large-flowered clematis over it to add colorful seasonal interest.

CULTURE: Plant in full sun in well-drained soil that has been amended with organic matter. Top-dress with compost annually. Fertilize in spring and after the first flowering with a complete organic fertilizer. For the first two or three years, little pruning is required: Just tie the canes to their support and deadhead spent blooms. Prune mature plants while dormant to remove deadwood and crowded canes; also choose young, stocky canes to replace older ones and reduce sideshoots to four buds. 'Parade' is an underused climber, highly recommended for all regions.

DISEASE AND PEST PROBLEMS: Like its 'New Dawn' parent, 'Parade' is disease-free. Sometimes rose slugs attack the new foliage. If so, spray with insecticidal soap.

Cultivar Name:	'Pascali'
Classification:	Hybrid tea
Parentage:	'Queen Elizabeth' × 'White Butterfly'
Introduced:	Lens, Belgium; 1963; Armstrong Nursery, United States; 1968 1969 All-America Rose Selection 1991 World's Favorite Rose
USDA Plant Hardiness Zones:	5 to 9

DESCRIPTION: Voted the world's favorite rose in 1991, 'Pascali' deserves the tribute for its elegant beauty and outstanding performance in gardens. It is simply the best white hybrid tea rose in the world. Everything about this rose is refined. Shapely, white buds tinged with green open in classic high-center form to exquisite medium-sized blooms of pure white. The lightly scented flowers are produced continuously, either singly or in sprays, atop slender, upright bushes that have thornless upper stems.

The vigorous bushes grow 5 feet tall and 2½ feet wide and are covered with dark, semiglossy leaves. It makes an excellent cut flower.

LANDSCAPE USES: 'Pascali' blends easily into mixed borders, where its lovely snow white flowers nod above its companions. Plant in groups of three or more for a mass of continuous bloom. A must for the cutting garden, it makes a long-lasting cut flower.

CULTURE: Plant in a sunny location in well-drained soil that has been amended with organic matter. Prune hard while dormant, removing dead and damaged canes, ridding plants of overwintering disease spores, and encouraging vigorous new growth. Fertilize after pruning in spring and after the first flowering with a complete organic fertilizer to promote repeat-flowering. Deadhead spent flowers by cutting back to at least the second five-leaflet node. Top-dress with compost in autumn. In Zone 5, mound mulch over the crowns as winter protection. 'Pascali' is highly recommended for all regions.

DISEASE AND PEST PROBLEMS: Like other hybrid tea roses, 'Pascali' is susceptible to black spot. For best results, apply fungicidal soap or garden sulfur combined with an antitranspirant as soon as leaves emerge; reapply as needed. Monitor the bushes for pests.

'Paulii Rosea', a sport of 'Paulii'

Cultivar Name:	'Paulii'
Classification:	Shrub
Parentage:	*Rosa arvensis* × *Rosa rugosa*
Introduced:	Paul, United Kingdom; 1903
USDA Plant Hardiness Zones:	3 to 8

DESCRIPTION: 'Paulii' bears clusters of single, white, fragrant flowers on a prostrate creeping shrub. It makes a trailing, once-blooming groundcover rose 2 to 3 feet high with an 8-foot spread well foliated with dark wrinkled, glossy foliage. This humble groundcover rose is worth growing for its vigor and its delicate blooms.

LANDSCAPE USES: 'Paulii' makes an excellent low-maintenance groundcover. Plant it on sunny slopes as a colorful alternative to juniper. It is a tough, useful choice for difficult situations including the seaside, hot-spot parking lot beds, highways, and industrial landscapes. It also relishes a good spill over a wall. To cover a slope or bed, plant bushes every 4 feet—plants will be touching in three years.

CULTURE: Plant in a sunny location in well-drained soil. Prune occasionally remove deadwood. Shear to keep in bounds if it begins to creep out of its bed. No other care is required. This is an offbeat once-blooming rose recommended for the adventurous gardener.

DISEASE AND PEST PROBLEMS: 'Paulii' is typically disease-free. Sometimes mildew develops. Spray with horticultural oil to eradicate the problem.

RELATED CULTIVARS: 'Paulii Rosea' (probably a 'Paulii' sport; Paul, United Kingdom; 1912) is identical to the parent except that its flower is pink with a white eye filled with yellow stamens.

'Pascali'

'Peace'

Cultivar Name:	'Peace'
Classification:	Hybrid tea
Parentage:	[('George Dickson' × 'Souvenir de Claudius Pernet') × ('Joanna Hill' × 'Charles P. Kilham')] × 'Margaret McGredy'
Introduced:	Meilland, France; Conard-Pyle, United States; 1945 1946 All-America Rose Selection
USDA Plant Hardiness Zones:	5 to 9

DESCRIPTION: 'Peace' is universally recognized for the beauty of its flowers. It is the best known of all roses and is grown throughout the world. Large, yellow buds open in classic high-center form to full, scented blooms of yellow edged in pink. Flowers are produced abundantly in spring with good repeat bloom. It makes an upright bush to 3½ feet tall and 2½ feet wide, with distinctive, glossy leaves. Unfortunately, cloning for half a century seems to have created a loss of vigor, and new bushes of 'Peace' are not as vigorous as the original.

LANDSCAPE USES: The beautiful color of its large flowers makes 'Peace' a wonderful addition to borders and mixed beds, where it blends easily with both cool and hot color schemes. It is a must for the cutting garden.

CULTURE: Plant in a sunny location in well-drained soil that has been amended with organic matter. Unlike most hybrid teas, 'Peace' does not respond well to hard pruning. Prune lightly in early spring, removing dead and damaged canes. Fertilize after pruning in spring and after

first flowering with a complete organic fertilizer to promote repeat flowering. Deadhead spent flowers by cutting back to at least the second five-leaflet node. Top-dress with compost in autumn. In Zone 5, mound mulch or pine needles over the crown of the plants in late autumn as winter protection.

DISEASE AND PEST PROBLEMS: 'Peace' and its kin are prone to black spot and mildew in regions where these diseases are common. For best results, apply fungicidal soap or garden sulfur combined with an anti-transpirant as soon as leaves emerge; monitor plants and reapply as needed. Monitor the bushes for pests, and apply insecticidal soap or neem extract as needed.

RELATED CULTIVARS: 'Climbing Peace' (climbing hybrid tea; Conard-Pyle, United States; 1950; sport of 'Peace') produces abundant spring bloom followed by autumn repeat bloom. The upright canes have glossy foliage and reach 6 to 10 feet tall.

Pearl Meidiland™

Cultivar Name:	Pearl Meidiland™
Classification:	Shrub
Parentage:	('Sea Foam' × 'MEIsecaso') × 'Sea Foam'
Introduced:	Meilland, France; 1989; Conard-Pyle, United States; 1989
USDA Plant Hardiness Zones:	4 to 9

DESCRIPTION: Pearl Meidiland™ is among the best of the series of Meidiland™ landscape roses. It bears sprays of small, pearly pink, double flowers that resemble sweetheart roses. They open flat and age to creamy white. Profuse late-spring bloom is followed by summer and autumn repeat bloom. It makes a trailing, mounding groundcover to 2½ feet tall and 6 feet wide with small, dark green, glossy leaves.

LANDSCAPE USES: Pearl Meidiland™ makes an excellent low-maintenance groundcover rose. Plant it on sunny slopes as a colorful alternative to juniper. It is a good choice for difficult situations like parking lot beds and industrial landscapes. It also looks great spilling over a wall or cascading from a large planter. To cover a bank or bed, set plants every 4 feet—they will be touching in three years.

CULTURE: Plant in a sunny location in well-drained soil. Top-dress with compost annually, or fertilize with a complete organic fertilizer. Prune occasionally to remove deadwood. Shear to keep the plant in bounds if it begins to creep out of its bed. This rose is highly recommended for all regions.

DISEASE AND PEST PROBLEMS: Pearl Meidiland™ has excellent disease resistance and is disease-free in some regions. Its U.S. introducer, the Conard-Pyle Company, recommends three sprays to keep all the Meidiland™ roses looking their best. Apply fungicidal soap or garden sulfur combined with an antitranspirant once in spring as leaves emerge, once in early summer, and again in midsummer to prevent black spot. Pearl Meidiland™ is highly recommended for all regions.

RELATED CULTIVARS: Alba Meidiland™ (*Rosa sempervirens* × 'Marthe Carron'; Meilland, France; 1985) is similar to Pearl Meidiland™ but bears pure white, double flowers. Trailing canes grow 2½ feet tall and 6 feet wide. The glossy, green foliage changes to yellow in autumn.

Scarlet Meidiland™ ('MEItriaca' × Clair Matin®; Meilland, France; 1987) is among the best of the series of Meidiland™ landscape roses. It bears semidouble blooms of cherry red with light crimson on the back of the petals. Vigorous, trailing canes have dark, glossy foliage and mound 3 feet tall and 6 feet wide. Shrubs are typically disease-free; they provide good repeat bloom and tolerate light shade. This rose is highly recommended for all regions.

Fuchsia Meidiland™ (Meilland, France; 1993) bears clusters of small, mauve-pink, semidouble flowers on a creeping shrub. The stems grow 2½ feet tall and 4 to 5 feet wide. The plant is covered with small, coppery, glossy leaves. It makes a mounding landscape shrub similar to Scarlet Meidiland™. This rose is recommended for all regions.

White Meidiland™ ('Temple Bells' × 'MEIguramai'; Meilland, France; 1986) bears the largest flowers in the Meidiland™ series and is one of the best for continuous bloom. Blooms are pure white, double, very full, and carried in clusters. The spreading shrub grows 2 feet tall and 6 feet wide and is covered with dark, glossy leaves. The flowers do not drop off, so the bushes will become unsightly unless deadheaded. This cultivar is susceptible to black spot and should be treated with three recommended preventive sprays for best results.

'Penelope'

Cultivar Name:	'Penelope'
Classification:	Hybrid musk
Parentage:	'Ophelia' × unnamed seedling
Introduced:	Pemberton, United Kingdom; 1924
USDA Plant Hardiness Zones:	5 to 9

DESCRIPTION: One of the best hybrid musk roses, 'Penelope' bears clusters of very fragrant, loosely double flowers of blush pink fading to creamy white. Large sprays of flowers are produced abundantly in spring with excellent repeat bloom. Flowers are followed by small, pink hips. Upright, spreading bushes are covered with copper-tinted young leaves that change to glossy, crisp dark green. Pruned shrubs mound to 5 feet tall and wide. Bushes are less vigorous and more compact due to winter dieback in Zone 5.

LANDSCAPE USES: 'Penelope' makes a wonderful specimen, mass, or informal hedge. You can make a beautiful garden scene by massing the shrubs with the floppy spikes of 'Dropmore' blue catmint (*Nepeta* × *faassenii* 'Dropmore'). In mixed borders, accent the soft blush flowers of 'Penelope' with lovely blue-flowered perennials and silver-leaved plants.

CULTURE: Site 'Penelope' in sun or light shade from deciduous trees. Plant in well-drained soil that has been amended with organic matter. Prune while dormant to keep shrubs in bounds, removing about one-third of the top growth and periodically cutting out older canes. Deadhead to encourage repeat bloom. Fertilize in spring and again after spring bloom with a complete organic fertilizer to encourage repeat bloom. To form a hedge, set bushes every 4 feet—plants will be touching in three years. This rose is recommended for all regions.

DISEASE AND PEST PROBLEMS: 'Penelope' is resistant to black spot and mildew. For extra protection, spray new foliage with fungicidal soap or garden sulfur combined with an antitranspirant; monitor plants and reapply if needed.

Cultivar Name:	**'Playboy'**
	(also called 'Cheerio')
Classification:	Floribunda
Parentage:	'City of Leeds' × ('Chanelle' × 'Piccadily')
Introduced:	Cocker, United Kingdom; 1976
USDA Plant Hardiness Zones:	5 to 9

DESCRIPTION: When in bloom, 'Playboy' is dazzling. Well-shaped, scarlet buds open to reddish orange flowers branded with a large, golden eye filled with orange stamens. The blooms are produced almost continuously in large sprays that are excellent for cut flowers. 'Playboy' forms a bushy, spreading shrub to 3 feet tall and less wide, with glossy leaves.

LANDSCAPE USES: Use 'Playboy' as a shrub mass, foundation planting, medium hedge, or container specimen. In mixed borders, its fiery flowers mix easily with bright perennials, and other roses in flame shades. Plant it in drifts of three or more bushes to make a mass of all-season bloom.

CULTURE: Plant 'Playboy' in a sunny location in well-drained soil that has been amended with organic matter. Prune hard while dormant to rid plants of overwintering disease spores and to encourage vigorous new growth. Fertilize after pruning and again after the first bloom with a complete organic fertilizer. Top-dress with compost annually. Deadhead spent blooms through the season. This rose is recommended for all regions.

DISEASE AND PEST PROBLEMS: 'Playboy' is moderately disease-resistant. Apply fungicidal soap or an antitranspirant as soon as leaves emerge in spring to prevent disease problems; reapply as needed.

RELATED CULTIVARS: 'Playgirl' ('Playboy' × 'Angel Face'; Moore, United States; 1986) produces bright pink, single flowers with prominent yellow stamens on bushy shrubs 3 feet tall and less wide.

'Playtime' ('Playboy' × 'Old Master'; Moore, United States; 1989) produces orange-red, single flowers on bushy shrubs that grow 3 feet tall and less wide.

'Ralph's Creeper' ('Papoose' × 'Playboy'; Moore, United States; 1988) is a groundcover rose that produces semidouble, orange-red blooms with a distinctive yellow eye and yellow on the back of the petals. Large sprays of flowers with a fruity fragrance cover bushes in spring, with good repeat bloom. Mounding, prostrate shrubs grow 1 foot tall and 5 feet wide.

'Playboy'

'Popcorn'

Cultivar Name:	**'Popcorn'**
Classification:	Miniature
Parentage:	'Katharina Zeimet' × 'Diamond Jewel'
Introduced:	Morey, United States; Pixie Treasures; 1973
USDA Plant Hardiness Zones:	5 to 9

DESCRIPTION: Rarely out of bloom, 'Popcorn' produces charming single to semidouble, pure white flowers that look like popped corn. This cultivar also resembles a dwarf wild rose with its tiny, few-petaled blooms that have a sweet fragrance. Plants are compact and bushy, 15 inches tall and less wide, with small, semiglossy foliage.

LANDSCAPE USES: 'Popcorn' is a versatile rose that is great as an edging, dwarf hedge, container specimen, or hanging basket plant. It is also wonderful in a rock garden and looks particularly attractive displayed in raised planters or cascading over a wall. Its dwarf size makes it a good candidate for indoor culture under lights.

CULTURE: Plant in a sunny location in well-drained soil that has been amended with organic matter. Prune hard in late winter or early spring to rid plants of overwintering disease spores and to encourage vigorous new growth. Fertilize after pruning and again after the first bloom with a complete organic fertilizer. Top-dress with compost annually. Shear after each bloom period through the season to avoid a leggy appearance. 'Popcorn' is recommended for all regions.

DISEASE AND PEST PROBLEMS: This rose has excellent disease resistance, but mites sometimes bother the plants. If so, wash the leaves with a strong spray of water to knock off the pests. If feeding persists, apply insecticidal soap.

RELATED CULTIVARS: 'Gourmet Popcorn' ('Popcorn' sport; Desamero, United States; 1986) bears large clusters of fragrant, pure white, anemone-like flowers. The flowers are semidouble, with more size and substance and a deeper butter yellow center than the original. The somewhat-cascading bushes grow 2 feet tall and less wide. This rose is highly recommended for all regions.

'Prairie Princess'

Cultivar Name:	**'Prairie Princess'**
Classification:	Shrub
Parentage:	'Carrousel' × ('Morning Stars' × 'Suzanne')
Introduced:	Buck, United States; Iowa State University; 1972
USDA Plant Hardiness Zones:	4 to 9

DESCRIPTION: 'Prairie Princess' is one of the first of the excellent, hardy, repeat-flowering shrubs raised by Griffith Buck at the University of Iowa. It is an important parent to many of the later great cultivars, including Carefree Beauty™. It is covered with clusters of large, semidouble, coral-pink flowers in late spring, with good repeat bloom. The flowers have a light perfume. Shrubs are upright and vigorous, growing 4 feet tall and less wide, with dark, leathery leaves.

LANDSCAPE USES: Use 'Prairie Princess' as an attractive mass, hedge, or specimen. Its old-fashioned flowers mix easily with antique and modern roses and perennials.

CULTURE: 'Prairie Princess' is a robust, hardy shrub that's easy to grow in full sun in any well-drained soil. Top-dress with compost annually, and fertilize in spring with a complete organic fertilizer. Prune annually while dormant, removing older canes and one-third of the top growth and thinning out crowded stems. To form a hedge, set bushes every 3 feet—plants will be touching in three years.

DISEASE AND PEST PROBLEMS: 'Prairie Princess' is noted for its disease resistance. For extra protection, apply fungicidal soap or garden sulfur combined with an antitranspirant as soon as leaves emerge in spring; reapply as needed. This rose is recommended for all regions.

RELATED CULTIVARS: 'Country Dancer' ('Prairie Princess' × 'Johannes Beottner'; Buck, United States; 1973) produces large, deep pink, fragrant blooms throughout the season. Bushes are upright and vigorous, reaching 3 feet tall and wide, with dark, leathery leaves.

'Earth Song' ('Music Maker' × 'Prairie Star'; Buck, United States; 1975) is classified as a grandiflora. It bears large, fragrant, cupped, deep rose-pink, double flowers in sprays. Bushes are upright, bushy, and vigorous, reaching 4½ to 5 feet tall and less wide, with glossy, dark leaves.

'Hawkeye Belle' (['Queen Elizabeth' × 'Pizzicato'] × 'Prairie Princess'; Buck, United States; 1975) bears fragrant, large, high-center, double flowers that are white, tinted with blush pink. The upright, bushy shrubs grow 4 feet tall and wide.

Cultivar Name:	**'Pristine'**
Classification:	Hybrid tea
Parentage:	'White Masterpiece' × 'First Prize'
Introduced:	Warriner, United States; Jackson & Perkins; 1978
USDA Plant Hardiness Zones:	5 to 9

DESCRIPTION: 'Pristine' is a special rose of rare, elegant charm. Its long, pointed, crimson buds open in classic high-center form. The large, double, scented blooms are pale blush-white and produced abundantly throughout the season. It makes an upright, bushy shrub 5 to 5½ feet tall and 3 feet wide. Its thick, purplish canes are well armed with red thorns and covered with large, dark, leathery leaves. It is an excellent exhibition and cut flower.

LANDSCAPE USES: The pale blush color of its large flowers makes 'Pristine' a wonderful addition to borders and mixed beds, where it blends easily with cool color schemes. It is a must for the cutting garden.

CULTURE: Plant in a sunny location in well-drained soil that has been amended with organic matter. Unlike most hybrid teas, 'Pristine' does not respond well to hard pruning. Prune lightly in early spring, removing dead and damaged canes. Fertilize after pruning in spring and after the first flush of blooms with a complete organic fertilizer to promote repeat flowering. Deadhead spent flowers by cutting back to at least the second five-leaflet node. Top-dress with compost in autumn. In Zone 5, mound mulch or pine needles over the crown of the plants in late autumn as winter protection.

DISEASE AND PEST PROBLEMS: 'Pristine' has above-average disease resistance. For extra protection, apply fungicidal soap or garden sulfur combined with an antitranspirant as soon as leaves emerge; reapply as needed. Monitor bushes for pests, and apply insecticidal soap or neem extract as needed.

'Pristine'

'Purple Pavement'

Cultivar Name:	**'Purple Pavement'** (also called 'Rotes Meer')
Classification:	Hybrid rugosa
Parentage:	Not recorded
Introduced:	Baum, Germany; 1984
USDA Plant Hardiness Zones:	3 to 8

DESCRIPTION: 'Purple Pavement' forms a dense, bushy, compact shrub about 2½ feet tall and wide. The semidouble flowers are deep magenta-pink, opening to reveal golden stamens. The elegant flowers are produced abundantly and almost continuously throughout the season. Large, red hips ripen in late summer, as the foliage turns an attractive golden bronze. To promote fruit set, plant a companion rugosa. Harvest fresh hips to make jam, or dry for use as an herbal tea rich in vitamin C.

LANDSCAPE USES: A fine low hedge, groundcover, mass, or specimen, 'Purple Pavement' is a multipurpose landscape plant. The nearly continuous bloom creates a bright spot in the mixed border, where it mixes well with perennials and herbs. This tough, hardy shrub is tolerant of seaside conditions and urban landscapes.

CULTURE: Plant 'Purple Pavement' in full sun in any well-drained soil. It tolerates reflected heat from paving. To form a hedge, set bushes every 2 feet—plants will be touching in three years. Prune mature specimens and hedges in late winter. Remove about one-third of the top growth to shape the plants. Periodically remove older canes to encourage vigorous new growth.

DISEASE AND PEST PROBLEMS: 'Purple Pavement' is a tough, disease-free rose. However, the summer flowers sometimes attract Japanese beetles. Pick off the adult beetles and treat lawn areas with milky disease

spores to control grubs. It is also susceptible to rose stem girdler. To discourage pests, keep plants free of deadwood; prune out and destroy infected canes.

RELATED CULTIVARS: Roses in the 'Pavement' series are welcome additions to the hybrid rugosa family because of their dwarf size, hardiness, handsome foliage, repeat bloom, bright hips, and fragrant, semidouble flowers. These bushy, spreading shrubs grow to 2½ feet tall and wide.

'Foxi Pavement' ('Foxi'; Uhl, Germany; 1989) bears deep pink, semidouble, fragrant blooms followed by red hips.

'Scarlet Pavement' ('Rote Foxi'; Uhl, Germany; 1991) is similar to 'Foxi' but has light crimson flowers.

'Pierette Pavement' ('Pierette'; Uhl, Germany; 1987) produces continuously blooming, semidouble, dark pink flowers, followed by red hips.

'Snow Pavement' ('Schneekoppe'; Baum, Germany; 1984) supplies a steady stream of semidouble, white blooms with a lavender tint and prominent golden stamens. Its red hips ripen in late summer.

'White Pavement' (Uhl, Germany; 1989) produces pure white, semidouble flowers continuously. The light red hips ripen in late summer.

'Queen Elizabeth'

Cultivar Name:	**'Queen Elizabeth'**
Classification:	Grandiflora
Parentage:	'Charlotte Armstrong' × 'Floradora'
Introduced:	Lammerts, United States; 1954 1955 All-America Rose Selection
USDA Plant Hardiness Zones:	5 to 9

DESCRIPTION: The grandiflora class was created for the royal debut of cherished 'Queen Elizabeth', the All-America Rose Selection for 1955. It bears clear pink, high-centered, double flowers either singly or in sprays. The everblooming, tall shrubs are upright and bushy, reaching 5 to 6 feet tall and 2½ to 3 feet wide, with dark, leathery leaves. 'Queen Elizabeth' blooms have a light tea scent and make excellent cut flowers.

LANDSCAPE USES: Use 'Queen Elizabeth' as an accent of all-season bloom in mixed borders. Position it near the back of the border, and camouflage its stiff hybrid tea habit by planting informal shrub roses and perennials in front of it. It is a must for the cutting garden for its fragrant, long-lasting blooms. It can also be used as a tall, everblooming hedge.

CULTURE: Plant this rose in a sunny location in well-drained soil that has been amended with organic matter. Prune hard in late winter or early spring to rid plants of damaged canes and overwintering disease spores. Fertilize after pruning and again after first bloom with a complete organic fertilizer. Top-dress with compost annually. Deadhead spent blooms to encourage repeat bloom. Apply a mound of mulch as winter protection in Zone 5.

DISEASE AND PEST PROBLEMS: 'Queen Elizabeth' has above-average disease resistance. For extra protection, spray new foliage with fungicidal soap or garden sulfur combined with an antitranspirant; reapply as needed. Monitor the plants for insect damage.

Cultivar Name:	**'Reine des Violettes'**
Classification:	Hybrid perpetual
Parentage:	'Pius XI' seedling
Introduced:	Millet-Malet, France; 1860
USDA Plant Hardiness Zones:	5 to 9

DESCRIPTION: A free-flowering shrub, 'Reine des Violettes' produces pale violet flowers with heavy perfume. The floppy, smooth-stemmed shrub grows 5 feet tall and less wide and has gray-green leaves. The double, many-petaled blooms open flat and quartered with a buttonlike center. 'Reine des Violettes' produces one of the only true violet-colored flowers in any rose class, making a stunning display in full bloom. Not reliably repeat-blooming, it seems to require cool nights to repeat its bloom.

LANDSCAPE USES: 'Reine des Violettes' combines well with perennials and antique roses in mixed borders and provides some height when trained up. It's easy to train as a pillar or short climber because its canes are thornless. Plant with 'Little Nell' clematis (*Clematis viticella* 'Little Nell'), which will weave its airy, small, pink, nodding blooms through the soft purple roses. This rose also responds well to pegging.

CULTURE: Plant in well-drained soil in full sun. Prune out older canes to encourage vigorous new growth, shortening laterals to four buds. Top-dress with compost in autumn and fertilize in spring with a complete organic fertilizer. 'Reine des Violettes' is highly recommended for all regions.

DISEASE AND PEST PROBLEMS: 'Reine des Violettes' has above-average disease resistance for a hybrid perpetual. Apply fungicidal soap or garden sulfur combined with an antitranspirant as soon as leaves emerge in spring to prevent black spot; reapply as needed.

'Reine des Violettes'

'Rise 'n' Shine'

'Rhonda'

Cultivar Name:	'Rhonda'
Classification:	Large-flowered climber
Parentage:	'New Dawn' × 'Spartan'
Introduced:	Lissemore, United States; Conard-Pyle, United States; 1968
USDA Plant Hardiness Zones:	5 to 9

Cultivar Name:	'Rise 'n' Shine'
Classification:	Miniature
Parentage:	'Little Darling' × 'Yellow Magic'
Introduced:	Moore, United States; Sequoia Nursery; 1977 1978 Award of Excellence
USDA Plant Hardiness Zones:	5 to 9

DESCRIPTION: 'Rhonda' has deep rose-pink blooms that are large, double, and lightly fragrant. They are produced abundantly in spring, intermittently through summer, and generously again in autumn. It has a bushy, upright habit, growing 10 to 12 feet or more, with glossy foliage.

LANDSCAPE USES: 'Rhonda' is worth growing for its abundant flower display. It makes an excellent climber to cover a wall, arch, or trellis and looks particularly fine with blue or pink flowers and silver-leaved perennials.

CULTURE: Plant in full sun in well-drained soil that has been amended with organic matter. Top-dress with compost annually. Fertilize in spring and after the first flowering with a complete organic fertilizer. For the first two or three years, little pruning is required: Just tie the canes to their support and deadhead spent blooms. Prune mature plants in late winter each year, removing deadwood and crowded canes, choosing young, stocky canes to replace older ones, and reducing sideshoots to four buds.

DISEASE AND PEST PROBLEMS: 'Rhonda' is disease-resistant. For extra protection, apply fungicidal soap, garden sulfur combined with an antitranspirant, or an antitranspirant alone when leaves emerge in spring; reapply as needed.

DESCRIPTION: Rarely out of bloom, 'Rise 'n' Shine' produces fragrant, high-centered, double flowers of clear yellow. Shrubs are upright and bushy, growing 18 to 24 inches tall and less wide, with small, semiglossy foliage. One of the best yellow miniatures, it makes a good cut flower.

LANDSCAPE USES: This is a versatile rose, suitable for edging, dwarf hedges, and rock gardens. It looks particularly attractive displayed in hanging baskets or raised planters or cascading over a wall. Its dwarf size makes it a good candidate for indoor culture under lights.

CULTURE: Plant in a sunny location in well-drained soil that has been amended with organic matter. Prune hard in late winter or early spring to rid plants of overwintering disease spores and to encourage vigorous new growth. Fertilize after pruning and again after the first bloom with a complete organic fertilizer. Top-dress with compost annually. Shear after each bloom period to avoid a leggy appearance. This rose is recommended for all regions.

DISEASE AND PEST PROBLEMS: 'Rise 'n' Shine' is moderately disease-resistant. Apply a preventive spray of fungicidal soap or garden sulfur combined with an antitranspirant to ward off black spot early in the season; reapply as needed. If mites appear, wash leaves with a strong spray of water to knock off the pests. If mites continue to be a problem, apply insecticidal soap.

RELATED CULTIVARS: 'Rainbow's End' ('Rise 'n' Shine' × 'Watercolor'; Saville, United States; 1984; 1986 Award of Excellence) produces deep yellow, red-tipped flowers in hybrid tea form. The bushes are upright, dense, and covered with dark, glossy leaves.

'Robusta'

Cultivar Name:	**'Robusta'**
Classification:	Shrub
Parentage:	Seedling × *Rosa rugosa*
Introduced:	W. Kordes Söhne, Germany; 1979
USDA Plant Hardiness Zones:	4 to 9

DESCRIPTION: 'Robusta' forms a tough, thorny shrub worthy of its name. The fragrant, five-petaled flowers are scarlet and filled with yellow stamens. The single flowers are produced throughout the growing season. The upright, vigorous shrubs reach 4 to 5 feet tall and nearly as wide.

LANDSCAPE USES: 'Robusta' is a knockout with its red flowers set against dark, glossy foliage. Use it as an everblooming hedge, mass, or specimen. It can brighten a dull corner and mixes well with both cool and hot color schemes in mixed borders. It tolerates hot spots characterized by reflected heat from paving and thrives in seaside gardens.

CULTURE: Plant 'Robusta' in full sun in any well-drained soil. Prune mature specimens and hedges while dormant. Remove about one-third of the top growth to shape the plants. Periodically remove older canes to encourage vigorous new growth. Top-dress with compost annually, and fertilize in early spring with a complete organic fertilizer. In climates where this rose suffers from winter injury, prune it back and let it resprout to produce its lovely flowers on new wood.

DISEASE AND PEST PROBLEMS: 'Robusta' is moderately resistant to black spot. If desired, apply a preventive spray of fungicidal soap or garden sulfur combined with an antitranspirant to protect the foliage.

RELATED CULTIVARS: 'Pink Robusta' (['Zitronenfalter' × 'Grammerstorf Climbing'] × 'Robusta'; W. Kordes Söhne, Germany; 1987) is similar to the original but has semidouble flowers of clear pink.

Rosa banksiae var. banksiae

Species Name:	*Rosa banksiae var. banksiae*
Common Name:	White Lady Banks rose
Classification:	Species
Origin:	Central and western China
Introduced:	Aiton; 1807
USDA Plant Hardiness Zones:	8 to 10

DESCRIPTION: White Lady Banks rose bears an abundance of small, fragrant, double, white blooms on slender, smooth stems that reach 20 feet or more. It is a rampant scrambler in southern gardens.

LANDSCAPE USES: White Lady Banks rose can be used to cover unsightly structures, to scramble into large trees, and to cover large pergolas. It is a fine rose for naturalizing.

CULTURE: Plant this rose in a sunny, well-drained site with average soil and give it something to climb on. Little care is required once the canes have wound themselves over their support.

DISEASE AND PEST PROBLEMS: White Lady Banks rose is disease- and pest-free.

RELATED VARIETIES AND CULTIVARS: Yellow Lady Banks rose (*Rosa banksiae* var. *lutea*; Lindley; 1824) is a double-flowered, yellow variety with no scent.

'Fortuniana' (thought to be *Rosa banksiae* × *Rosa laevigata*; 1850) bears well-scented, large, double, white flowers. Its relatively smooth canes stretch to 20 feet and are covered with dark green, shiny, three-leaflet leaves. It is an excellent climber for southern gardens and a bit more tame than white Lady Banks rose.

Rosa blanda

Species Name:	Rosa blanda
Common Name:	Meadow rose
Classification:	Species
Origin:	Northern North America
Introduced:	Aiton; 1773
USDA Plant Hardiness Zones:	2 to 7

DESCRIPTION: Meadow rose bears light pink, single, fragrant flowers in abundance in late spring or early summer, followed by the best hip display of any native wild rose. The glistening red hips are showy well into winter and are attractive to birds. Meadow rose forms a vigorous, suckering, mounded shrub 4 to 5 feet tall and less wide with smooth red stems covered with blue-green leaves.

LANDSCAPE USES: Meadow rose's extreme hardiness, fragrant flowers, and excellent hip display make it a useful ornamental for northern gardens. Use it as freestanding specimen shrub, mass, or informal hedge, or naturalize it in meadow gardens.

CULTURE: Plant in any well-drained soil in a sunny site. Prune to keep in bounds and to remove deadwood. Rejuvenate overgrown shrubs by cutting them to the ground and allowing them to resprout.

DISEASE AND PEST PROBLEMS: Meadow rose is susceptible to black spot late in the season. However, defoliation makes its bright red hips more prominent, and they give a fantastic show well into winter.

RELATED CULTIVARS: 'Betty Bland' (*Rosa blanda* × a hybrid perpetual; Skinner, Canada; 1926) produces double, deep pink, fragrant blooms in early summer, with no repeat bloom. The bushes are 5 to 6 feet tall and less wide, with handsome red stems.

Rosa eglanteria

Species Name:	Rosa eglanteria (also called *Rosa rubiginosa*)
Common Name:	Sweetbriar; Eglantine rose
Classification:	Species
Origin:	Europe; naturalized in North America
Introduced:	Linnaeus; cultivated before 1550
USDA Plant Hardiness Zones:	4 to 8

DESCRIPTION: Sweetbriar is one of the most common and cherished European wild roses. It has been grown in North America since colonial times and is often found naturalized in meadows. Fragrant, single, rose-pink flowers are produced in abundance in late spring, followed by oval, scarlet hips that attract birds and last into winter. The aromatic foliage provides a scent of freshly cut apples as it emerges in spring and whenever it is wet, bruised, or crushed. It makes a dense shrub 6 to 8 feet tall and wide, armed with hooked prickles and covered with small, leathery, dark green leaves.

LANDSCAPE USES: Sweetbriar is at home in the herb garden, where its fragrant flowers, apple-scented foliage, and red hips provide multi-seasonal interest. It makes an excellent impenetrable hedge. Use it as a free-standing specimen shrub or mass, or naturalize it in meadow gardens. In mixed borders, place it near the back, where it will fade into the green background when not in bloom.

CULTURE: Plant in well-drained soil in a sunny site. Prune to keep in bounds; remove deadwood and occasionally older canes. Prune hedges while dormant to shape and neaten. To form a hedge, plant bushes every 4 feet—plants will be touching in three years.

DISEASE AND PEST PROBLEMS: Sweetbriar is usually disease- and pest-free.

RELATED CULTIVARS: There are many excellent hybrid sweetbriar roses. Most are similar in habit to the species, with one flush of bloom and aromatic foliage. They are all highly recommended.

'Amy Robsart' (*Rosa eglanteria* × a hybrid perpetual; Penzance, United Kingdom; 1894) produces large, fragrant, semidouble, deep pink flowers followed by red hips.

'Goldbusch' ('Golden Glow' × *Rosa eglanteria*; W. Kordes Söhne, Germany; 1954) is blessed with sweetbriar's hardiness, apple-scented foliage, and long canes. From its parent 'Golden Glow', it inherited an aptitude for vigorous, upright growth. Large, semidouble, yellow flowers are borne in clusters. Its fragrant, old-fashioned flowers bloom with abandon for several weeks in late spring and are followed by orange hips. Vigorous canes easily scale 8 to 10 feet and are covered with large prickles and light green leaves. 'Goldbusch' is generally used as a hardy climber trained up pillars, trellises, walls, or fences. In the coldest regions, 'Goldbusch' can be grown as a tall shrub. It is highly recommended for all regions.

'Greenmantle' (Penzance, United Kingdom; 1895) bears single, fragrant, crimson flowers with a prominent white eye.

'Hebe's Lip' (*Rosa damascena* × *Rosa eglanteria*; Lee, United Kingdom; 1846; reintroduced by Paul, United Kingdom; 1912) is sometimes classified as a damask, but it bears a greater resemblance to its sweetbriar parent in overall appearance. It produces cupped, semidouble, bicolored flowers with musk fragrance. The blooms are soft white, edged with crimson, and filled with a center of golden stamens. The hips ripen in late summer. The prickly shrubs reach 4 feet high and less wide. The sweetbriar-type foliage has a light apple scent. This cultivar is highly recommended for all regions.

'Lady Penzance' (*Rosa eglanteria* × *Rosa foetida* var. *bicolor*; Penzance, United Kingdom; 1894) bears fragrant, single flowers of salmon pink with prominent golden stamens. It has strongly aromatic leaves.

'Lord Penzance' (*Rosa eglanteria* × 'Harison's Yellow'; Penzance, United Kingdom; 1894) bears abundant, lovely, single flowers of apricot-yellow. The blooms are fragrant. This cultivar does not set hips. The shrubs are clothed in strongly aromatic foliage. This rose is highly recommended for all regions.

'Manning's Blush' (cultivated before 1799) is a compact form, growing 4 to 5 feet tall and wide, covered with scented, blush-white, full, double flowers. The foliage has a strong apple scent.

Species Name:	*Rosa filipes*
Common Name:	Himalayan musk rose
Classification:	Species
Origin:	Western China
Introduced:	Rehder and Wilson; 1908
USDA Plant Hardiness Zones:	6 to 8

DESCRIPTION: One of the most massive wild roses, Himalayan musk rose reaches 15 to 30 feet tall and bears fragrant, single, white flowers in large, loose clusters. Its round, scarlet hips ripen in late summer. It has hooked prickles, smooth stems, and large, matte green leaflets.

LANDSCAPE USES: Allow Himalayan musk rose to climb into a large tree, or use it to cover unsightly structures in the garden. Its cultivated form, 'Kiftsgate', is a superior rambler for landscape use.

CULTURE: Plant in full sun in well-drained soil. To train Himalayan musk rose to climb into a tree, plant the bush 3 feet away from the trunk and guide it along a bamboo stake. Once trained up the trunk to the first branch, this rambler will pull itself up by its prickles and scramble into the upper branches as it grows toward the light. No pruning is required except occasional removal of unsightly deadwood.

DISEASE AND PEST PROBLEMS: Himalayan musk rose is disease- and pest-free.

RELATED SPECIES AND CULTIVARS: 'Kiftsgate' (cultivar of Himalayan musk rose named for the famous English garden where it was discovered; Murrell, United Kingdom; 1954) bears enormous clusters of pure white, fragrant flowers. It tops its parent in size, growing as tall as 60 feet and as wide as 40 feet in England and moderate climates in the United States. It is more impressive than the parent and recommended for all regions. At the edge of its hardiness in Zone 6, it reaches about 20 feet and is kept in bounds because it withstands some winter dieback.

Rosa sinowilsonii (China; Hemsley; 1904) is noted for its large clusters of single, white flowers borne in early summer, followed by round, red hips. Vigorous, well-armed, flexible canes scramble 50 feet in mild climates. Its cultivar 'Wedding Day' is a superior, hardy form.

'Wedding Day' (rambler; *Rosa sinowilsonii* × seedling; Stern, United Kingdom; 1950) produces fantastic trusses of fragrant, single flowers that start out a soft yellow and fade to white-tinged pink. Vigorous, prickly canes stretch to 20 feet.

'Kiftsgate', a cultivar of *Rosa filipes*

Rosa soulieana (rambler; Crepin, western China; 1896) produces gray-green leaves and clusters of white flowers, followed by orange red hips, held on long, flexible, prickly canes to 12 feet tall. Its cultivars 'Chevy Chase' and 'Kew Rambler' are superior, hardy ramblers.

'Chevy Chase' (rambler; *Rosa soulieana* × 'Eblouissant'; Hansen, United States; 1939) bears fragrant, small, dark crimson red, many-petaled flowers that are held in sizable clusters of one to two dozen blooms. Vigorous canes, 12 to 15 feet tall, are covered with light green, crinkled foliage. Winner of the 1941 American Rose Society Dr. W. Van Fleet Medal, 'Chevy Chase' is highly recommended.

'Kew Rambler' (rambler; *Rosa soulieana* × 'Hiawatha'; United Kingdom; 1913) produces clusters of small, five-petaled, pink flowers. Vigorous, prickly canes growing 12 to 15 feet tall are covered with blue-green leaves.

Rosa foetida var. *bicolor*

Species Name:	**Rosa foetida**
Common Name:	**Austrian briar**
Classification:	Species
Origin:	Asia
Introduced:	Miller; before 1542
USDA Plant Hardiness Zones:	3 to 8

DESCRIPTION: Austrian briar is treasured for its bright, sulfur yellow flowers and extreme hardiness. The five-petaled flowers have a cloying sweet scent and are borne on arching canes 7 to 9 feet tall. The plant has few prickles but many dull green, aromatic leaves. The spring bloom is followed by red hips in late summer. Support the canes or allow them to spread to make a bush 5 to 7 feet high and less wide.

LANDSCAPE USES: The bright yellow flowers of Austrian briar are a welcome sight in the spring garden in mixed borders and shrub beds. Combine Austrian briar with its varieties *bicolor* and *persiana* to create a vibrant collection of wild roses. Use it to fill a position at the back of the border, and plant late-flowering shrubs such as bluebeard (*Caryopteris × clandonensis*), butterfly bush (*Buddleia × davidii*), and repeat-blooming roses in the foreground. Place it where it will blend into surrounding greenery after it blooms because it develops black spot and drops its leaves. Austrian briar can also be trained as a short climber with its arching canes supported on pillars or walls.

CULTURE: Austrian briar thrives in a sunny location in dry soil. Prune only to remove deadwood. Top-dress with compost annually.

DISEASE AND PEST PROBLEMS: Austrian briar and its varieties are notoriously susceptible to black spot. Apply fungicidal soap or garden sulfur combined with an antitranspirant as soon as leaves emerge in early spring. Reapply occasionally through the season to cut down on the problem. It's worth looking after this rose to enjoy the annual vivid flower display.

RELATED VARIETIES: *Rosa foetida* var. *bicolor* (also called 'Austrian Copper'; Willmott; before 1590) produces five-petaled flowers that are coppery red with yellow on the back of the petals; it is unmatched in its vivid coloring.

Rosa foetida var. *persiana* (also called 'Persian Yellow'; Rehder; 1837) bears double, sulfur yellow flowers. It is the parent of modern roses in the yellow and orange-red color range. It is recommended particularly for northern gardens, where few other many-petaled yellow roses can survive.

burgundy, creating a handsome contrast to the red stems. Its small, starlike, lightly scented flowers are pink with a white eye and bloom in clusters along the canes in early June. Mahogany red fruits ripen in late summer, and the leaves turn yellow in autumn. The red stems remain attractive throughout winter. This graceful, loose shrub reaches 4 to 6 feet tall and 3 to 4 feet wide. A European mountain species well loved by rose enthusiasts and flower arrangers alike, redleaved rose is a four-star specimen plant that deserves greater use in U. S. gardens. Its extreme winter hardiness should appeal to northern gardeners.

LANDSCAPE USES: Redleaved rose is a valuable specimen rose. Its blue-gray foliage also stands out in shrub beds or mixed borders, where it combines beautifully with many perennials. For an interesting planting, combine redleaved rose with the shiny leaves of New England shining rose (*Rosa nitida*) and the airy lavender globes of star of Persia (*Allium christophii*). This loose shrub can also be espaliered against a wall or fence to highlight its exquisite foliage. Redleaved rose looks especially good when planted in groups.

CULTURE: Plant in a cool, well-drained site in soil that has been amended with organic matter, and provide some afternoon shade. Redleaved rose establishes slowly where summers are hot, so plant three bushes close together to make an immediate impact. Hot, dry, full sun situations can cause redleaved rose to change color early and drop its leaves in late summer; however, the stems remain attractive throughout the year. Allow this handsome shrub to attain its graceful, arching habit: No hard pruning is necessary. Periodically remove older canes to encourage vigorous growth and new shoots from the base. Top-dress with compost or rotted manure in spring. No other care is required.

Species Name:	**Rosa glauca** (also called *Rosa rubrifolia*)
Common Name:	**Redleaved rose**
Classification:	Species
Origin:	Central and southern Europe
Introduced:	Pourret; cultivated prior to 1830
USDA Plant Hardiness Zones:	2 to 8

DESCRIPTION: Redleaved rose, an excellent specimen shrub in all seasons, is known for its distinctive foliage. The remarkably beautiful blue-gray leaves are tinged with

Rosa glauca

DISEASE AND PEST PROBLEMS: Redleaved rose has excellent disease resistance. In a hot spot, it can become infested with mites. Prevent problems by planting in a spot with afternoon shade. No other pests have been noted.

RELATED CULTIVARS: 'Carmenetta' (*Rosa glauca* × *Rosa rugosa*; 1923) strongly resembles its red-leaved rose parent, but has larger features. The blue-gray, burgundy-tinted leaves and pink, starlike flowers are larger thanthe species; the red hips are similar. This vigorous shrub reaches 7 feet tall and wide and is more upright and coarser than the species. Its excellent heat tolerance makes 'Carmenetta' ideal for regions with hot summers.

Rosa helenae

Species Name:	*Rosa helenae*
Common Name:	Helen rose
Classification:	Species
Origin:	Central China
Introduced:	Rehder and Wilson; 1907
USDA Plant Hardiness Zones:	5 to 8

DESCRIPTION: Helen rose is a vigorous scrambler that stretches 12 to 18 feet and carries masses of small, white, scented flowers in dense clusters followed by large, distinctive, orange-red hips. It is a lovely sight in full bloom in early summer and again when fruits ripen in late summer and autumn. The canes are covered with hooked prickles.

LANDSCAPE USES: Helen rose looks beautiful when trained to climb a crab apple, cherry, or other tree. One of the best uses of Helen rose is to train it up through a purple-leaved plum tree, where the rose flowers and hips

create interesting seasonal contrasts against the backdrop of maroon leaves. You can also use Helen rose to cover an unsightly structure, such as a garage.

CULTURE: Plant in well-drained soil with as much sun as you can give it. To train it to climb a tree, plant the bush 3 feet away from the tree and guide it along a bamboo stake to the trunk. Once trained up the trunk to the first branch, the rambler pulls itself up by its prickles and scrambles into the upper branches as it grows toward the light. No pruning is required except occasional removal of unsightly deadwood.

DISEASE AND PEST PROBLEMS: Helen rose is disease-free.

RELATED CULTIVARS: 'Lykkefund' (*Rosa helenae* seedling × 'Zéphirine Drouhin'; Olesen, Denmark; 1930) is a vigorous, thornless rambler that produces fragrant, semidouble, creamy yellow flowers that fade to white. Vigorous canes grow 10 to 15 feet and have glossy, dark leaves.

'Cantabrigiensis', a cultivar of *Rosa hugonis*

Species Name:	*Rosa hugonis*
Common Name:	Father Hugo's rose (also called Golden rose of China)
Classification:	Species
Origin:	Central China
Introduced:	Hemsley; 1899
USDA Plant Hardiness Zones:	4 to 8

DESCRIPTION: Father Hugo's rose is a well-known garden favorite noted for its exquisite yellow flowers. The cupped, single blooms are lemon yellow with pronounced golden stamens. They are produced in abundance in late spring. The fine-textured, bluish green foliage turns bronzy orange in fall. Upright, arching shrubs reach 6 feet tall and nearly as wide, with ornamental, red-brown canes.

LANDSCAPE USES: The lemon flowers of Father Hugo's rose are a welcome sight in the spring garden, where they combine well with old roses and perennials in mixed borders. It looks particularly beautiful when combined with companion blue flowers of false indigo (*Baptisia tinctoria*) and 'Persimmon' Siberian iris (*Iris sibirica* 'Persimmon'). Plant late-flowering shrubs such as bluebeard (*Caryopteris* × *clandonensis*) and repeat-blooming roses such as 'The Fairy' in the foreground, where they will attract attention once Father Hugo's rose ceases blooming. Or use this rose alone as an informal hedge.

CULTURE: Father Hugo's rose prefers full sun and well-drained, poor soils, but it also thrives in good garden soil high in organic matter. Occasionally remove older canes on mature specimens to encourage vigorous new canes. Otherwise, allow the shrub to attain its full height and graceful habit.

DISEASE AND PEST PROBLEMS: Father Hugo's rose is not usually bothered by diseases. It is susceptable to rose stem girdler. Remove and destroy any infected canes.

RELATED SPECIES AND CULTIVARS: 'Cantabrigiensis' (*Rosa hugonis* × *Rosa sericea*, Cambridge Botanic Gardens, United Kingdom; 1931) bears large, pale lemon, single flowers on an arching shrub 5 to 7 feet tall and as broad covered with small, fernlike foliage.

'Canary Bird' (probably *Rosa xanthina* × *Rosa hugonis*; 1907) produces deep yellow, single flowers with prominent yellow stamens followed by purple hips. Shrubs are 6 to 8 feet tall and nearly as broad with prickly, brown stems with dark green, tiny, fernlike foliage.

Rosa primula (incense rose; Turkestan to N. China; Boulenger; 1919) is a small shrub growing 2 to 4 feet tall with a similar spread. Slender, flexible stems are armed with tiny red prickles and bear small, glossy, incense-scented leaves. Flowers are pale yellow, single, and about 1½ inches across. This rose is worth growing for its early yellow flowers and aromatic foliage; it is an appropriate candidate for herb gardens. Its culture, hardiness, and disease resistance are similar to those of Father Hugo's rose. *Rosa primula* is usually not bothered by rose stem girdler.

Rosa laevigata

Species Name:	**Rosa laevigata**
Common Name:	**Cherokee rose**
Classification:	Species
Origin:	China; naturalized in southeastern North America
Introduced:	Michaux; 1759
USDA Plant Hardiness Zones:	7 to 9

DESCRIPTION: Cherokee rose is found growing throughout the Southeast, where it has become widely naturalized in the two centuries since its introduction. Its beginnings in North America are obscure; American rose expert Leonie Bell suggested that it arrived from China as seed in rice shipments. It bears fragrant, single, pure white flowers with prominent, yellow stamens. It blooms abundantly for several weeks in spring. Trained as a vigorous scrambler, its floppy canes stretch to 15 feet and are covered with handsome, shiny, green foliage, divided into three-point leaflets. As a mounded shrub, expect it to grow 5 to 6 feet tall and nearly twice as wide.

LANDSCAPE USES: In the South, Cherokee rose has been commonly planted in hedgerows, and it is a good candidate for use in erosion control, highway plantings, and natural areas. It makes an excellent climber, espalier, and mounding shrub. It scales trees with ease and looks good cascading over a wall.

CULTURE: Plant in well-drained soil with as much sun as you can give it. To train it to climb a tree, plant the bush 3 feet away from the tree and guide it along a bamboo stake to the trunk. Once trained up the trunk to the first branch, Cherokee rose pulls itself up by its prickles and scrambles into the upper branches as it grows toward the light. No pruning is required except to occasionally remove unsightly deadwood or to keep it from growing out of bounds.

DISEASE AND PEST PROBLEMS: Cherokee rose is disease-free.

Species Name:	**Rosa moschata**
Common Name:	**Musk rose**
Classification:	Species
Origin:	Southern Europe; northern Africa
Introduced:	Herrmann; 1540
USDA Plant Hardiness Zones:	6 to 9

DESCRIPTION: Many important reblooming roses trace their ancestry to the musk rose. Its five-petaled, sweetly scented flowers resemble small, white stars branded with golden centers. They are held in small clusters on wiry-stemmed bushes that reach 6 feet tall and half as wide. The smooth stems are covered with glossy, pointed leaves. Musk rose is often grown as a climber on a sheltered wall, where it reaches 10 feet or more. Flowers usually appear late in the season and are in bloom from midsummer until autumn.

LANDSCAPE USES: Use musk rose on a pillar, as a climber, or in a mass, hedge, or specimen planting. Its sweet fragrance makes it a good choice for the herb garden.

CULTURE: Plant in full sun in well-drained soil. Prune in early spring to remove deadwood and to shape the plant.

DISEASE AND PEST PROBLEMS: Musk rose is susceptible to black spot in many regions. For best results, apply fungicidal soap or garden sulfur combined with an antitranspirant as soon as leaves emerge in early spring; reapply as needed.

RELATED CULTIVARS: 'Nastarana' (Noisette; also called *Rosa moschata* var. *nastarana*, 'Persian Musk Rose'; an early *Rosa chinensis* × *Rosa moschata* hybrid; 1879) produces clusters of pure white, single flowers with yellow stamens. The fragrant blooms are produced continuously, followed by small red hips in autumn. It makes a shrub 3 to 4 feet tall and less wide with narrow, glossy foliage. In mild climates, it is often trained as a climber that reaches 6 to 8 feet. It is recommended for all regions in Zones 6 to 9.

'Paul's Himalayan Musk Rambler' is a vigorous rose with long, flexible canes reaching 30 feet. It bears large clusters of pink, fully double flowers on slender stems.

'The Garland' (*Rosa moschata* × *Rosa multiflora*; Wells, United Kingdom; 1835) produces fragrant, white, semidouble flowers tinged with yellow and pink. Blooms are held in large clusters atop climbing stems reaching 8 to 10 feet.

'Nastarana', a cultivar of *Rosa moschata*

Rosa moyesii

Species Name:	*Rosa moyesii*
Common Name:	Moyes rose
Classification:	Species
Origin:	Western China
Introduced:	Hemsley & Wilson; 1894; reintroduced 1903
USDA Plant Hardiness Zones:	5 to 8

DISEASE AND PEST PROBLEMS: Moyes rose is typically disease- and pest-free. In some climates, foliage is affected by mildew. Spray with fungicidal soap or horticultural oil to control the problem.

RELATED CULTIVARS: 'Geranium' (*Rosa moyesii* seedling; Wisley, Royal Horticultural Society, United Kingdom; 1938) is the most compact of the hybrid Moyes roses. The single blooms are geranium red, filled with creamy stamens. The blooms are followed by large, flask-shaped, scarlet hips. The arching canes are covered with light green leaves. Plants grow about 8 feet tall and less wide. This rose is highly recommended for all regions.

'Highdownensis' (*Rosa moyesii* seedling; Stear, United Kingdom; 1928) produces single, crimson flowers followed by excellent orange-red, flask-shaped hips. Shrubs grow 10 feet tall and less wide with a bushy, more dense habit than the species.

'Sealing Wax' (*Rosa moyesii* seedling; Wisley, Royal Horticultural Society, United Kingdom; 1938) takes its name from its especially large, scarlet hips. This arching shrub grows 8 to 10 feet tall and less wide and is covered with single, pink flowers in June.

DESCRIPTION: Aristrocratic Moyes rose is a four-star specimen shrub named for the missionary Reverend Moyes. Blood red, single flowers filled with distinctive golden stamens are borne in small clusters at the same time modern roses bloom. Outstanding, flask-shaped, orange-red hips ripen in late summer and are effective for several months. Arching, reddish canes armed with straight prickles rise 7 to 10 feet tall and nearly as wide to form an open, vase-shaped shrub. The large, light green leaves have many distinctly rounded leaflets.

LANDSCAPE USES: Moyes rose and its superior cultivars are useful specimen shrubs. They also add all-season interest to mixed flower borders, shrub borders, foundations, and accent plantings. Noted for its fantastic fruit display, Moyes rose also has reddish stems that provide interest in the winter garden.

CULTURE: Plant Moyes rose and its relatives in well-drained soil. Give it as much sun as you can to promote prolific flowering and fruit set. Top-dress with compost annually, and fertilize in early spring with a complete organic fertilizer. Prune only to remove crowded stems and, occasionally, older canes. Allow this attractive shrub to assume its upright, open habit.

Species Name:	*Rosa multiflora*
Common Name:	Multiflora rose
Classification:	Species
Origin:	Eastern Asia; naturalized in North America
Introduced:	Thunberg; 1784
USDA Plant Hardiness Zones:	5 to 9

DESCRIPTION: Multiflora rose produces its blooms in large, pyramidal, tightly packed clusters. This familiar flower form is transmitted to its offspring, which include polyantha, hybrid musk, and floribunda roses. Multiflora rose's small, white, five-petaled flowers have distinctive golden stamens and a fruity fragrance that carries in the air on warm June days. The blooms are followed by small, round, red hips that are attractive to birds. From a trunklike base, long canes emerge and mound on themselves or scale the nearest tree, easily scrambling 15 feet or more. These canes are equipped with curved prickles and covered with large, matte green leaves. There is a distinct hairlike fringe at the base of each leaf stalk, or stipule.

Introduced into the United States in 1810, multiflora rose was widely planted in this century and promoted as a blooming fence for use in hedgerows. Since then it has effectively naturalized itself throughout the country. It is difficult to eradicate and has been declared a noxious weed in many states. Nevertheless, this rampant species has made important contributions to modern roses. A thornless form is commonly used as a rootstock in the commercial production of budded roses.

LANDSCAPE USES: Although the species is rarely planted today, hybrid multiflora ramblers have inherited its perfume, vigor, and disease resistance, as well as its aptitude for scrambling. They are easily trained to carpet slopes, hug fences, and drape garden structures, gazebos, posts and chains, pergolas, and walls. They effortlessly cover unsightly buildings and scramble into medium-sized trees, enhancing the garden with annual garlands of fragrant flowers. Like the species, they are also useful for impenetrable, freestanding shrub masses.

'Trier', a cultivar of *Rosa multiflora*

CULTURE: Plant hybrid multiflora ramblers in well-drained soil in as much sun as you can give them, although, like the species, they tolerate light shade. Those trained to climb into trees or over buildings can mostly be left alone, with the occasional removal of dead-wood and older canes. Prune plants neatly trained on pillars, arches, and pergolas annually after the flowers have faded in summer. Remove the canes that carried the flowers to make room for the vigorous new shoots. Tie these new shoots to their supports to form the scaffolding for the next season's flower display.

DISEASE AND PEST PROBLEMS: Multiflora rose is typically disease- and pest-free. Most of the recommended cultivars are resistant to black spot, but a few are bothered by powdery mildew. The scentless old cultivar 'Crimson Rambler' is not recommended because it is particularly prone to mildew. Full sun, good air circulation, and annual removal of crowded stems help prevent mildew on susceptible cultivars.

RELATED VARIETIES AND CULTIVARS: *Rosa multiflora* var. *carnea* (Thory; 1804) is a double-flowered form bearing clusters of fragrant, light pink, pompon flowers on prickly canes reaching 15 to 20 feet tall. The foliage is disease-resistant.

'Bobbie James' (Sunningdale Nursery, United Kingdom; 1961) is a vigorous rambler perfect for covering unsightly buildings and training up into trees. It produces huge clusters of exceptionally fragrant, small, cupped, semi-double, white flowers that open to reveal yellow stamens. Vigorous, prickly canes scramble 15 to 20 feet. The narrow, glossy leaves of 'Bobbie James' are disease-resistant.

'Goldfinch' ('Helene' × seedling; Paul, United Kingdom; 1907) is a rambler prized for its yellow buds and semidouble flowers filled with golden stamens. The yellow blooms fade to creamy white and have a strong, fruity fragrance. They are followed by attractive orange hips. The thornless canes are covered with shiny, green leaves and grow 8 to 10 feet tall; they are easy to wrap on a pillar. 'Goldfinch' can also be used as a floppy shrub. It is extremely disease-resistant.

'Hiawatha' ('Crimson Rambler' × 'Paul's Carmine Pillar'; Walsh, United States; 1904) produces large clusters of lightly scented, single flowers that are crimson with a white eye. Vigorous canes grow 10 to 15 feet tall. The glossy foliage of this rambler has good black spot resistance but is sometimes bothered by mildew.

'Russelliana' ('Russell's Cottage Rose'; before 1837) bears very double, crimson-magenta flowers that open flat and quartered and have a strong old-rose fragrance. The prickly, purplish stems reach 10 to 15 feet tall and are covered with rough, dark leaves. This hybrid rambler is extremely disease-resistant.

'Seagull' (Pritchard, United Kingdom; 1907) is like an improved wild form. Huge clusters of fragrant, pure white, single blooms open to reveal distinctive golden stamens. Vigorous, arching canes are well-armed with prickles. It easily scrambles to 15 feet in a medium-sized tree. In full bloom, it is simply glorious. 'Seagull' is usually disease-free.

'Seven Sisters' (*Rosa multiflora* var. *platyphylla*) is a variable selection of the species with broad leaves. It has been cultivated for centuries in China and was introduced into England in 1817. The fragrant, double flowers are larger than the species and produced in huge clusters on arching canes that easily reach 10 to 15 feet tall. As the rose-pink flowers age, many tints are discernible in one flower cluster—pink, rose, purple, crimson, and white. A popular curiosity in Victorian times, 'Seven Sisters' is worth growing for its spectacular bloom and disease resistance.

'Tausendschon' (also called 'Thousand Beauties'; 'Daniel Lacombe' × 'Weisser Herumstreicher'; Kiese, Germany; 1906) is a snap to train on a pillar or fence because it is thornless. The double, cupped, pompon flowers are rose-pink with a swirl of white petals that quickly fade. The large flower clusters appear polka-dotted with rose-pink, light pink, and white blossoms. Canes covered with glossy foliage spread 8 to 10 feet as a groundcover and fill a similar space when trained up. It is somewhat susceptible to mildew; provide good air circulation to prevent problems.

'Thalia' (also called 'White Rambler'; *Rosa multiflora* × 'Paquerette'; Schmitt, France; 1895) produces small, snow white, double flowers in large clusters. Masses of perfumed blooms are produced on prickly canes that reach 10 to 12 feet tall. 'Thalia' has excellent disease resistance.

'Trier' ('Aglaia' seedling; Lambert, France; 1904) is an important rose because it is reblooming—a characteristic it inherits from its Noisette grandparent 'Reve d'Or'. It is also the distinguished parent of the wonderful hybrid musk roses. Like many of its famous offspring, including 'Penelope' and 'Cornelia', it makes an excellent short climber to cover a fence, wall, or trellis. Fragrant, semi-double flowers are white with a golden yellow eye and held in medium clusters. Clumps of smooth, purple-tinged canes stretch 10 feet tall and wide and are covered with leaves similar to the species. This rose has good disease resistance and is prized for its repeat bloom.

'Veilchenblau' (also called 'Blue Rambler'; 'Crimson Rambler' × 'Erinnerung an Brod'; Schmidt, Germany; 1909) bears large, fragrant clusters of semidouble flowers. The color is irresistible: Reddish purple buds open to violet flowers streaked with white and filled with yellow stamens. Smooth canes grow 10 to 15 feet tall and are covered with matte green foliage. It is a good candidate for training to climb into a tree. It looks particularly fine sharing a support with the yellow rose 'Goldfinch'. Mildew sometimes blemishes the leaves; provide good air circulation to prevent problems.

Rosa nitida

Species Name:	**Rosa nitida**
Common Name:	**New England shining rose**
Classification:	Species
Origin:	Northeastern North America: Newfoundland to southern New England
Introduced:	Willdenow; cultivated 1807
USDA Plant Hardiness Zones:	3 to 7

DESCRIPTION: New England shining rose, the smallest of the eastern North America native roses, grows to only 2 feet in the wild. In gardens, it can easily reach 3 feet tall and 3 feet wide from creeping stems. Deep rose-pink, single flowers with light fragrance are produced in June; small red fruits ripen in late summer. Small, pointed, glossy leaves turn brilliant red-purple and scarlet in autumn. In fact, New England shining rose is worth growing for its striking autumn color alone.

LANDSCAPE USES: This rose's dwarf size makes it an excellent choice for use as a low groundcover, foreground shrub, or rock garden specimen. Its handsome foliage enhances mixed borders, and it looks attractive with old roses and perennial companions. In the wild, New England shining rose is found in many harsh situations; it is a bog species as well as a colonizer of windswept grassy cliffs overlooking the sea.

CULTURE: Easy to grow in regular garden soil, this rose also thrives in wet sites, in rock gardens, and on dry slopes. In Zones 3 to 5, plant New England shining rose in full sun. In Zones 6 to 7, where summers are very hot and humid, it appreciates some afternoon shade. Thin and prune out older canes periodically. If the plant becomes overgrown, rejuvenate by cutting the bushes to the ground and allowing them to regrow.

DISEASE AND PEST PROBLEMS: New England shining rose is not usually bothered by disease or pests.

RELATED CULTIVARS: 'Aylsham' (*Rosa nitida* × 'Hansa'; Wright; 1948) forms a prickly shrub reaching 5 feet tall. Its double flowers are large, deep pink, and fragrant. The disease-resistant, glossy foliage turns scarlet in autumn after the hips ripen to deep red.

'Corylus' (*Rosa nitida* × *Rosa rugosa* var. *rubra*; LeRougetel; 1988) is more heat-tolerant than the species. The flowers are single, medium pink, and fragrant, followed by medium, round, red hips that ripen in late summer. The glossy, elongated, pointed foliage resembles that of New England shining rose and has scarlet autumn color. This handsome shrub grows to about 3 feet tall and wide.

'Defender' (1971) is a prostrate, spreading cultivar of New England shining rose. It is useful as a groundcover, mounding to 3 feet tall and 6 feet wide.

'Lydia Morris' (*Rosa nitida* seedling; Morris Arboretum; Heritage Roses; 1994) bears deep pink, fragrant, semidouble flowers and has hips and foliage like the species. Upright bushes are 3 to 4 feet tall and wide and have yellow autumn foliage color.

'Metis' (*Rosa nitida* × 'Thérèse Bugnet'; Harp; 1967) produces soft pink, double flowers on an upright shrub 3 to 4 feet tall and wide with small, glossy leaves.

Species Name:	**Rosa palustris**
Common Name:	Swamp rose
Classification:	Species
Origin:	North America: Nova Scotia to Minnesota; south to Florida; Mississippi
Introduced:	Marshall; 1726
USDA Plant Hardiness Zones:	3 to 7

DESCRIPTION: Swamp rose is a common American native. Unlike most roses, it is at home in wet as well as normal soil. In average garden soil, it forms an upright, suckering shrub to about 5 feet tall and 3 feet wide, covered with excellent glossy foliage. Fragrant, single, pink blooms are produced later than most species—from late June and early July depending on region; orange-red hips ripen in late summer. In autumn, the foliage turns orange-red. The mahogany red canes retain their color through winter.

LANDSCAPE USES: Swamp rose is an all-season ornamental shrub with its fragrant flowers, showy fruits, and colorful foliage and stems. Swamp rose thrives in wet sites and bog gardens, where it looks attractive with perennials and shrubs including irises, hollies, and native azaleas. Like other North American natives, swamp rose is useful for naturalizing in wild gardens.

CULTURE: In the wild, swamp rose is extremely adaptable. It accepts an edge of the woodland position in the high shade of deciduous trees or feels at home in sunny meadows. It colonizes bogs and wet sites and also thrives on dry ridges. This is a dependable shrub for tough situations. Prune out older canes to encourage new shoots from the base. Trim the plant to fit its spot in the garden, or allow it to grow as a wild, suckering mass. Cut overgrown plants to the ground and allow them to resprout.

DISEASE AND PEST PROBLEMS: Swamp rose is not usually bothered by diseases or pests.

RELATED VARIETIES: *Rosa palustris* var. *plena* is a form with double flowers. *Rosa palustris* var. *nuttalliana* bears larger flowers and sporadic bloom through fall.

Rosa palustris var. *nuttalliana*

Rosa roxburghii

Species Name:	*Rosa roxburghii*
Common Name:	Chestnut rose
Classification:	Species
Origin:	China, Japan
Introduced:	Trattinnick; cultivated prior to 1814
USDA Plant Hardiness Zones:	6 to 9

DESCRIPTION: Chestnut rose buds open to double, lilac-pink flowers about 2½ inches across. Flowers are freely produced in late spring and repeat sporadically throughout the season. The prickly fruit is green and changes to orange. Both flower buds and fruits are covered with prickles like chestnut fruits, hence the common name. It makes a vigorous, upright to arching shrub from 5 to 7 feet tall and half as wide. The peeling, tan to light brown bark provides year-round interest.

LANDSCAPE USES: Chestnut rose makes a unique specimen shrub for all-season interest in the garden. Use it as an accent in mixed borders and shrub borders. It can be also be planted to make an informal hedge, and it responds well to shearing.

CULTURE: Plant chestnut rose in full sun in well-drained garden soil. Prune out deadwood and periodically remove older canes to make room for young shoots. This rose is recommended for all regions within Zones 6 to 9.

DISEASE AND PEST PROBLEMS: Chestnut rose is disease- and pest-free.

RELATED VARIETIES: *Rosa roxburghii* var. *normalis* ('Single Chestnut Rose'; Rehder and Wilson; 1908) was discovered later than the double-flowered one and therefore given the name 'normal'. It is the most common form of the species. Buds covered with prickles open to single, lilac-pink flowers filled with yellow stamens. Flowers are about 2½ to 3 inches across. *Rosa roxburghii* var. *normalis* blooms less heavily and has no repeat bloom. However, it is hardier and more vigorous than the double-flowered form, which can be tender at the edge of its hardiness in Zone 6. Its beautiful peeling bark and prickly fruits are identical to those of chestnut rose.

Species Name:	*Rosa rugosa*
Common Name:	Rugosa rose
Classification:	Species
Origin:	Siberia, northern China, Korea, and Japan
Introduced:	Thunberg; cultivated prior to 1799
USDA Plant Hardiness Zones:	2 to 8

Rosa rugosa var. alba

DESCRIPTION: Rugosa rose is a thorny, dense, upright to arching shrub with leathery, wrinkled, dark green foliage that turns golden bronze in autumn. Fragrant, large, single, mauve-pink flowers with distinctive yellow stamens appear in late spring and summer. Numerous large hips ripen to brilliant tomato red in late summer and autumn along with autumn blooms. A seaside colonizer, rugosa rose is also tolerant of tough, urban landscapes characterized by poor, compacted soils, salt spray from de-icing agents, and reflected heat. It has become naturalized in northeastern North America and northern Europe, especially near the seaside. In garden soils, rugosa rose makes an upright, arching shrub from 4 to 6 feet tall and 4 feet wide. Rugosa rose is extremely hardy and disease-resistant and has been used extensively in the development of hardy shrub roses; its kin are classed as hybrid rugosa roses. These are superior specimens for garden use.

LANDSCAPE USES: Tough, hardy rugosa rose makes an excellent impenetrable hedge, screen, or windbreak. It's also a good choice for highway plantings. Rugosa rose grows as far north as Siberia, so the extreme winter hardiness of it and its kin should appeal to northern gardeners.

CULTURE: Rugosa rose thrives in full sun and even flourishes in hot spots characterized by reflected heat from sand, macadam, or paving. This durable shrub is not fussy about soil but does resent poor drainage. Single-flowered forms produce the best hips, but you need to plant at least two to get fruit. Prune in late winter, removing about one-third of the older canes and reducing remaining canes by about one-third their length. No other care is required.

DISEASE AND PEST PROBLEMS: Typically not bothered by diseases or pests, rugosa rose and its closely related kin are susceptible to rose stem girdler. Prune out and destroy infected canes.

RELATED VARIETIES AND CULTIVARS: *Rosa rugosa* var. *alba* produces the loveliest single flowers of all of the rugosa varieties and hybrids. Pale pink buds open to large, pure white flowers with golden stamens. Flowers are well scented, repeat bloom is good, and the crop of large, tomato red hips is excellent. This vigorous shrub reaches 4 to 4½ feet tall and wide.

Rosa rugosa var. *rubra* is rarely out of bloom. Its brilliant magenta-purple flowers, the largest of the single-flowered forms, are followed by superb fruit set. Shrubs reach 4 to 4½ feet tall and wide.

'Scabrosa' is similar to *Rosa rugosa* var. *rubra*. The large, single flowers are deep mauve followed by tomato red hips; bushes are compact, growing 3 feet tall and wide.

Hybrid rugosa roses include: 'Belle Poitevine', 'Blanc Double de Coubert', 'Dart's Dash', 'Frau Dagmar Hartopp', 'F. J. Grootendorst', 'Fimbriata', 'Hansa', 'Purple Pavement, 'Roseraie de l'Hay', 'Schneezewerg', 'Thérèse Bugnet', and 'Topaz Jewel'.

Rosa sericea var. pteracantha

Species Name:	*Rosa sericea* var. *pteracantha*
Common Name:	Wingthorn four-petal rose
Classification:	Species
Origin:	Western China
Introduced:	Franchet; 1890
USDA Plant Hardiness Zones:	5 to 8

DESCRIPTION: The wingthorn four-petal rose is grown for its attractive thorns and delicate, fernlike foliage. Spectacular winged thorns of translucent scarlet arm the new growth and make a beautiful and effective display through summer. Among the earlier of the Asian species to bloom, it produces small, white, four-petaled flowers. This rose forms an upright, vase-shaped specimen shrub, 6 to 7 feet tall and 4 feet wide.

LANDSCAPE USES: Wingthorn four-petal rose provides a striking form in all seasons and makes an excellent specimen. It looks attractive with old roses and perennials in mixed borders and contributes seasonal interest and novelty to shrub borders. It is a tough shrub rose tolerant of seaside conditions, harsh urban sites, and tough roadside conditions.

CULTURE: Wingthorn four-petal rose grows in any well-drained soil in full sun. Prune mature specimen shrubs by thinning out older canes to encourage vigorous new growth (on which the red thorns are carried). Remove outside older canes to maintain the upright, vase-shaped habit and to save space in the garden.

DISEASE AND PEST PROBLEMS: This rose is not bothered by diseases and pests.

RELATED CULTIVARS: 'Redwing' (probably *Rosa sericea* var. *pteracantha* × *Rosa hugonis*) is similar to wingthorn four-petal rose but has golden yellow flowers. It is armed with extremely large, red thorns.

Rosa setigera

Species Name:	*Rosa setigera*
Common Name:	Prairie rose
Classification:	Species
Origin:	North America
Introduced:	Michaux; 1810
USDA Plant Hardiness Zones:	4 to 9

DESCRIPTION: A late-blooming North American species, prairie rose bears single, pink flowers. The lighter, creamy white center is branded with a golden eye of yellow stamens. Prickly, reddish canes can grow 10 to 15 feet tall and are covered with rough, green leaves. Freestanding shrubs usually form mounds about 4 to 5 feet tall and wide. Flowers bloom for a few weeks in summer during July and August. Blooms are followed by bunches of red hips that remain attractive through winter. The leaves turn scarlet in autumn. The vigor of this species has been transmitted to some American climbing roses, including 'Baltimore Belle'. Prairie rose was bred with memorial rose (*Rosa wichuraiana*) to produce the popular climber 'American Pillar'.

LANDSCAPE USES: Prairie rose is not a good choice for small gardens, although it can be wrapped on a pillar and kept tidy with annual pruning. It is much more attractive growing unpruned in a hedgerow, draping a dead tree, or cascading down a slope or over a wall. It is a four-star specimen shrub for larger gardens. Prairie rose is also useful for naturalizing and highway plantings.

CULTURE: Plant in well-drained soil in full sun. If you're growing prairie rose on a pillar, prune out old stems annually while the plant is dormant, leaving only a few canes to wrap around the support.

DISEASE AND PEST PROBLEMS: Prairie rose is usually not bothered by diseases or pests.

RELATED CULTIVARS: 'Baltimore Belle' (hybrid of *Rosa setigera*; probably *Rosa setigera* × a Noisette; Feast, United States; 1843) is a handsome rambler that bears double, fragrant, blush pink flowers in clusters. It can be grown as a freestanding shrub, wrapped on a pillar, or trained horizontally on a fence. Expect it to grow about 8 to 10 feet tall. Surround it with tall summer and fall perennials that will grow up and camouflage its moderately disease-susceptible leaves.

Rosa spinosissima

Species Name:	*Rosa spinosissima* (also called *Rosa pimpinellifolia*)
Common Name:	Scotch briar (also called burnet rose)
Classification:	Species
Origin:	Europe and Western Asia; naturalized in the northeastern United States
Introduced:	Linnaeus; cultivated before 1600
USDA Plant Hardiness Zones:	4 to 8

DESCRIPTION: One of the most widely distributed of all wild roses, Scotch briar is found from as far north as Iceland, east to Siberia and from southern Europe to central Asia. It is native to the British Isles and has become naturalized in North America. Typically found growing on dunes and in dry pastures, it forms a mounding, suckering shrub. The canes are densely armed with straight prickles and bristles and covered with small, fernlike leaves. Given its wide distribution, it is not surprising that the plant is extremely variable, sometimes growing only 12 inches on windswept dunes and arching or mounding to 5 feet tall in more hospitable situations. Fragrant, single flowers are usually creamy white (occasionally yellow or pink) and followed by distinctive black hips. In the garden, bushes usually grow 4 to 5 feet tall and wide, depending on the climate and site. Cherished for its scented flowers, Scotch briar covers itself with masses of single blooms in May and early June. There are countless varieties and described forms for which the nomenclature is often inconsistent.

LANDSCAPE USES: Scotch briar is charming as a specimen, mass planting, informal hedge, or mounding groundcover. Low-growing varieties can be trained to cascade down a slope or over a wall. English garden writer Gertrude Jekyll recommends planting Scotch briar to drape a rock wall to enjoy the flowers at eye level. Many of its vigorous, showy cultivars hold their own in the mixed border, and a few provide repeat bloom. Scotch briar is also suitable for roadside plantings and naturalizing.

CULTURE: Plant in well-drained soil in full sun to partial shade. It accepts extremely poor soils and thrives on neglect. Occasionally prune out dead and crowded canes.

DISEASE AND PEST PROBLEMS: Scotch briar is usually not bothered by diseases or pests. Some of the hybrid cultivars are occasionally marred by mildew; provide a sunny location with good air circulation to prevent problems.

RELATED VARIETIES AND CULTIVARS: *Rosa spinosissima* var. *altaica* (Western Asia; Wildenow; 1820) is noted for its large, pale yellow to creamy white, five-petaled flowers filled with distinctive gold stamens. Vigorous bushes covered with gray-green foliage grow 5 to 6 feet tall and less wide. One of the first species to bloom in late spring, its flowers are followed by maroon hips. It is a lovely and particularly hardy variety that has been used in breeding hardy modern shrub roses, including 'Fruhlingsmorgen'.

Rosa spinosissima var. *hispida* (Koehne; cultivated before 1781) bears large, creamy white, fragrant flowers. Bushes grow 5 feet tall and less wide. The canes are densely covered with bristles but have few prickles.

Rosa spinosissima var. *lutea* (Bean) bears bright yellow, single flowers that cover 4-foot bushes.

Rosa spinosissima var. *nana* (Andrews) bears small, white, semidouble flowers on compact bushes. This variety looks particularly fine cascading over a wall.

'Aicha' ('Souvenir de Jacques Verschuren' × 'Guldtop'; Petersen, Denmark; 1966) produces fragrant, large, yellow, semidouble flowers on vigorous bushes that typically reach 6 feet tall. It can be trained as a short climber or pillar rose.

'Double Blush Burnet' (before 1846) is a hybrid noted for its pink, globular flowers with white on the back of the petals. It grows about 3 to 4 feet tall and wide.

'Double Dark Marbled' ('Petite Red Scotch'; before 1822) is a hybrid that bears small, fragrant, semidouble flowers that are red splashed with purple on bushes 3 to 4 feet tall and wide.

'Double White Burnet' is a hybrid that bears very fragrant, pure white, pompon flowers on vigorous bushes 4 to 6 feet tall and wide.

'Hazeldean' (*Rosa spinosissima* var. *altaica* × 'Persian Yellow'; Wright, Canada; 1948) produces semidouble, sulfur yellow flowers similar to 'Persian Yellow' on bushes growing 4 to 5 feet tall and less wide. It is fragrant and extremely hardy (to Zone 2).

'Kakwa' (Wallace, 1973) is a hybrid that covers itself with extremely fragrant, blush pink, double flowers on a bushy, mounding shrub 4 to 5 feet tall and wide.

'Karl Forster' ('Frau Karl Druschki' × *Rosa spinosissima* var. *altaica*; W. Kordes Söhne, Germany; 1931) is a modern cultivar particularly prized for its repeat bloom. It bears masses of lightly scented, pure white, double flowers on attractive bushes to 5 feet tall and less wide. The canes are covered in wrinkled, gray-green leaves. This rose is recommended in Zones 4 to 8.

'Mary Queen of Scots' (old *Rosa spinosissima* hybrid) produces masses of scented, single, cream-colored blooms that are tinted with crimson and lilac and have prominent stamens. From a distance, the flowers appear deep pink. The flowers are followed by purple-black hips. Compact bushes grow 3 feet tall and wide.

'William III' (old *Rosa spinosissima* hybrid) bears abundant fragrant, semidouble, crimson-plum flowers that fade to lilac-gray. The compact bushes grow 2 to 3 feet tall and wide and have tiny gray-green foliage.

For additional hybrid spinosissima shrubs, see the entries 'Fruhlingsmorgen' and 'Stanwell Perpetual'.

Rosa virginiana

Species Name:	*Rosa virginiana*
Common Name:	Virginia rose
Classification:	Species
Origin:	Eastern North America
Introduced:	Miller; prior to 1807
USDA Plant Hardiness Zones:	3 to 7

DESCRIPTION: Virginia rose forms a suckering shrub from 3 to 5 feet tall and 3 feet wide with excellent glossy foliage. Single, pink flowers are produced in June; red hips ripen on the red stems in late summer and are attractive through winter. The autumn foliage color is a bright orange-red.

LANDSCAPE USES: Virginia rose is an all-season ornamental shrub with its delicate flowers, showy fruits, bright foliage, and colorful red stems. It combines well with antique roses, perennials, and herbs. It is right at home in the herb garden, as its fruits can be harvested and dried for use as a tea. Virginia rose is a useful plant for naturalizing in wild gardens, too, where it looks attractive with wildflowers and wild shrubs. Its abundant, small hips attract birds to the garden.

CULTURE: Virginia rose will grow on the edge of a woodland in the high shade of deciduous trees, but for maximum flower and fruit production, place it in a sunny location in any well-drained soil. Allow Virginia rose to attain its graceful, arching habit, or, for small gardens, prune it to maintain a more compact plant of about 3 feet. Selectively remove canes to prevent crowding and to encourage vigorous new shoots. Rejuvenate by cutting all canes to the ground and encouraging suckers to resprout.

DISEASE AND PEST PROBLEMS: Virginia rose is not usually bothered by diseases or pests.

RELATED SPECIES AND CULTIVARS: 'Rose d'Amour' (*Rosa virginiana* var. *plena*; prior to 1759) is considered a hybrid of *Rosa virginiana*. It bears double, pink flowers on a bush that grows to 7 feet tall and 5 feet wide. It is valued for its late bloom.

Rosa carolina (pasture rose; Linnaeus; cultivated before 1826) is an eastern North American native similar to *Rosa virginiana*, but its foliage is not shiny. It grows as a suckering shrub 3 to 6 feet tall and tends to form thickets. The five-petaled, medium pink flowers are followed by persistent red fruits. The green leaves turn reddish in autumn. Pasture rose is useful for naturalizing in Zones 4 to 9.

Rosa carolina var. *alba* (Rehder; cultivated before 1880) bears single, white flowers.

Rosa carolina var. *plena* (Marshall) bears double, pink flowers.

'Silver Moon', a climbing cultivar of *Rosa wichuraiana*

Species Name:	*Rosa wichuraiana*
Common Name:	Memorial rose
Classification:	Species
Origin:	East Asia
Introduced:	Crepin; 1891
USDA Plant Hardiness Zones:	5 to 9

DESCRIPTION: Memorial rose is so called because it was frequently planted to adorn graves early in this century. It is a semi-evergreen, trailing or prostrate shrub that produces 15-foot canes armed with large, hooked prickles and covered with glossy, dark green leaves. Clusters of pure white, single flowers branded with a yellow eye cover bushes in summer; they are sweetly scented and followed by orange-red hips. Late autumn foliage color is yellow.

The long, trailing canes tend to root easily wherever a tip touches the ground. This trait makes memorial rose a natural choice as a groundcover, and it has been used in the development of modern trailing groundcover roses. It is best known, however, in its role as the ancestor of modern climbers, especially 'Dr. W. Van Fleet' and its everblooming sport 'New Dawn'. Memorial rose has been used extensively in breeding diverse groups of modern roses and typically contributes glossy, disease-resistant foliage to its offspring.

LANDSCAPE USES: Memorial rose and its hardy creeping forms are used as groundcovers to carpet sunny slopes. Its excellent hybrid ramblers and climbers can be grown as groundcovers and mounding shrubs but are usually trained to climb trellises, fences, pillars, pergolas, arches, trees, or unsightly buildings.

CULTURE: Plant memorial rose in well-drained soil in as much sun as you can give it, although it tolerates some light shade. It is tolerant of both sandy and heavy clay soils and thrives on neglect. Clean up hybrid ramblers and climbers trained into trees or over buildings by occasionally removing deadwood. Prune those neatly trained on pillars, arches, and pergolas annually after the flowers have faded in summer. Remove the canes that carried the summer flower display to make room for the vigorous new shoots. Tie these new shoots to their supports to form the scaffolding for the next season's bloom. Top-dress climbers and ramblers with compost annually.

DISEASE AND PEST PROBLEMS: Memorial rose is disease-free. Most of the memorial rose hybrids are also extremely disease-resistant, although some of the ramblers are susceptible to mildew. To prevent problems, plant in full sun on a freestanding pillar, arch, or tripod rather than against a wall, and annually prune out older canes to allow for good air circulation.

RELATED VARIETIES AND CULTIVARS: *Rosa wichuraiana* var. *poterifola* is similar to the species except for its smaller leaves and flowers. Its slender canes spread to 15 feet. It blooms sporadically all summer.

'Albéric Barbier' (*Rosa wichuraiana* × 'Shirley Hibberd'; Barbier, France; 1900) is one of the most beautiful and gratifying of the memorial rose climbers you can grow. Yellow buds open to large, scented, loosely double, creamy white flowers with a swirl of lemon color at the center. Prickly canes stretch to 15 feet and are covered with dark green, glossy foliage. Trained up a trellis, pillar, or tripod or across chains positioned at the rear of a border, its glossy foliage makes a handsome seasonal backdrop. It can be trained in nearly any situation and accepts some light shade. It is extremely disease-resistant and deserves greater attention in American gardens.

'Albertine' (*Rosa wichuraiana* × 'Mrs. Arthur Robert Waddell'; Barbier, France; 1921) produces vigorous canes covered in dark, glossy foliage. Beautiful coppery apricot buds open to large, fragrant, cupped, loosely double, coppery pink flowers held in clusters. It is an unforgettable sight in full bloom. Trained on a large pergola, this climber reaches 15 to 18 feet tall. As an unsupported shrub, expect it to grow 6 feet high and 15 feet wide, filling a quiet corner of the garden with a mass of June blooms.

'American Pillar' (*Rosa wichuraiana* × *Rosa setigera*; Van Fleet, United States; 1902) is one of the most popular climbers of all time. Its single flowers are carmine-pink branded with a white eye and held in huge clusters; they are followed by red hips. Vigorous, prickly, hardy canes stretch 15 to 20 feet tall. The dark green, leathery foliage is subject to mildew after the bloom but is resistant to black spot. Today 'American Pillar' is rarely found in U.S. gardens except on Nantucket; however, it is still commonly grown in the great gardens of Europe. This must have been the feeling that prompted English garden writer Vita Sackville-West to note that 'American Pillar' was overused and overrated and that its flower color was difficult to blend with other plants. She was right; yet it is a glorious, wonderful sight in full bloom. The best display of 'American Pillar' in this country can be seen at Longwood Gardens in Kennett Square, Pennsylvania, where it is grown to perfection on magnificent arches spanning a huge semicircular arena. It's worth the trip in mid-June.

'Debutante' (*Rosa wichuraiana* × 'Baroness Rothschild'; Walsh, United States; 1902) is a rambler that produces pink, double, pompon flowers in fragrant clusters. Prickly canes growing 10 to 15 feet tall are covered with glossy, dark green foliage, which is sometimes marred by mildew.

'Dorothy Perkins' (*Rosa wichuraiana* × 'Madame Gabriel Luizet'; Jackson & Perkins; 1901) is the most famous of the wichuraiana ramblers and can still be found on old garden sites and homesteads all over the United States. It produces small, many-petaled, rose-pink flowers in large clusters. Vigorous, 15-foot, pliable canes are armed with nasty prickles and covered with dark green, glossy foliage. It can be trained to climb, sheared as a hedge, or grown as a groundcover. It is susceptible to mildew; a location in full sun discourages this disease.

'Dr. W. Van Fleet' ([*Rosa wichuraiana* seedling × 'Sarfano'] × 'Souvenir du President Carnot'; Van Fleet, United States; 1902) is one of the first and most important large-flowered climbers because it sported everblooming 'New Dawn'—parent to many of the best repeat-flowering modern climbers. Even without this claim, it is a wonderful rose. Pink buds open to large hybrid tea–type blooms of blush pink. The fragrant blooms are carried in sprays on long stems and are followed by red hips. Vigorous, prickly canes easily reach 15 feet and are covered with dark green, glossy foliage. Train this rose on a sturdy trellis or fence twined with a large-flowered clematis. 'Dr. W. Van Fleet' is hardy and disease-free.

'Evangeline' (Rosa wichuraiana × 'Crimson Rambler'; Walsh, United States; 1906) is a rambler that bears large clusters of single, fragrant, blush pink blossoms with golden stamens, followed by small, red hips. Vigorous prickly canes grow 12 to 15 feet and are covered with light green leaves. 'Evangeline' can be kept on a pillar, arch, or trellis if you prune out older canes annually. Or let it scramble into an old crab apple tree or cascade down a slope. Plant in a sunny location to discourage mildew.

'Excelsa' ('Red Dorothy Perkins'; Rosa wichuraiana × a polyantha; Walsh, United States; 1909) bears huge clusters of cupped, double, pompon flowers that are red to light crimson and fade lighter. Prickly, flexible, 15-foot canes are covered with glossy, dark green foliage. Use this rambler as a groundcover or to climb a pergola, arch, or pillar. Like 'Dorothy Perkins', 'Excelsa' was enormously popular in its day and can still be found in old gardens and homesteads. Grow it in full sun to deter mildew.

'Gardenia' (Rosa wichuraiana × 'Perle des Jardins'; Manda, United States; 1899) produces pale yellow buds that open to creamy white, double flowers with a yellow center. The fragrant blooms are carried in small sprays along vigorous, prickly canes. The canes of this rambler grow to 15 feet long and are covered with small, glossy foliage.

'Minnehaha' (Rosa wichuraiana × 'Paul Neyron'; Walsh, United States; 1905) was compared favorably to 'Dorothy Perkins' in its heyday because it produces a wonderful mass of pink blooms. Large clusters of small, pink, pompon flowers fade to white. Prickly canes grow to 15 feet tall and are covered with glossy, dark green leaves. Plant this rambler in full sun to deter mildew.

'Petite Pink' (also called 'Petite Pink Scotch') is a wichuraiana hybrid and a wonderful little shrub or groundcover rose for the organic gardener. It produces clusters of small, pink, pompon flowers that fade to white in a big June show with no repeat. Prickly canes mound 2 to 3 feet tall and about 3 feet wide. The canes are covered with tiny, glossy, dark green leaves. The foliage is disease-free and nearly evergreen. Use 'Petite Pink' as a carpet or specimen. It accepts light shade.

'Red Cascade' ([Rosa wichuraiana × 'Floradora'] × 'Magic Dragon'; Moore, United States; 1976; 1976 American Rose Society Award of Excellence) is a climbing miniature that forms an excellent vigorous, everblooming groundcover. Clusters of small, red, cupped, pompon flowers cover the bushes from June until frost. When grown as a groundcover, 'Red Cascade' usually mounds 2 to 3 feet tall and 5 to 6 feet wide; the slender, prickly canes are covered with tiny, shiny leaves. It can also be grown as a pillar or trained on a fence or trellis, where it easily reaches 6 to 10 feet or more, depending on the climate. In northern climates, grow this rose cascading from an urn or hanging basket. It is disease-resistant. Periodically remove older wood to keep it attractive.

'Running Maid' (Rosa multiflora × [Rosa wichuraiana × 'Violet Hood']; Lens, Belgium; 1982) is a hybrid multiflora, with memorial rose adding its prickles, rampant trailing habit, and shiny, healthy foliage. Fragrant, single flowers of mauve-red are produced in big clusters in June, followed by orange-red hips. This shrub or groundcover rose forms a sprawling mound 2 to 3 feet tall and 4 to 6 feet wide.

'Sanders' White Rambler' (Sanders & Sons, United Kingdom; 1912) bears huge sprays of pure white pompon flowers that have a rich fragrance. Long, prickly canes grow 15 to 20 feet long and are covered with healthy, glossy foliage. This hybrid is frequently used as a groundcover in England and can be trained to cover a pergola, fence, tripod, or tree.

'Silver Moon' ([Rosa wichuraiana × 'Devoniensis'] × Rosa laevigata; Van Fleet, United States; 1910) is a lovely, rampant, large-flowered climber. Pure white buds open to huge, semidouble flowers filled with a center of golden stamens. The prickly canes grow 15 to 20 feet tall and are covered with dark green, leathery, healthy foliage. Grow 'Silver Moon' on a sturdy trellis or fence, and plant a large-flowered clematis to climb over it to extend the season of bloom.

'Snow Carpet' ('New Penny' × 'Temple Bells'; McGredy, New Zealand; 1980) is one of the best creepers for walls and rock gardens. Low-growing plants are covered in tiny, white, double blooms all season.

'Temple Bells' (Rosa wichuraiana × 'Blushing Jewel'; Morey; United States; 1971) was introduced by McGredy into Britain in 1976; there it has remained a popular prostrate miniature and progenitor of the 'Bells' series of miniature groundcovers. It is like a miniature version of memorial rose: Small, single, white flowers are produced in June and sporadically thereafter on trailing, prickly canes that mound to 2 feet tall and 4 feet wide. Its tiny, shiny leaves are extremely disease-resistant.

The 'Bells' series of trailing miniatures—'Pink Bells', 'Red Bells', and 'White Bells'—were bred by Poulsen of Denmark using 'Temple Bells' × 'Mini-Poul' and introduced by Mattock into Britain in 1983. These prostrate, trailing miniature roses are covered with clusters of small, double flowers in June with sporadic repeat bloom until frost. Their habit, foliage, and size are similar to 'Temple Bells'. Roses in the 'Bells' series make excellent groundcovers to carpet sunny or lightly shaded slopes and are fine rock garden creepers.

Rosa woodsii

Species Name:	**Rosa woodsii**
Common Name:	**Mountain rose**
Classification:	Species
Origin:	Western North America
Introduced:	Lindley, 1820; cultivated in 1880
USDA Plant Hardiness Zones:	4 to 8

DESCRIPTION: Mountain rose is prized for its fragrant blooms and excellent scarlet autumn foliage color. Rich pink, single flowers held on short, smooth stems bloom in June and July, followed by round, red, currantlike hips that are effective through autumn. Upright to arching canes covered with glossy leaves and armed with straight prickles and bristles form suckering shrubs to 3 feet tall.

LANDSCAPE USES: Include mountain rose in shrub borders and hedgerows. It is also suitable for naturalizing in meadows, wild gardens, and roadside plantings or along the edge of a woodland.

CULTURE: Plant in well-drained soil in full sun to partial shade. Top-dress with compost annually. Occasionally prune out dead and crowded canes in maintained garden areas.

DISEASE AND PEST PROBLEMS: Mountain rose is typically disease- and pest-free.

RELATED VARIETIES AND SPECIES: *Rosa pisocarpa* (Gray; circa 1882) is a western North American native that produces clusters of small, dark pink, single blooms followed by persistent, round, red hips. Upright, mahogany-brown canes with few prickles grow 3 to 4 feet tall. The suckering shrubs are covered with handsome foliage that has a matte gray-green finish. It is recommended in Zones 6 to 9.

Rosa woodsii var. *fendleri* (Rehder; cultivated in 1888) is more attractive than the typical species and produces tall, graceful, slender canes with gray-green leaves and few thorns. It makes a suckering shrub 3 to 5 feet high and less wide. Single, lilac-pink flowers are followed by persistent, large, round, red hips. Autumn color is a showy orange-scarlet. Its range extends farther south than the species, and it is recommended for use in Zones 4 to 8.

'Rose de Rescht'

Cultivar Name:	**'Rose de Rescht'**
Classification:	Portland (damask perpetual)
Parentage:	Not recorded
Introduced:	Brought to England from Persia by Nancy Lindsay; 1940s
USDA Plant Hardiness Zones:	4 to 8

DESCRIPTION: As a group, damask perpetual roses are known for their fragrance, hardiness, and a long flowering season. Their tidy habit makes them well suited to small gardens. 'Rose de Rescht' is one of the best and most compact of these unsung heros. The scented flowers are fuchsia-red, with many packed petals that fade to purple as they age. Its bright flowers are held on short, bristly stems in a rosette of rough, medium green leaves atop compact bushes reaching 3 feet tall and less wide. Flowers are produced freely in late spring, with a generous autumn repeat.

LANDSCAPE USES: Use this rose as an attractive mass, drift, or container plant. 'Rose de Rescht' looks best in groups of three or five plants blended with soft blue and lavender flowers and silver foliage to set off its deep red blooms. For a stunning combination, plant fountain buddleia (*Buddleia alternifolia*) to provide a background fountain of lavender blooms.

CULTURE: 'Rose de 'Rescht' is easy to grow. It thrives in a sunny situation in well-drained, loamy soil. Fertilize after spring pruning and again after flowering in early summer with a complete organic fertilizer to encourage repeat bloom. Top-dress with manure, compost, or Milorganite annually. Prune while dormant to shape plants. Deadhead spent flowers to encourage growth and to promote autumn bloom. This rose is highly recommended for all regions.

DISEASE AND PEST PROBLEMS: 'Rose de Rescht' has good disease resistance. For extra protection, apply a preventive spray of fungicidal soap or garden sulfur combined with an antitranspirant as leaves emerge in spring.

RELATED CULTIVARS: 'Rose du Roi' (Lelieur, France; 1815) produces fragrant, double, crimson flowers shaded with purple on a spreading shrub to 3 feet tall and wide. It is an important parent to modern roses because its dark red flower color was transmitted to hybrid perpetuals and through them to hybrid teas. Unfortunately, it is highly susceptible to black spot.

Cultivar Name:	**'Rose Parade'**
Classification:	Floribunda
Parentage:	'Sumatra' × 'Queen Elizabeth'
Introduced:	Williams, Howard Rose Co., United States; 1974 1975 All-America Rose Selection
USDA Plant Hardiness Zones:	5 to 9

DESCRIPTION: The full, cupped flowers of 'Rose Parade' are coral-pink and open flat in charming old rose form. They are produced continuously in large, showy

clusters. Bushy shrubs grow 3 feet tall and 2 feet wide and are covered with glossy foliage.

LANDSCAPE USES: 'Rose Parade' is an excellent compact floribunda for use as a mass or low everblooming hedge. Plant a group of 'Rose Parade' near the front of mixed borders to provide a drift of all-season color. This rose also makes an excellent container specimen.

CULTURE: 'Rose Parade' thrives in a sunny situation in well-drained, loamy soil. Fertilize after spring pruning and again after flowering in early summer with a complete organic fertilizer to encourage repeat blooms. Top-dress with manure, compost, or Milorganite annually. Prune hard at bud break to remove dead and damaged wood and to rid plants of overwintering disease spores. Deadhead spent flowers to encourage vigorous and repeat bloom. 'Rose Parade' is highly recommended for all regions.

DISEASE AND PEST PROBLEMS: 'Rose Parade' has good disease resistance. For extra protection, spray shrubs with a fungicidal soap or garden sulfur combined with an antitranspirant as leaves emerge in spring.

'Rose Parade'

attack, pick off the adults, and treat lawn areas with milky disease spores to control grubs. This rose is also susceptible to rose stem girdler. Keep plants free of deadwood; prune out and destroy infested canes.

'Roseraie de l'Hay'

Cultivar Name:	'Roseraie de l'Hay'
Classification:	Hybrid rugosa
Parentage:	Not recorded
Introduced:	Cochet-Cochet, France; 1901
USDA Plant Hardiness Zones:	4 to 8

DESCRIPTION: 'Roseraie de l'Hay', named for the world-renowned rose garden near Paris, produces plentiful, intensely fragrant, large, double flowers of crimson-purple in late spring with excellent repeat bloom. It makes a dense, prickly shrub with wrinkled, dark green, leathery foliage that colors to a handsome bronze yellow in autumn. It does not set much fruit. The arching to rounded shrub grows to 5 feet tall with a similar spread. You may dry the fragrant flower petals for use in potpourri.

LANDSCAPE USES: 'Roseraie de l'Hay' is a superb specimen shrub. It also combines well with perennials and herbs and is a good candidate for mixed borderss or herb gardens. The vigorous shrub also makes an excellent hedge, screen, or windbreak.

CULTURE: Plant rugosa hybrids in full sun in any well-drained soil. They will tolerate arid and poor soils as long as they are very well drained. To form a hedge, plant bushes every 3 feet—plants will be touching in three years. Prune mature specimens and hedges in late winter to shape the plants, taking off about one-third of the top growth. Periodically remove older canes to keep plants growing vigorously. No other care is required. This rose is recommended for all regions.

DISEASE AND PEST PROBLEMS: 'Roseraie de l'Hay' is a tough, disease-free rose. However, summer flowers sometimes attract Japanese beetles. If beetles

'Roulettii'

Cultivar Name:	'Roulettii' (also called *Rosa roulettii*)
Classification:	China
Parentage:	*Rosa chinensis* var. *minima* selection; cultivated before 1818
Introduced:	Correvon; 1922
USDA Plant Hardiness Zones:	6 to 9

DESCRIPTION: An important ancestor of modern miniature roses, 'Roulettii' produces masses of tiny, rose-pink, double flowers on wiry bushes to 12 inches tall and wide. Rarely out of bloom, the small bushes have few thorns and are covered with tiny, semiglossy, pointed foliage.

LANDSCAPE USES: A versatile rose, 'Roulettii' is suitable for use as an edging or dwarf hedge. It also looks good in a rock garden as a container plant. When planted in groups, it is useful as a low perennial drift in mixed borders. Its dwarf size makes it a good candidate for indoor culture under lights.

CULTURE: Plant in a sunny location in well-drained soil that has been amended with organic matter. Prune hard at bud break in late winter or early spring to rid plants of dead and damaged canes and overwintering disease spores. Like its modern miniature offspring, 'Roulettii' responds well to severe pruning to encourage vigorous new growth. Fertilize after pruning and again after the first bloom with a complete organic fertilizer. Top-dress with compost annually. Shear after each bloom period to encourage continued bloom. 'Roulettii' is highly recommended for all regions.

DISEASE AND PEST PROBLEMS: This rose has good disease resistance. For extra protection, apply a preventive spray (of fungicidal soap or garden sulfur combined with an antitranspirant) early in the season to ward off black spot, or allow plants to fend for themselves. Mites sometimes bother the plants. Wash leaves with a strong spray of water to knock off the pests. If mites continue to be a problem, apply insecticidal soap.

'Salet'

Cultivar Name:	'Salet'
Classification:	Moss
Parentage:	Not recorded
Introduced:	Lacharme, France; 1854
USDA Plant Hardiness Zones:	4 to 8

DESCRIPTION: The mossy buds of 'Salet' open to clear pink, full flowers that are packed with petals and exude a wonderful perfume. Prolific early-summer bloom is followed by some late-summer repeat bloom. The prickly, bristly shrubs grow 4 feet tall and less wide and are covered with coarse foliage. You may dry petals for use in potpourri.

LANDSCAPE USES: 'Salet' is superb as a specimen shrub. It also looks wonderful in herb gardens or with perennials in the middle of mixed borders.

CULTURE: Plant in a sunny location in well-drained soil that has been amended with organic matter. Prune while dormant to shape the plant; deadhead after the first bloom to encourage later flowers. Top-dress with compost annually. 'Salet' is recommended for all regions.

DISEASE AND PEST PROBLEMS: 'Salet' has above-average disease resistance. If mildew develops, apply fungicidal soap or horticultural oil (at a rate of 1 to 2 tablespoons per 1 gallon of water) to control the problem.

RELATED CULTIVARS: 'Alfred de Dalmas' (Laffay, France; 1855) is a repeat-flowering moss rose that produces well-shaped mossy buds opening to cupped, blush pink, well-scented flowers. Prickly shrubs grow 3 to 4 feet tall and less wide and are covered with pale green leaves.

'Sarabande'

Cultivar Name:	'Sarabande'
Classification:	Floribunda
Parentage:	'Cocorico' × 'Moulin Rouge'
Introduced:	Meilland, France; 1957; Conard-Pyle, United States; 1959 1960 All-America Rose Selection
USDA Plant Hardiness Zones:	5 to 9

DESCRIPTION: 'Sarabande' has semidouble flowers that are orange-red, opening flat to reveal yellow stamens. They're produced continuously in large, showy clusters.

Bushy shrubs grow 3 feet tall and 2 feet wide and have glossy foliage.

LANDSCAPE USES: 'Sarabande' is an excellent compact floribunda for use as a mass or low everblooming hedge. Plant a group of 'Sarabande' near the front of mixed borders to provide a drift of all-season color. It also makes an excellent container specimen.

CULTURE: 'Sarabande' thrives in a sunny location in well-drained, loamy soil. Fertilize after spring pruning and again after flowering in early summer with a complete organic fertilizer to encourage repeat bloom. Top-dress with manure, compost, or Milorganite annually. Prune hard at bud break to remove dead and damaged wood and to rid plants of overwintering disease spores. Deadhead spent flowers to encourage vigorous and repeat bloom. This rose is highly recommended for all regions. Apply winter protection in Zone 5.

DISEASE AND PEST PROBLEMS: 'Sarabande' is one of the most disease-resistant floribunda roses. For extra protection, spray with fungicidal soap or garden sulfur combined with an antitranspirant as leaves emerge in spring.

Cultivar Name:	**'Scarlet Knight'**
Classification:	Grandiflora
Parentage:	('Happiness' × 'Independence') × 'Sutter's Gold'
Introduced:	Meilland, France; 1966; Conard-Pyle, United States; 1967 1968 All-America Rose Selection
USDA Plant Hardiness Zones:	5 to 9

DESCRIPTION: 'Scarlet Knight' has striking, nearly black buds that open to large, cupped, crimson-red flowers with a light tea scent. Blooms are produced singly or in sprays, over dark green leaves. The everblooming shrubs are upright and bushy, reaching 5 feet tall and 2½ feet wide. The blooms make excellent cut flowers.

LANDSCAPE USES: Use a grouping of 'Scarlet Knight' as an accent of all-season bloom in flower borders where hot colors dominate. Position it near the back, and camouflage its stiff hybrid tea habit by planting informal shrub roses and perennials in front of it. It is a must for the cutting garden for its dark, long-lasting blooms.

CULTURE: Plant in a sunny location in well-drained soil that has been amended with organic matter. Prune hard in late winter or early spring to rid plants of damaged canes and overwintering disease spores. Fertilize after pruning and again after the first bloom with a complete organic fertilizer. Top-dress with compost annually. Deadhead spent blooms to encourage repeat bloom. Apply a mound of mulch as winter protection in Zone 5.

DISEASE AND PEST PROBLEMS: Like other grandifloras, 'Scarlet Knight' is susceptible to diseases. Protect new foliage with an application of fungicidal soap or garden sulfur combined with an antitranspirant to prevent black spot; reapply monthly. Monitor the plants for insect damage.

'Scarlet Knight'

'Schneezwerg'

Cultivar Name:	**'Schneezwerg'** (also called 'Snow Dwarf')
Classification:	Hybrid rugosa
Parentage:	*Rosa rugosa* × *Rosa bracteata*
Introduced:	Lambert, Germany; 1912
USDA Plant Hardiness Zones:	3 to 8

DESCRIPTION: 'Schneezwerg' forms a dense, bushy, compact shrub about 4 feet tall and wide. Its semidouble white flowers open to reveal a center of golden yellow stamens. The fragrant flowers are produced in abundance and almost continuously throughout the season. Bushes are covered with small, dark green, glossy foliage. Small, orange-red hips ripen in late summer. To make sure plants set fruit, grow at least two for cross-pollination. Harvest fresh hips to make an excellent jam, or dry them for use as an herbal tea rich in vitamin C.

LANDSCAPE USES: A fine hedge, groundcover, or specimen, 'Schneezwerg' is an excellent compact landscape plant. The nearly continuous bloom creates a bright spot in mixed borders, where it looks attractive with perennials and herbs. This tough, hardy shrub is tolerant of seaside conditions and urban landscapes.

CULTURE: Plant 'Schneezwerg' in full sun in any well-drained soil. Rugosa hybrids tolerate hot spots characterized by reflected heat from paving and thrive in seaside gardens. To form a hedge, plant bushes every 3 feet—plants will be touching in three years. Prune mature specimens and hedges in late winter. Remove about one-third of the top growth to shape the plants. Periodically remove older canes to encourage vigorous new growth. This rose is recommended for all regions.

DISEASE AND PEST PROBLEMS: 'Schneezwerg' is a durable, disease-free rose. However, the summer flowers sometimes attract Japanese beetles. If beetles attack, pick off the adults, and treat lawn areas with milky disease spores to control grubs. 'Schneezwerg' is also susceptible to rose stem girdler. Keep plants free of deadwood; prune out and destroy infested canes.

RELATED CULTIVARS: 'David Thompson' (['Schneezwerg' × 'Frau Dagmar Hartopp'] × seedling; Svejda, Canada; 1979) is a compact, small-leaved rugosa hybrid that is rarely out of bloom from spring through frost. Its reddish pink, semidouble to double, fragrant flowers open to reveal golden stamens.

'Jens Munk' ('Schneezwerg' × 'Frau Dagmar Hartopp'; Svejda, Canada; 1974) bears clear pink, semidouble blooms with a wonderful perfume. Arching to rounded shrubs attain a height of 5 feet with a similar spread and flower profusely in spring with excellent repeat bloom. This rose does not set many hips. 'Jens Munk' is particularly susceptible to rose stem girdler. Prune out and destroy infested canes.

Cultivar Name:	**'Sea Foam'**
Classification:	Shrub
Parentage:	Three crosses with 'White Dawn' × 'Pinocchio'
Introduced:	Schwartz, Conard-Pyle, United States; 1964
USDA Plant Hardiness Zones:	5 to 9

DESCRIPTION: 'Sea Foam' is an excellent care-free, low-spreading shrub. It bears abundant creamy white, double flowers in clusters in June, followed by excellent repeat flowering. In fact, the shrubs bloom almost continuously. The vigorous, prostrate plants reach 3 feet tall and 6 feet wide and are covered with small, shiny, leathery, dark foliage.

LANDSCAPE USES: Use this shrub as an attractive mass, groundcover, low hedge, climber, or specimen. Its clusters of white flowers mix easily with antique and modern roses and perennials. It is a good choice for cascading over a wall, draping a fence, or tumbling down a sunny slope.

CULTURE: 'Sea Foam' is a robust, hardy shrub that's easy to grow in full sun in any well-drained soil. Top-dress with compost annually, and fertilize in spring with a complete organic fertilizer. Prune while dormant to keep in bounds, and occasionally remove older canes and thin out crowded stems. To make a hedge, plant bushes every 4 feet—plants will be touching in three years. 'Sea Foam' is highly recommended for all regions.

DISEASE AND PEST PROBLEMS: 'Sea Foam' is noted for its disease resistance. In wet seasons, it occasionally develops black spot in some regions. For best results, apply fungicidal soap or garden sulfur combined with an antitranspirant as soon as leaves emerge in spring to ward off the disease.

RELATED CULTIVARS: 'Fiona' ('Sea Foam' × 'Picasso'; Meilland, France; 1979) produces dark red, double flowers in clusters. It is repeat-flowering and similar in habit to 'Sea Foam'.

'Two Sisters' ('Sea Foam' × 'The Fairy'; Williams, United States; 1992) is an interesting mix of the best groundcover shrub roses. Double flowers open pink and age to white. The mounding shrubs reach 4 feet tall and wide and are covered with small, glossy foliage.

'Seashell'

Cultivar Name:	'Seashell'
Classification:	Hybrid tea
Parentage:	Seedling × 'Color Wonder'
Introduced:	W. Kordes Söhne, Germany; Jackson & Perkins, United States; 1976 1976 All-America Rose Selection
USDA Plant Hardiness Zones:	5 to 9

DESCRIPTION: 'Seashell' is an excellent ever-blooming hybrid tea in the tangerine color range. Pointed, burnt-orange buds open to high-centered, double blooms of soft apricot-orange that have a light tea scent. Bushes are vigorous and upright, reaching 4 to 5 feet tall and 2½ feet wide. The dark, matte green leaves are tinted with copper.

LANDSCAPE USES: The tangerine blooms of 'Seashell' blend easily with hot color schemes. Place this rose in the middle of a border, where low-growing perennials and shrubs will hide its stiff hybrid tea frame.

CULTURE: Give 'Seashell' a sunny location in well-drained soil that has been amended with organic matter. Top-dress with compost annually. Prune hard in late winter or early spring to rid bushes of damaged canes and overwintering disease spores. Fertilize after pruning and again after the first flowering with a complete organic fertilizer. Deadhead spent flowers to encourage repeat bloom. Apply a mound of mulch as winter protection in Zone 5. This rose is highly recommended for all regions.

DISEASE AND PEST PROBLEMS: 'Seashell' is susceptible to black spot in some regions. For best results, apply fungicidal soap or garden sulfur combined with an antitranspirant as leaves emerge in spring. Reapply monthly.

'Sea Foam'

'Secret'

Cultivar Name:	'Secret'
Classification:	Hybrid tea
Parentage:	'Pristine' × 'Friendship'
Introduced:	Tracy, United States; 1992; Conard-Pyle, United States 1994 All-America Rose Selection
USDA Plant Hardiness Zones:	5 to 9

DESCRIPTION: The elegant, urn-shaped buds of this rose open to high-centered, classic, double flowers that are light pink edged with deep pink. The blooms, carried on long stems, have a wonderful perfume. The everblooming shrubs are upright and bushy, reaching 4 to 5 feet tall and 2½ feet wide, with large, semiglossy, dark green leaves. A vigorous bush with exquisite blooms, 'Secret' takes after its lovely 'Pristine' parent. It makes an excellent cut flower.

LANDSCAPE USES: Use a group of 'Secret' for an accent of all-season bloom in mixed borders. Position it near the back of the border, and camouflage its stiff hybrid tea habit by planting informal shrub roses and perennials in front of it. It is a must for the cutting garden for its long-lasting blooms.

CULTURE: Plant in a sunny location in well-drained soil that has been amended with organic matter. Prune hard in late winter or early spring to rid plants of damaged canes and overwintering disease spores. Fertilize after pruning and again after the first bloom with a complete organic fertilizer. Top-dress with compost annually. Deadhead spent blooms to encourage repeat bloom. Apply a mound of mulch as winter protection in Zone 5.

DISEASE AND PEST PROBLEMS: Like other hybrid teas, 'Secret' is susceptible to diseases. Protect new foliage with an application of fungicidal soap or garden sulfur combined with an antitranspirant to prevent black spot; repeat monthly. Monitor the plants for insect damage.

Sexy Rexy®

Cultivar Name:	Sexy Rexy®
Classification:	Floribunda
Parentage:	'Seaspray' × 'Dreaming'
Introduced:	McGredy, New Zealand; 1984
USDA Plant Hardiness Zones:	5 to 9

DESCRIPTION: Rarely out of bloom, Sexy Rexy® covers itself with large clusters of clear rose-pink double blooms that are lightly tea-scented. Vigorous bushes grow to 3½ feet tall and less wide, and are covered with small, glossy, leathery leaves.

LANDSCAPE USES: Sexy Rexy® makes a superb mass, foundation planting, low everblooming screen, and container rose. In mixed borders its abundant floral display provides an accent easily combined with antique and modern roses, perennials, and shrubs. Plant it in drifts of three or more bushes to make a mass of season-long bloom.

CULTURE: Plant Sexy Rexy® in a sunny location in well-drained soil that has been amended with organic matter. Prune hard in late winter or early spring to encourage vigorous new growth. Fertilize after pruning and again after the first bloom with a complete fertilizer. Top-dress with compost annually. Deadhead spent blooms throughout the season.

DISEASE AND PEST PROBLEMS: Sexy Rexy® demonstrates excellent resistance to black spot and mildew. Apply garden sulfur combined with an antitranspirant to protect new foliage in spring, and monitor thereafter. Watch for signs of insect damage.

'Showbiz'

Cultivar Name:	**'Showbiz'**
Classification:	Floribunda
Parentage:	Not recorded
Introduced:	Tantau, Germany; 1981
	1985 All-America Rose Selection
USDA Plant Hardiness Zones:	5 to 9

DESCRIPTION: 'Showbiz' shows off its semidouble, cupped flowers of bright scarlet in large sprays. Rarely out of bloom, 'Showbiz' makes a bushy, compact, vigorous shrub 2½ to 3 feet tall and less wide and has semiglossy, leathery foliage.

LANDSCAPE USES: Use this bold, everblooming floribunda to brighten up a dull, sunny spot in the garden. It makes an excellent everblooming mass, foundation planting, edging, or container specimen. Plant it in drifts of three or more bushes to make a mass of all-season bloom. Its red blooms are a welcome addition to mixed borders and look attractive with shrubs and perennials in yellow, red, and orange. One classic combination is bright red 'Showbiz' with drifts of lemon yellow 'Moonshine' yarrow (*Achillea* × 'Moonshine').

CULTURE: Plant 'Showbiz' in a sunny location in well-drained soil that has been amended with organic matter. Prune hard in late winter or early spring to rid plants of overwintering disease spores and to encourage vigorous new growth. Fertilize after pruning and again after the first bloom with a complete organic fertilizer. Top-dress with compost annually. Deadhead the spent blooms through the season. Apply a mound of mulch to protect the graft union from winter injury in Zone 5. This rose is highly recommended for all regions.

DISEASE AND PEST PROBLEMS: 'Showbiz' has good disease resistance. For extra protection, apply fungicidal soap or garden sulfur combined with an antitranspirant as soon as leaves emerge in spring to prevent black spot. Monitor plants and reapply as needed.

'Shropshire Lass'

Cultivar Name:	**'Shropshire Lass'**
Classification:	English rose
Parentage:	'Madame Butterfly' × 'Madame Legras de St. Germain'
Introduced:	Austin, United Kingdom; 1968
USDA Plant Hardiness Zones:	5 to 9

DESCRIPTION: The large, single, blush-white flowers of 'Shropshire Lass' open to reveal an eye of yellow stamens. This rose is famous for its rich perfume and wonderful, abundant spring bloom. The vigorous, upright shrubs reach 8 feet tall and less wide and are covered with blue-green foliage. Trained as a climber, it stretches to 15 feet.

LANDSCAPE USES: Grow this lovely rose as a once-blooming shrub or climber or on a pillar. Use it to fill a position in the back of the mixed border, where its handsome flowers will nod above companion plants and the leafy stems can fade into the background when they are not in bloom. 'Shropshire Lass' can also be trained along a fence or wall or permitted to climb into a small tree.

CULTURE: Give this rose a sunny location in well-drained soil that has been amended with organic matter. Top-dress with compost annually. Fertilize with a complete organic fertilizer. Prune after flowers fade in early summer. Thin out about one-third of the older canes, and reduce the stems that have just flowered by two-thirds of their length. In spring, neaten bushes by removing wayward growth. 'Shropshire Lass' is recommended for all regions.

DISEASE AND PEST PROBLEMS: This rose is disease-resistant, but its breeder recommends applying a preventive spray for best results. Spray new foliage with fungicidal soap or garden sulfur combined with an antitranspirant; reapply as needed.

'Sissinghurst Castle'

Cultivar Name:	'Sissinghurst Castle' (also called 'Rose des Maures')
Classification:	Gallica
Parentage:	Not recorded
Introduced:	Reintroduced by Vita Sackville-West in 1947
USDA Plant Hardiness Zones:	4 to 8

DESCRIPTION: 'Sissinghurst Castle' is an old gallica that was found growing in the garden at Sissinghurst Castle in Kent by Vita Sackville-West. It is one of the most richly colored gallicas. Its fragrant, semidouble flow-

ers are deep plum with gold stamens. The vigorous, upright bushes grow 4 feet tall and less wide and are covered with rough, gray-green foliage.

LANDSCAPE USES: This is an excellent once-blooming shrub for small gardens. Use it in the middle of a border, where you can appreciate its fragrant, shapely blooms. Its rich violet flowers are nicely complemented by pink flowers and silver-leaved plants such as artemisias (*Artemisia* spp.) and lamb's-ears (*Stachys byzantina*).

CULTURE: This rose is easy to grow in a sunny location. Plant in well-drained soil that has been amended with organic matter. Top-dress liberally with compost. Fertilize in spring with a complete organic fertilizer. Prune while dormant to thin out crowded stems and to shape bushes. 'Sissinghurst Castle' is highly recommended for all regions.

DISEASE AND PEST PROBLEMS: 'Sissinghurst Castle' is usually resistant to black spot. Surround it with later-blooming plants to hide any mildew that might develop. 'Sissinghurst Castle' is best left to fend for itself.

Cultivar Name:	'Sombreuil'
Classification:	Climbing tea
Parentage:	'Gigantesque' seedling
Introduced:	Robert, France; 1850
USDA Plant Hardiness Zones:	6 to 9

DESCRIPTION: A graceful, free-flowering climber, 'Sombreuil' has long been admired for its lovely flowers. It bears clusters of full, shapely, creamy white blooms that open flat, sometimes revealing a blush tint. The flowers have a rich tea fragrance. An abundant spring bloom is followed by dependable repeat bloom. The vigorous, upright canes, growing 8 to 10 feet tall, are armed with prickles and covered with glossy, leathery leaves that make a handsome contrast to the snowy blooms. The blooms make top quality cut flowers. The plant itself is the hardiest of the climbing tea roses.

LANDSCAPE USES: A superb climber for covering a pillar, wall, arch, fence, or trellis, 'Sombreuil' makes a vigorous, showy specimen. It blends well with perennials in mixed borders, providing some height. Try weaving dainty violet *Clematis viticella* up through it to provide interesting contrast to the creamy white flowers.

CULTURE: Plant 'Sombreuil' in well-drained soil in a sunny location. Remove the deadwood and occasionally prune out older canes to encourage vigorous new growth. Top-dress with compost in autumn. Fertilize in spring and again after flowering with a complete organic fertilizer to encourage repeat bloom. Deadhead spent blooms through the season. Give it a warm wall for protection in Zone 6. Even when some of the canes are winterkilled, vigorous shoots quickly grow up from the base and set buds the first season. This rose is highly recommended for all regions.

DISEASE AND PEST PROBLEMS: 'Sombreuil' has good disease resistance. However, the leaves are sometimes skeletonized by rose slugs early in the season. At the first sign of damage, spray the leaves with insecticidal soap.

'Souvenir de la Malmaison'

Cultivar Name:	**'Souvenir de la Malmaison'**
Classification:	Bourbon
Parentage:	'Madame Desprez' × a tea rose
Introduced:	Beluze, France; 1843
USDA Plant Hardiness Zones:	6 to 9

DESCRIPTION: Introduced in 1843 to commemorate the famous rose garden established by Josephine I near Paris, 'Souvenir de la Malmaison' brings the best of the French Bourbons to your landscape. It is the most reliable Bourbon rose for continuous bloom. Many-petaled, blush pink flowers open flat and quartered. They have a wonderful perfume and cover the bush throughout the season. This rose makes a compact bush, 2½ feet tall and wide, with dark, semiglossy foliage. It may grow larger in mild climates.

LANDSCAPE USES: 'Souvenir de la Malmaison' is an excellent compact Bourbon, resembling a low floribunda in northern gardens. It is one of the best repeat-flowering roses for small gardens. Grow a group of several plants near the front of a border to provide a drift of all-season color. It also makes an excellent container specimen.

CULTURE: This vigorous shrub is easy to grow in full sun in any well-drained soil. Top-dress with compost annually, and fertilize in spring with a complete organic fertilizer. Prune while dormant, removing damaged canes, thinning out crowded stems, and reducing canes by one-half their length. This rose is highly recommended for all regions.

DISEASE AND PEST PROBLEMS: 'Souvenir de la Malmaison' is moderately resistant to disease. For best results, apply fungicidal soap or garden sulfer combined with an antitranspirant as soon as leaves emerge in spring; reapply if needed.

'Sombreuil'

RELATED CULTIVARS: 'Souvenir de la Malmaison Climbing' (climbing sport; Bennett, United Kingdom; 1893) produces the same excellent flowers on vigorous canes to 12 feet tall. It is once-blooming.

'Kronprinzessin Viktoria' ('Souvenir de la Malmaison' sport; Vollert; 1887) bears pure white flowers tinged with lemon yellow. It is like its wonderful parent in all other aspects.

'Souvenir de St. Anne's' ('Souvenir de la Malmaison' sport; before 1916; reintroduced Hilling, United Kingdom; 1950) bears large, semidouble, blush pink flowers that age to pure white. More strongly scented than its parent, this rose produces flowers continuously on a shapely bush that normally grows 3 to 4 feet tall and wide. Expect it to grow taller in warm climates. It is highly recommended for all regions.

CULTURE: Plant 'Sparrieshoop' in a sunny location in well-drained soil that has been amended with organic matter. To form a hedge, plant bushes every 4 feet—plants will be touching in three years. Prune while dormant to thin out crowded stems and to keep plants in bounds. Fertilize after pruning with a complete organic fertilizer. Top-dress with compost annually. This rose is highly recommended for all regions.

DISEASE AND PEST PROBLEMS: 'Sparrieshoop' has good disease resistance. For extra protection, spray the new leaves with fungicidal soap or garden sulfur combined with an antitranspirant; reapply as needed.

'Sparrieshoop'

'Stanwell Perpetual'

Cultivar Name:	'Sparrieshoop'
Classification:	Shrub
Parentage:	('Baby Chateau' × 'Else Poulsen') × 'Magnifica'
Introduced:	W. Kordes Söhne, Germany; 1953
USDA Plant Hardiness Zones:	4 to 9

Cultivar Name:	'Stanwell Perpetual'
Classification:	Hybrid spinosissima
Parentage:	*Rosa damascena* var. *semperflorens* × *Rosa spinosissima*
Introduced:	Lee, United Kingdom; 1838
USDA Plant Hardiness Zones:	3 to 8

DESCRIPTION: In full bloom, 'Sparrieshoop' makes a magnificent display. The vigorous bushes are blanketed with huge five-petaled, light pink blossoms filled with golden stamens. The flower show is repeated through frost. Tall, arching, dense shrubs, growing to 5 feet tall with a similar spread, are modestly armed with prickles and covered with leathery foliage.

LANDSCAPE USES: 'Sparrieshoop' serves wonderfully as an accent in mixed borders. It is also good in a mass or as a screen or hedge.

DESCRIPTION: 'Stanwell Perpetual' produces charming blush pink, double flowers that open flat to reveal golden stamens. The highly fragrant blooms appear regularly until frost. Its prickly stems are covered with gray-green leaves. It forms a mound about 3½ feet tall by 3½ feet wide.

LANDSCAPE USES: 'Stanwell Perpetual' makes a fine mounding groundcover or informal low hedge. It also looks wonderful cascading over a wall. It mixes beautifully with other antique shrub roses and perennials in an informal border. English garden writer Gertrude Jekyll recommends planting three bushes spaced 1 foot apart if you'd like a more upright look.

CULTURE: Plant in well-drained soil in full sun or dappled shade. To form an informal hedge, set the bushes every 4 feet—plants will be touching in three years. Prune out older canes to encourage vigorous new growth. Prune hedges lightly in late winter to shape them. Top-dress with compost in spring. No other care is required.

DISEASE AND PEST PROBLEMS: 'Stanwell Perpetual' is not usually bothered by diseases and pests.

'Starina'

Cultivar Name:	'Starina'
Classification:	Miniature
Parentage:	('Dany Robin' × 'Fire King') × 'Perla de Montserrat'
Introduced:	Meilland, France; 1965
USDA Plant Hardiness Zones:	5 to 9

DESCRIPTION: 'Starina' is a world-class miniature. It produces small, vermilion-red, high-centered, double blooms nonstop from spring through frost. It makes an upright, bushy shrub, 12 to 15 inches tall and 12 inches wide, with glossy leaves. The blooms make excellent cut flowers.

LANDSCAPE USES: 'Starina' is suitable for edging, in a mass or rock garden, or as a container specimen. Plant it in drifts of three or more bushes to make a mass of all-season bloom.

CULTURE: Plant in a sunny location in well-drained soil that has been amended with organic matter. Prune hard in late winter or early spring to rid plants of overwintering disease spores and to encourage vigorous new growth. Fertilize after pruning and again after the first bloom with a complete organic fertilizer. Top-dress with compost annually. Deadhead spent blooms through the season. This rose is highly recommended for all regions.

DISEASE AND PEST PROBLEMS: 'Starina' has good disease resistance. For extra protection, apply fungicidal soap or garden sulfur combined with an antitranspirant as soon as leaves emerge in spring to prevent black spot. Monitor the plants and reapply at least monthly thereafter. Mites sometimes bother the small-leaved plants. If the bugs appear, wash the leaves with a sharp spray of water. If feeding persists, apply insecticidal soap.

'Sunsprite'

Cultivar Name:	'Sunsprite' (also called 'Friesia')
Classification:	Floribunda
Parentage:	'Spanish Sun' × seedling
Introduced:	W. Kordes Söhne, Germany; 1977
USDA Plant Hardiness Zones:	5 to 9

DESCRIPTION: The best of the yellow floribunda roses, 'Sunsprite' has it all: nonstop bloom, fragrance, vigor, and above-average disease resistance. Well-shaped, golden buds open to deep yellow, double flowers held in clusters. The flowers are large, flat, and exude a wonderful fruity perfume. The bushes are vigorous and upright, with light green, semiglossy foliage. They grow 3 to 4 feet tall and 2 feet wide.

LANDSCAPE USES: 'Sunsprite' makes a superb mass, foundation planting, or specimen. In mixed borders, its abundant floral display looks wonderful with antique and modern roses, perennials, and shrubs. Plant it in drifts of three or more bushes to make a mass of all-season bloom. This four-star specimen is a must for those who cherish yellow roses.

CULTURE: Plant in a sunny location in well-drained soil that has been amended with organic matter. Prune hard in late winter or early spring to encourage vigorous new growth. Fertilize after pruning and again after the first bloom with a complete organic fertilizer. Top-dress with compost annually. Deadhead spent blooms through the season.

DISEASE AND PEST PROBLEMS: 'Sunsprite' has above-average resistance to black spot and mildew. For extra protection, apply fungicidal soap or garden sulfur combined with an antitranspirant to protect new foliage in spring; reapply if needed. Check often for insect damage.

RELATED CULTIVARS: 'Sunflare' ('Sunsprite' × seedling; Warriner, Jackson & Perkins, United States; 1982; 1983 All-America Rose Selection) is a useful low floribunda that bears clusters of medium yellow flowers that fade to pale yellow. Small, glossy foliage covers compact bushes that reach 2 feet tall and wide and are rarely out of bloom.

'Sun Flare Climbing' ([also called 'Yellow Blaze'] 'Sun Flare' sport; Burks, Co-Operative Rose Growers, United States; 1987–88) produces semidouble, medium yellow flowers that fade to pale yellow. Long canes covered with small, glossy leaves reach 8 to 10 feet tall. This cultivar is a hardy, repeat-blooming pillar rose or short climber.

Cultivar Name:	'Sweet Chariot'
Classification:	Miniature
Parentage:	'Little Chief' × 'Violette'
Introduced:	Moore, United States; 1984
USDA Plant Hardiness Zones:	5 to 9

DESCRIPTION: One of the most fragrant miniature roses, 'Sweet Chariot' bears small, lavender, double blooms in clusters. It makes a spreading, bushy shrub, reaching 15 to 18 inches tall and wide, with matte green leaves. This rose is an excellent choice for hanging baskets.

LANDSCAPE USES: 'Sweet Chariot' is suitable for edging or for use in a mass, rock garden, or container. It looks especially good in a hanging basket. In the garden, grow it in drifts of three or more bushes to make a mass of all-season bloom.

CULTURE: Plant 'Sweet Chariot' in a sunny location in well-drained soil that has been amended with organic matter. Prune hard in late winter or early spring to rid plants of overwintering disease spores and to encourage vigorous new growth. Fertilize after pruning and again after the first bloom with a complete organic fertilizer. Top-dress with compost annually. Deadhead or shear spent blooms through the season. This rose is highly recommended for all regions.

DISEASE AND PEST PROBLEMS: 'Sweet Chariot' has good disease resistance. For extra protection, apply fungicidal soap or garden sulfur combined with an antitranspirant as soon as leaves emerge in spring; reapply at least monthly. Mites sometimes bother the plants. If the bugs appear, wash the leaves with a strong spray of water. If mites continue to be a problem, apply insecticidal soap.

'Sweet Chariot'

'Sweet Sunblaze'

Cultivar Name:	**'Sweet Sunblaze'** (also called 'Pink Symphony')
Classification:	Miniature
Parentage:	'Darling Flame' × 'Air France'
Introduced:	Meilland, France; 1987
USDA Plant Hardiness Zones:	5 to 9

DESCRIPTION: 'Sweet Sunblaze' produces clear pink, double flowers that are held in clusters. The lightly tea-scented blooms are produced nonstop from spring through frost. The plant makes an upright, bushy shrub, 18 to 24 inches tall and 12 inches wide, with glossy leaves. The blooms make excellent cut flowers.

LANDSCAPE USES: 'Sweet Sunblaze' is suitable for edging or for use in a mass, rock garden, or container. It is particularly well suited for a low hedge. In borders, plant it in drifts of three or more bushes to make a mass of all-season bloom.

CULTURE: Plant 'Sweet Sunblaze' in a sunny location in well-drained soil that has been amended with organic matter. Prune hard in late winter or early spring to rid plants of overwintering disease spores and to encourage vigorous new growth. Fertilize after pruning and again after the first bloom with a complete organic fertilizer. Top-dress with compost annually. Deadhead or shear spent blooms through the season. This rose is highly recommended for all regions.

DISEASE AND PEST PROBLEMS: 'Sweet Sunblaze' has good disease resistance. For extra protection, apply fungicidal soap or garden sulfur combined with an antitranspirant as soon as leaves emerge in spring;

reapply at least monthly. Mites sometimes bother the plants. If the pests appear, wash the leaves with a strong spray of water. If mites continue to be a problem, apply insecticidal soap.

RELATED CULTIVARS: Many of the Sunblaze series of miniature roses make excellent everblooming, dwarf garden and patio shrubs. Their compact, uniform growth habit makes them particularly useful as edging or low hedges.

'Debut' (also called 'Sweet Symphony'; 'Coppelia' × 'Magic Carrousel'; Meilland, France; 1988; 1989 All-America Rose Selection) is a lovely bicolor red miniature. Flowers are red, blended with creamy yellow at the base.

'Orange Sunblaze' ('Parador' × ['Baby Bettina' × 'Duchess of Windsor']; Meilland, France; 1982) bears orange-red, cupped blooms.

'Royal Sunblaze' (seedling × seedling; Schwartz, United States; 1987) bears double, lemon yellow flowers on upright, bushy shrubs.

'Scarlet Sunblaze' ('Tamango' × ['Baby Bettina' × 'Duchess of Windsor']; Meilland, France; 1982) produces semidouble, scarlet flowers on bushy plants.

'Thérèse Bugnet'

Cultivar Name:	**'Thérèse Bugnet'**
Classification:	Hybrid rugosa
Parentage:	Complex cross involving *Rosa acicularis* and *Rosa rugosa*
Introduced:	Bugnet, Canada; 1950
USDA Plant Hardiness Zones:	2 to 8

DESCRIPTION: 'Thérèse Bugnet' produces many intensely fragrant, large, double pink flowers in late spring, followed by excellent repeat bloom. However, you won't find many hips on the plant. It makes a dense, prickly shrub with blue-green foliage, coloring to a handsome yellow-orange in autumn. Its shiny, red canes are striking in winter. Arching to rounded shrubs reach 5 to 6 feet with a similar spread. Dry the fragrant petals for use in potpourri.

LANDSCAPE USES: This superb specimen rose also looks attractive with perennials and herbs in mixed borders or herb gardens. It also makes an excellent hedge, screen, or windbreak.

CULTURE: Plant 'Thérèse Bugnet' in full sun in any well-drained soil. It will tolerate arid and poor soils as long as they are sharply drained. To form a hedge, plant bushes every 4 feet—plants will be touching in three years. Prune mature specimens and hedges in late winter to shape the plants, taking off about one-third of the top growth. Remove the older canes periodically to keep the plants growing vigorously. No other care is required. This rose is recommended for all regions.

DISEASE AND PEST PROBLEMS: 'Thérèse Bugnet' is an easy-care plant that is normally disease-free. However, the summer flowers sometimes attract Japanese beetles. Pick off adult beetles, and treat lawn areas with milky disease spores to control grubs. 'Thérèse Bugnet' is also susceptible to rose stem girdler. Keep plants free of deadwood; prune out and destroy infested canes.

Cultivar Name:	**'Tuscany'** (also called 'The Old Velvet Rose')
Classification:	Gallica
Parentage:	Not recorded
Introduced:	Before 1820
USDA Plant Hardiness Zones:	4 to 8

DESCRIPTION: 'Tuscany' is a very old gallica rose, known since the sixteenth century. It bears one of the deepest, most richly colored flowers. The blooms are fragrant, semidouble, and deep violet with prominent gold stamens. The vigorous, upright bushes grow 3 feet tall and less wide and are covered with rough, gray-green foliage.

LANDSCAPE USES: This is an excellent once-blooming shrub for small gardens. Use it in the middle of borders, where you can appreciate the fragrant, shapely blooms. Its rich violet flowers look best when they're contrasted with pink flowers and silver-leaved plants, such as artemisias (*Artemisia* spp.) and lamb's-ears (*Stachys byzantina*).

CULTURE: 'Tuscany' is easy to grow in any sunny location. Plant it in well-drained soil that has been amended with organic matter. Top-dress liberally with compost. Fertilize in spring with a complete organic fertilizer. Prune while dormant to thin out crowded stems and to shape bushes. This rose is highly recommended for all regions.

DISEASE AND PEST PROBLEMS: 'Tuscany' is usually resistant to black spot, and is best left to fend for itself.

RELATED CULTIVARS: 'Superb Tuscan' (also called 'Tuscany Superb'; 'Tuscany' seedling; before 1837) bears large, full flowers on a more vigorous bush to 4 feet tall and less wide.

'Tuscany'

'Vick's Caprice'

Westerland®

Cultivar Name:	'Vick's Caprice'
Classification:	Hybrid perpetual
Parentage:	'Archiduchesse Elisabeth d'Autriche' sport
Introduced:	Vick, United States; 1891
USDA Plant Hardiness Zones:	5 to 9

Cultivar Name:	Westerland®
Classification:	Floribunda
Parentage:	'Friedrich Worlein' × 'Circus'
Introduced:	W. Kordes Söhne, Germany; 1969
USDA Plant Hardiness Zones:	5 to 9

DESCRIPTION: 'Vick's Caprice' is a reliable, repeat-blooming hybrid perpetual boasting large, pink flowers striped with white and deep pink. Cupped, fragrant blooms cover vigorous shrubs that reach 4 feet tall and less wide.

LANDSCAPE USES: Use 'Vick's Caprice' as an accent in mixed borders, where you can enjoy its bloom in June and again in autumn.

CULTURE: Plant 'Vick's Caprice' in well-drained soil in full sun. Prune shrubs hard in early spring, cutting back canes to healthy wood, reducing their length by about two-thirds and thinning out the centers. Deadhead spent blooms after flowering to encourage repeat bloom. Apply compost, well-rotted manure, or Milorganite liberally to these heavy-feeding antique roses. Fertilize after spring pruning and again after flowering in early summer with a complete organic fertilizer to encourage repeat bloom. This rose is highly recommended for all regions.

DISEASE AND PEST PROBLEMS: 'Vick's Caprice' is susceptible to black spot and powdery mildew. For best results, spray new leaves with fungicidal soap or garden sulfur combined with an antitranspirant; reapply as needed.

DESCRIPTION: Westerland® is one of the best and most beautiful roses to use as a repeat-blooming climber or pillar. Its perfumed blooms are large, apricot-orange, cupped, loosely double, and produced in abundance with excellent repeat bloom. This vigorous shrub generally grows 6 feet tall and wide and has large, semiglossy leaves. Trained as a climber, it will easily reach 8 feet.

LANDSCAPE USES: This free-flowering shrub can be used in a mass, on a pillar, or as a climber. It looks particularly fine surrounded with purple-leaved plants, such as 'Royal Purple' smokebush (*Cotinus coggygria* 'Royal Purple'). In hot-colored mixed borders, its handsome flowers mingle easily with yellow- or orange-flowered perennials.

CULTURE: Give Westerland® a sunny location in well-drained soil that has been amended with organic matter. Top-dress with compost annually. Prune while dormant, and deadhead after flowering to encourage repeat bloom. Fertilize with a complete organic fertilizer.

DISEASE AND PEST PROBLEMS: Westerland® is extremely disease-resistant. However, for best results, apply an antitranspirant as leaves emerge; reapply as needed.

'White Cockade'

Cultivar Name:	'White Cockade'
Classification:	Large-flowered climber
Parentage:	'New Dawn' × 'Circus'
Introduced:	Cocker, United Kingdom; 1969
USDA Plant Hardiness Zones:	5 to 9

DESCRIPTION: 'White Cockade' is the best repeat-blooming white climber. Its pure white flowers are fragrant, high-centered, and double. It makes a short climber or pillar, reaching 8 feet tall, with glossy foliage. The repeat bloom is excellent.

LANDSCAPE USES: 'White Cockade' is an excellent pillar or climber to cover a pillar, trellis, wall, or arch. It can also be grown as a mounding shrub. Try growing a large- or small-flowered blue clematis with it. A handsome combination at the Morris Arboretum near Philadelphia, Pennsylvania, features 'White Cockade' grown on a pillar with lavender-blue 'Mrs. Cholmondeley' clematis (*Clematis* 'Mrs. Cholmondeley') woven through it, surrounded by yellow roses.

CULTURE: Plant in well-drained soil in full sun. Young plants need little pruning. Manage older plants by cutting out old canes to encourage vigorous new growth and shortening sideshoots to four buds. Top-dress with compost in autumn. Fertilize in spring and again after flowering with a complete organic fertilizer to encourage repeat bloom.

DISEASE AND PEST PROBLEMS: 'White Cockade' is disease-free.

RELATED CULTIVARS: 'Compassion' ('White Cockade' × 'Prima Ballerina'; Harkness, United Kingdom; 1973) produces lovely hybrid tea–type blooms of salmon pink tinged with apricot and orange. They are fragrant and produced continuously on upright canes growing to 10 feet tall and covered with glossy, dark green foliage. This rose is useful as a short climber or shrub or on a pillar.

Wife of Bath®

Cultivar Name:	Wife of Bath®
Classification:	English rose
Parentage:	'Madame Caroline Testout' × ('Ma Perkins' × Constance Spry®)
Introduced:	Austin, United Kingdom; 1969
USDA Plant Hardiness Zones:	5 to 9

DESCRIPTION: The double, cupped, light pink blooms of Wife of Bath® are produced in profusion in late spring, followed by reliable repeat bloom. It makes a vigorous, bushy, spreading shrub, 3 feet tall and wide, with dark, glossy foliage.

LANDSCAPE USES: This free-flowering shrub can be used as a mass, hedge, foundation planting, or specimen. Plant a group of a few bushes to provide some substance. Use Wife of Bath® in the middle of mixed borders, where its handsome flowers mingle easily with perennials.

CULTURE: Give this rose a sunny location in well-drained soil that has been amended with organic matter. Top-dress with compost annually. Prune hard while dormant and again after the first bloom to shape the plant and to encourage repeat bloom. Fertilize with a complete organic fertilizer. Apply winter protection in Zone 5.

DISEASE AND PEST PROBLEMS: Wife of Bath® has variable disease resistance. The breeder recommends applying preventive sprays for best results. Spray with fungicidal soap or garden sulfur combined with an antitranspirant as soon as leaves emerge in spring; reapply as needed.

RELATED CULTIVARS: Heritage® (seedling × [Wife of Bath® × 'Iceberg']; Austin, United Kingdom; 1984) bears blush pink, cupped flowers on bushes 4 to 5 feet tall and less wide.

'Yankee Doodle'

Cultivar Name:	**'Yankee Doodle'**
Classification:	Hybrid tea
Parentage:	'Color Wonder' × 'King's Ransom'
Introduced:	W. Kordes Söhne, Germany; 1965 1976 All-America Rose Selection
USDA Plant Hardiness Zones:	5 to 9

DESCRIPTION: 'Yankee Doodle' has urn-shaped buds that open to very full, double flowers. The apricot-peach blooms have a light tea perfume and are carried on long stems. The everblooming, tall shrubs are upright and bushy, growing 5 to 6 feet tall and 2½ feet wide, with large, semiglossy, dark green leaves. A vigorous rose, it is one of the best garden cultivars, and makes an excellent cut flower.

LANDSCAPE USES: In mixed borders, use a group of 'Yankee Doodle' as an accent of all-season bloom. Position it near the back, and camouflage its stiff hybrid tea habit by planting informal shrub roses and perennials in front of it. Its long-lasting blooms make it a must for the cutting garden.

CULTURE: Plant in a sunny location in well-drained soil that has been amended with organic matter. Prune hard in late winter or early spring to rid plants of damaged canes and overwintering disease spores. Fertilize after pruning and again after the first bloom with a complete organic fertilizer. Top-dress with compost annually. Deadhead spent blooms to encourage repeat bloom. Apply a mound of mulch as winter protection in Zone 5.

DISEASE AND PEST PROBLEMS: 'Yankee Doodle' has above-average disease resistance. For extra protection, spray new foliage with fungicidal soap or garden sulfur combined with an antitranspirant; reapply monthly. Monitor the plants for insect damage.

'Zéphirine Drouhin'

Cultivar Name:	**'Zéphirine Drouhin'**
Classification:	Bourbon
Parentage:	Not recorded
Introduced:	Bizot, France; 1868
USDA Plant Hardiness Zones:	6 to 9

DESCRIPTION: 'Zéphirine Drouhin' is among the best known and most popular of the lovely Bourbon roses. Its long, pointed, deep pink buds open to large, cerise pink, semidouble flowers. The sweetly scented blooms are produced abundantly in late spring and repeat bloom can be expected in mild climates. Treasured wherever it is cultivated, 'Zéphirine Drouhin' has a floppy habit and thornless canes covered with light green foliage. When trained as a climber, 'Zéphirine Drouhin' scrambles 8 to 15 feet.

LANDSCAPE USES: 'Zéphirine Drouhin' makes an excellent climber to cover a pillar, trellis, wall, or arch. It can also be grown as a mounding shrub. It's a delight to train because its canes are thornless. This rose mixes beautifully with vines such as trumpet honeysuckle (*Lonicera sempervirens*) and large- or small-flowered clematis. A showy combination at the Morris Arboretum near Philadelphia, Pennsylvania, features 'Zéphirine Drouhin' grown on a pillar with sky blue 'Will Goodwin' clematis (*Clematis* 'Will Goodwin') woven through it. The repeat-blooming clematis provides autumn interest and also hides unsightly rose foliage in summer.

CULTURE: Plant in well-drained soil in full sun. Prune out older canes to encourage vigorous new growth, and shorten sideshoots to four buds. Top-dress with compost in autumn. Fertilize in spring and again after flowering with a complete organic fertilizer. This rose occasionally suffers some winter injury in Zone 6, but quickly covers its support again in one season.

DISEASE AND PEST PROBLEMS: Like many of the Bourbon roses, 'Zéphirine Drouhin' is prone to black spot. Apply fungicidal soap or garden sulfur combined with an antitranspirant as soon as leaves emerge in spring and at regular intervals thereafter. Or try weekly applications of baking soda combined with horticultural oil. In a no-spray solution, grow a vine over it to hide the bare canes, but remember that the fallen leaves from an infected rose provide a continual source of black spot inoculum, which aggravates the problem in disease-susceptible neighbors.

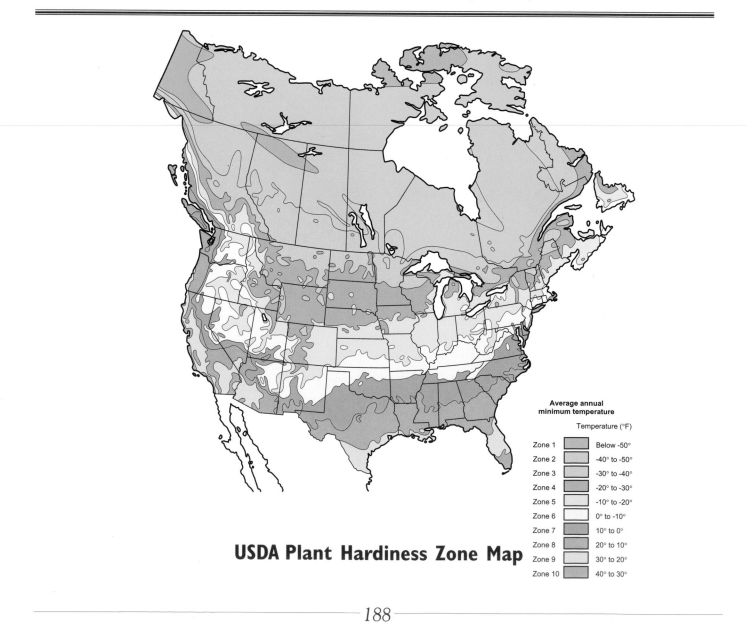

Average annual minimum temperature

Temperature (°F)

Zone 1		Below -50°
Zone 2		-40° to -50°
Zone 3		-30° to -40°
Zone 4		-20° to -30°
Zone 5		-10° to -20°
Zone 6		0° to -10°
Zone 7		10° to 0°
Zone 8		20° to 10°
Zone 9		30° to 20°
Zone 10		40° to 30°

USDA Plant Hardiness Zone Map

Recommended Reading

The American Rose Society. *The American Rose Annual*, 1916 - present.

Austin, David. *Old Roses and English Roses*. Woodbridge, Suffolk, England: Antique Collectors' Club, 1992.

——. *Shrub Roses and Climbers*. Woodbridge, Suffolk, England: Antique Collectors' Club, 1993.

Beales, Peter. *Classic Roses*. New York: Holt, Rinehart, and Winston, 1985.

Bell, Léonie. "The Autumn Damask Roses." *The American Rose Annual*. (1974): 47-58.

——. "More on Rosa Laevigata." *The Rose Letter*. 14(1): 6-7; February, 1989.

——. "Rose Signatures." *Morris Arboretum Bulletin*. 23(4): 59-66; December, 1972. Morris Arboretum of the University of Pennsylvania.

Buck, Griffith J. "Roses, Ltd.: Cold Tolerant Cultivars." *The American Rose Annual*. (1979): 124-133.

Dobson, Beverly and Peter Schneider. *Combined Rose List*. Rocky River, Ohio: Peter Schneider, 1994.

Druitt, Liz and G. Michael Shoup. *Landscaping with Antique Roses*. Newtown, CT: Taunton Press, 1992.

Epping, Jeffery E. and Edward R. Hasselkus. "Spotlight on Shrub Roses." *American Nurseryman*; 170(2): 27-39; July 15, 1989.

Gibson, Michael. *Growing Roses*. London & Canberra: Croom Helm, 1984.

——. *Shrub Roses, Climbers, & Ramblers*. London: Collins, 1981.

——. *Shrub Roses for Every Garden*. London: Collins, 1973.

Horst, R. K. *Compendium of Rose Diseases*. St. Paul, MN: American Phytopathological Society, 1983.

——. "New Promising Controls for Powdery Mildew and Blackspot of Roses." *Long Island Horticulture News*. April, 1992.

Horst, R K., S. O. Kawamoto, and L. L. Porter. "Effect of Sodium Bicarbonate and Oils on the Control of Powdery Mildew and Black Spot of Roses." *Plant Disease*. 76: 247-251; March, 1992. American Phytopathological Society.

Jekyll, Gertrude. *Color Schemes for the Flower Garden*. London: Country Life, 1908. Revised by Graham Stuart Thomas. Reprint. Salem, NH: Ayer Co., 1983.

—— and Edward Mawley. *Roses for English Gardens*. London: Country Life, 1902. Reprinted as *Roses*; revised by Graham Stuart Thomas. Salem, NH: Ayer Co., 1983.

Krüssmann, Gerd. *The Complete Book of Roses*. Translated and revised by Gerd Krüssmann and Nigel Raban. Portland, OR: Timber Press, 1981.

LeRougetel, Hazel. *A Heritage of Roses*. Owings Mill, MD: Stemmer House, 1988.

Marshall, H. H. and L. M. Collicutt. " 'Morden Amorette' and 'Morden Cardinette' Roses." *HortScience*. 20(2): 305-306; April, 1985. American Society for Horticultural Science.

McCann, Sean. *Miniature Roses*. New York: Prentice Hall Press, 1985.

McFarland, J. Horace, editor. *What Every Rose Grower Should Know*. Harrisburg, PA: The American Rose Society, 1931.

McKeon, Judith C. "Growing Roses in a City Garden." *Green Scene*. 18 (1):12-14; Sept/Oct, 1989. The Pennsylvania Horticultural Society.

——. "Species Roses and Their Hybrids." *Green Scene*. 18(6): 17-20; July/August, 1990.

Modern Roses 8: The International Check-list of Roses. Compiled by The International Registration Authority for Roses. The American Rose Society. Edited by Catherine Meikle. Harrisburg, PA: McFarland, 1980.

Modern Roses 9: The International Check-list of Roses. Edited by P. A. Haring. Shreveport, LA: The American Rose Society, 1986.

Modern Roses 10: The Comprehensive List of Roses. Edited by Thomas Cairns. Shreveport, LA: *The American Rose Society*, 1993.

Moore, Ralph S. "The Case for Own-Root Roses." *The American Rose Annual*. (1983): 21-24.

The Organic Gardeners' Handbook of Natural Insect and Disease Control. Edited by Barbara W. Ellis and Fern Marshall Bradley. Emmaus, PA: Rodale Press, 1992.

Osborne, Robert. *Hardy Roses*. Pownal, VT: Storey Communications, 1991.

Oster, Maggie. *The Rose Book*. Emmaus, PA: Rodale Press, 1994.

Rodale's All-New Encyclopedia of Organic Gardening. Edited by Fern Marshall Bradley and Barbara W. Ellis. Emmaus, PA: Rodale Press, 1992.

Sackville-West, Vita. *V. Sackville-West's Garden Book*. Edited by Philippa Nicolson. New York: Atheneum, 1983.

Scanniello, Stephen. *Climbing Roses*. New York: Prentice Hall, 1994.

—— and Tanya Bayard. *Roses of America: The Brooklyn Botanic Garden's Guide to Our National Flower*. New York: Henry Holt, 1990.

Schneider, Peter, editor. *Taylor's Guide to Roses*. Revised. Boston: Houghton Mifflin, 1995.

Shepperd, Roy. *History of the Rose*. New York, 1954. Facsimile reproduction. New York: Coleman, 1978.

Steen, Nancy. *The Charm of Old Roses*. 2nd edition. Washington, D.C.: Milldale Press, 1987.

Svejda, Felicitas. "Breeding for Improvement of Flowering Attributes of Winterhardy Rosa Kordesii (Wulff) Hybrids." *American Rose Annual*. (1978): 83-90.

——. "Canadian Explorer Roses." *American Rose Annual*. (1984): 70-82.

——. "'Henry Kelsey' Rose." *HortScience*. 20(3) 454-455; June, 1985.

——. "'William Baffin' Rose." *HortScience*. 18(6): 962; 1983.

Thomas, Graham Stewart. *Climbing Roses Old and New*. New York: St. Martin's Press, 1966.

——. *The Old Shrub Roses*. Revised edition. London: J. M. Dent & Sons, 1985.

——. *Shrub Roses of Today*. Revised edition. London: J. M. Dent & Sons, 1980.

Verrier, Suzanne. *Rosa Rugosa*. Deer Park, WI: Capability's Books, 1991.

Westcott, Cynthia. *Anyone Can Grow Roses*. New York: D. Van Nostrand Co., 1952.

——. *The Gardener's Bug Book*. Revised edition. Garden City, NY: Doubleday, 1956.

Wilson, Ernest H. *Aristocrats of the Garden*. Boston: Stratford Co., 1926.

——. *More Aristocrats of the Garden*. Boston: Stratford Co., 1928.

——. *Plantae Wilsonianae*, Vol III. Edited by Charles Sprague Sargent. Boston: Cambridge University Press, 1916. Reprint. Portland, OR: Dioscorides Press, 1988.

Mail Order
Sources
for Roses

(bareroot, budded bushes except where noted)

United States

Antique Rose Emporium
Rt. 5, Box 143
Brenham, TX 77833
own-root, bareroot, and container roses

The Roseraie at Bayfields
P. O. Box R
Waldoboro, ME 04572
hardy roses

Carroll Gardens
444 East Main Street
P. O. Box 310
Westminster, MD 21158
modern and antique roses

Edmunds' Roses
6235 SW Kahle Road
Wilsonville, OR 97070
hybrid tea roses

Forevergreen Farm
Royall River Roses
70 New Gloucester Road
North Yarmouth, ME 04097
hardy roses

Greenmantle Nursery
3010 Ettersburg Road
Garberville, CA 95542
own-root heritage roses

Heirloom Old Garden Roses
24062 Riverside Drive NE
St. Paul, OR 97137
own-root and container roses

Heritage Rose Gardens, Rosequus
40350 Wilderness Road
Branscomb, CA 95417
own-root roses

High Country Rosarium
1717 Downing Street
Denver, CO 80218
minimum order: 10 plants
own-root old garden roses

Historical Roses
1657 West Jackson Street
Painesville, OH 44077

Jackson & Perkins
One Rose Lane
Medford, OR 97501-0702
modern roses

Justice Miniature Roses
5947 SW Kahle Road
Wilsonville, OR 97070

Lowe's Own Root Roses
6 Sheffield Road
Nashua, NH 03062
own-root heritage roses

Moore Miniature Roses
Sequoia Nursery
2519 East Noble Avenue
Visalia, CA 93277

Nor'East Miniature Roses, Inc.
P. O. Box 307
Rowley, MA 01969

Oregon Miniature Roses, Inc.
8285 SW 185th Avenue
Beaverton, OR 97007-5742

The Rose Ranch
P. O. Box 10087
Salinas, CA 93912
own-root old and rare roses

Roses of Yesterday and Today
802 Brown's Valley Road
Watsonville, CA 95076

York Hill Farm
271 N. Haverhill Road
Kensington, NH 03833
heritage roses

Canada

Corn Hill Nursery, Ltd.
R. R. 5
Petitcodiac, N. B. E0A 2H0
hardy rose specialist; own-root roses

Hortico, Inc.
723 Robson Road
R. R. 1
Waterdown, Ontario L0R 2H1
European, hardy, and old roses

Pickering Nurseries, Inc.
670 Kingston Road
Pickering, Ontario L1V 1A6
antique and rare rose specialist;
English roses

Europe

Peter Beales Roses
London Road
Attleborough, Norfolk, NR17 1AY
England, UK
old garden rose specialist

Cants of Colchester, Ltd.
Nayland Road, Mile End
Colchester, Essex CO4 5EB
England, UK

Georges Delbard SA
16 Quai de la Megisserie
75038 Paris Cedex 01
France

W. Kordes Söhne
Rosenstraße 54
25365 Klein
Offenseth-Sparrieshoop, Germany
minimum order: 10-12 plants

Organizations

The American Rose Society
P. O. Box 30,000
Shreveport, LA 71130
membership includes subscription to
The American Rose magazine and
The American Rose Annual

The Canadian Rose Society
Anne Graber
10 Fairfax Crescent
Scarborough, Ontario M1L 1Z8

The Royal National Rose Society
The Secretary
Lt. Col. Kenneth J. Grapes
Chiswell Green
St. Albans, Hertfordshire AL2 3NR
England, UK

Other Useful
Addresses

The Combined Rose List
Peter Schneider
P. O. Box 677
Mantua, OH 44255

Import Permit:
Permit Unit
USDA, PPQ
Federal Building
Room 638
Hyattsville, MD 20782

Index

Italicized page numbers refer to photographs and illustrations.

Photography Credits

Front jacket: ©David Coppin
(left and right), ©Jerry Pavia
(center), ©Derek Fell (background)

Back jacket: ©Alan and
Linda Detrick

©Cathy Wilkinson Barash:
122(L), 185(L)

©David Coppin: 1(L&R),
7(L&R), 29, 47(R), 49,
73(C&R), 76, 79(R), 80,
82(L), 84(L), 85(L), 87(R),
90, 92, 93(L), 95(R), 98,
99(L), 100, 101, 103(R), 107,
110(L), 111, 116(L), 118,
119(L), 120(L), 124(L),
125(R), 130(L), 134, 135,

137, 138, 139(R), 140,
142(R), 144, 146, 147(R),
149(R), 150(R), 151(R),
153(L), 156, 159, 162(L),
166(R), 171(R), 172(R), 174,
175(L), 177(L), 179, 181(R),
183(R), 187(R)

©Alan and Linda Detrick: 3,
4, 7(C), 8, 9, 11, 12, 14, 28,
30, 32, 33(L), 34, 36, 37, 38,
47(C), 62, 74(R), 75,
77(R), 78, 81, 82(R), 87(L),
89, 94, 97(L), 103(L),
104(R), 105, 110(R), 112(R),
113(L), 114, 115(L), 116(R),
117, 119(R), 120(R), 121,
123, 126(R), 127, 128, 129,
131(L), 133(R), 141(L),
142(L), 143, 145(L), 147(L),
148, 149(R), 150(L), 153(R),

154, 155(R), 157, 158, 163,
164(R), 176(L), 180(R)

Envision: ©Tim Gibson/
Envision: 58; ©Emily
Johnson/Envision: 61, 162(R)
©Tony Kastel/ Envision: 60,

©Derek Fell: 10(L), 18,
33(R), 46, 48, 50, 54, 55,
56(R), 85(R), 86, 112(L),
170, 182, 185(R), 187(L)

©John Glover: 91, 97(R),
141(R), 184

©Mike Lowe/Lowe's Roses:
57, 96, 108(L), 130(L), 132,
139(L), 145(R), 151(L), 160,
164(L), 169(R), 171(L),
172(L), 176(R), 177(R), 186(R)

©Charles Mann: 56(L), 99(R),
102, 126(L)

©Bruce McCandless: 40(R)

©Judith McKeon: 47(L),
79(L), 83, 84(R), 88, 93(R),
104(L), 106, 109, 115(R),
133(L), 155(R), 161, 166(L),
175(R), 178, 186(L)

©Muriel Orans: 74(L),
124(R), 131(R), 180(L),
181(L)

©Jerry Pavia: 1(C), 5, 6,
10(R), 52, 72, 73(L), 77(L),
94(L), 122(R)

©Joanne Pavia: 108(R),
169(L), 173

©Richard Shiell: 136

Tony Stone Images: ©Sean
Arbabi/TSW: 15

Courtesy of The Conard-Pyle
Company: 113(R), 125(L),
183(L)

Illustrations: ©Susan
Kemnitz, 1995

Garden designs: ©Jennifer
Markson, 1995

Photo key: L = Left, R =
Right, C = Center